TRAVELER

D0064285

Fall Out of Heaven

Also by Alan Cheuse

Candace & Other Stories
The Bohemians
The Grandmothers' Club

FALL OUT OF HEAVEN

An Autobiographical Journey across Russia

ALAN CHEUSE

THE ATLANTIC MONTHLY PRESS
NEW YORK

First published in the United States of America in 1987 by Gibbs M. Smith, Inc.

First Atlantic Monthly Press edition, April 1989

Printed in the United States of America

Library of Congress Cataloging-in-Publication Data

Cheuse, Alan
Fall out of heaven : an autobiographical journey across Russia / Alan Cheuse. — 1st Atlantic Monthly Press ed.
ISBN 0-87113-300-8
1. Cheuse, Alan—Journeys—Soviet Union. 2. Authors, American—20th century—Biography. 3. Russian Americans—Social life and customs. 4. Soviet Union—Description and travel—1970– I. Title.
PS3558.H436Z467 1989 818′.5403—dc19[B] 88-39289

Design by J. Scott Knudsen

The Atlantic Monthly Press
19 Union Square West
New York, NY 10003

FIRST PRINTING

For Emma & Sonya

Short fiction by Alan Cheuse has appeared in *The New Yorker, New Letters, Quarterly West, Black Warrior Review,* and the *Texas Review*. He is book commentator for National Public Radio's evening newsmagazine, "All Things Considered," and producer and host of "The Sound of Writing," for the PEN Fiction Syndicate and N.P.R. He lives in Washington, D.C., and teaches at George Mason University.

Acknowledgments: The author would like to thank Robert Faber and Sarah Johnson of Faber Travel, Ann Arbor, Michigan, for their assistance. Thanks are also due the Corporation of Yaddo for space and time to write. The greatest and deepest thanks go to James and Denise Thomas, editors, friends.

Chapter fourteen first appeared in *Present Tense*, vol. 3, no. 4, 1976.

Portions of chapter 23 first appeared in slightly different form in *The Bennington Review*, Spring 1984.

Lines from Philip Levine excerpted from the poem "1933" in *Selected Poems*. Copyright © 1974, Philip Levine, reprinted with the permission of Atheneum Publishers, an imprint of Macmillan Publishing Company.

In the cities of the world
the streets darken with flies
all the dead fathers fall out of heaven
and begin again

Philip Levine, "1933"

Dark early hour of a cold winter weekday morning. I start from my bed in the room I have shared with my younger brother since memory began. I walk on the cool linoleum barefoot through the kitchen and down the hall and step onto the thick, soft, warm, wine-colored living room rug. I'm looking for my father, but under cover of darkness he has already gone, leaving nothing behind but the familiar odor of his sweat and sweet pipe tobacco, and his voice echoing in my head. I see my fresh-cheeked young mother and brother standing close to each other at the northwest corner window, and I silently move toward them, then hover just behind. They are watching a gangly, slightly stoop-shouldered boy wearing a dark pea coat and blue knit cap stride purposefully across the road. The boy I am watching them watch is me.

ONE

THE TRAIN ROLLS FORWARD THROUGH THE Finnish countryside—trees, trees, trees, and telephone poles, tidy little towns filled with cars and television antennas and warehouses and shops—and I feel the relentless power of our forward motion, eastward, eastward! I'm caught at the beginning of this journey in something like the gravitational pull of another planet. There's someone out there in the unknown territory ahead calling to me, calling.

But when did this journey really begin, this journey of father and son, sons and fathers? The day my old man went up in that new monoplane from that distant airfield in Khabarovsk? Or the day he crashed into the Volga? Or was it the fiery afternoon in the Kyzyl Kum Desert when he took his first bullets? Or the day that he was born? Or the bitter, snowy hour in the Russian winter of 1812 when a wounded French sergeant fell by the wayside and watched the grenadiers retreating to Paris without him? Or was it the morning that Eve and Adam first cleaved to one another?

I can wander in this journal a bit more randomly than our immediate itinerary will take me. But how far back must I go, and how far ahead, in order to join these lines together, notes from the present and stories of the past?

These are the first thoughts I enter as my son Josh and I rush forward through the forests of Scandinavia. Storm clouds are gathering to the south over the Gulf of Finland, and also far to the north where, according to the map I've brought with me, you can find Murmansk, Russia's ice-free port on the Barents Sea. This map, this journal, the stories we have on our minds, the books I carry, the books yet to be, Josh's cameras, our stimulated eyes and rushing blood—we're travelling light but we're encumbered, like all wanderers, with the ineffable but ever-present baggage of everything that's come before.

We buried my father in the little cemetery in central Jersey on a rainy winter afternoon nearly four years ago. And even as each of us—my brother, mother, my son, and I—stepped forward to chunk our small shovelfuls of dirt atop his coffin, I could hear the charge of his voice in my head. It was faint at first, like some radio signal from one of the near-planets that he liked to babble about in the childish manner he adopted toward the end of his life, in his enthusiasm about science and medical miracles, space travel and video phones. And then the sound became stronger, and I didn't know whether if in my grief I was throwing my own voice like some black-crepe-draped ventriloquist of the graveyard, or if it was the real noise of his spirit hovering above us, the survivors, in the cold January rain. But I remember much of what I heard: *Go to Khiva,* he told me. *Take your own son and go to Khiva, that little desert outpost in Uzbekistan where I spent my best youth, and I'll meet you there, and we'll see what happens next.*

And then it faded, and I was left alone in the crowd of rain-soaked mourners, eschewing an umbrella, eschewing prayer.

All my forty-some years I had been fighting with the man, the immigrant, the worker, the old soldier, the sour-faced oppressor, the aging patriot both Soviet and American, the sentimental dreamer, the Philistine, and now that he was gone I missed him as much as if I had been stripped of my skin and left to stand bone-naked in the icy downpour. I could go on arguing with him now that he was dead, but that would be talking into a hole in the ground. And as his voice disappeared I understood that I could no longer resist reading the manuscript that he had been working on during the last few years of his life, when his heart was fading but his imagination shed brighter and stronger light on the events of his wild and adventurous youth in the Soviet Union. *Read it,* the man had added to his charge. *Read my book and make it your own if you like. I wrote it for you, not just for myself.*

I read it, finally, after years of putting it off, after years of elbowing my father aside and ignoring his stupid hopes for his writing in a language not his own native tongue, after years of ferocious mental battle that followed a childhood of physical struggle with this man born into another culture, another time and place, a military man with an odd mixture in his person of iron will and sweet, syrupy sentiment about family and life. I had closed my eyes to his desperate hopes and imaginings about making his story known to the world, his desire for fame and recognition, and regarded him for long years with a coldness that took its toll in other aspects of my life as well as in our kinship. He was, after all, my own father, and I had closed my ears to his stories as though the tale of his life and how he came to this country after travelling such a great distance and surviving so many hardships and adventures was the addled raving of some stranger on a wine-soaked street.

He offered his manuscript to me and I literally tossed it into the trunk of my car without reading it. He had wanted me to help him revise it, to strip it of some of the more florid and sentimental passages, and to publish it under my own name as a book called *Tales My Father Told Me,* but before his death it had taken no longer than it takes to swat a fly or crush a mosquito to each time reject the story in my mind and put the book out of my heart. God help me, I nearly spit in his face. And the battle between us—old father, new son, man of Old World ways, and a boy trying to make an American life—raged on until his death.

But after his funeral I took the book up again in my arms and held it to me, and read it, not just for him, not just for myself, but for my own son who had helped me shovel dirt onto his grave, and for my daughters. And for whomever as offspring these children of mine might one day in their own loves and lunacies produce. And by the time I had finished reading it seriously for the first time I wept over its pages a storm's worth of grief. My father, in his story, was once again alive.

In April 1986 I began to make plans to go to the U.S.S.R. to see if such a journey would begin to allay my father's wandering soul, or at least fulfill that final part of the burial ceremony: his charge for me to see the places of his youth, the regions where he had first come to see himself as a man. I would travel with my son, who would take photographs, and we would walk the same streets where my father walked, poke our noses up at the same sky, breathe the same Russian air. *Khiva!* I became obsessed with the place where he had fought the battles of his youth. *Khiva! Khiva!* I wanted to see that desert outpost more than anything. By mid-July our travel plans were all in place, though we still did not have our Soviet visas. Day after day I made telephone calls, travel agents made telephone calls, but still no visas. By the end of the second week in August I was getting nervous. It seemed as though instead of trying to get *into* the Soviet Union we were trying to get *out!*

"It's difficult for them to think about individual travellers. They're used to dealing with groups," my travel agent in Michigan said. I got more nervous still, but kept a lid on things by recalling a story a historian friend of mine told about how he had waited like this for his visa to Russia only to receive it by messenger at his hotel in Finland the night before his train was to leave for Leningrad.

I picked up our visas at the travel office in New York City one day before our scheduled departure.

So how do you feel? You're excited?" my mother asked as we arrived at Kennedy airport.

I couldn't tell her how I felt. It was too complicated. All I could do was behave like my usual reclusive self (my role when I'm with her, it seems) and say that I wouldn't know until I wrote it down. And I think that's true. E. M. Forster said that once, and I agree. Except he said I never know what I *think* until I write it down.

ONE

In the SAS lounge we waited for Josh and his mother. They arrived a few minutes later than expected – traffic problems in Manhattan. Josh looked composed and ready for the trip, his Fila cap atilt on his stubby, dark brown hair. Wait till the Russians get a look at him, I thought to myself. They won't have seen anything like him, this flashy young artist from the West. Meme, his mother, was dressed for the occasion of farewells, looking more beautiful than she had seemed to me in years. She was sweet to my mother, as she always had been, and in a funny way we were again a family, survivors of divorces and deaths. She told me that her current husband had just gotten a terrific magazine job in Chicago. I wished them well. From the lounge I called my daughters in Albany. Emma, nearly ten, gave me a big, cheery goodbye. Sonya, seven, was a little confused by the call – she knew that I was going to Russia but thought that I was *calling* from there. I explained that our airplane would leave in about an hour, and then I spoke briefly to *their* mother.

These lovely children, the girls, Josh, their mothers once my loves, it all makes my head spin if I think about it too hard, all this, past and present, all these years. And now Josh and I are setting off on this odyssey to my father's homeland, a place whose literature I've loved since college, but which might as well be on the moon for all I know about it, for all I know about how it feels to live there.

"Oh, so you're making a 'roots' trip," somebody said to me last month. "My father went back to his village in the Ukraine a while ago, looking for his roots." Peace to you, Alex Haley. At least I don't have to explain too much about what we're up to because Haley's done it already. So has Nicholas Gage, who wrote *Eleni.* Each of them had a special mission to fulfill on his journey to the places of family origins. We've got ours.

Thoughts of the girls in Albany flick through my mind as I record this airport farewell scene. What if with all the airplanes we're taking we should crash? How could I do this to the girls, give them the rest of their childhood without a father? And Josh? He's going to celebrate his twenty-first birthday while we're in Russia. What a horrifying thought, that he might be snuffed out on the verge of his prime, *because* of his father.

We leave our compartment and head for the dining car where there is none of the fabled Russian scarcity. We eat black as well as red caviar sandwiches, we drink Stolichnaya vodka. There's also delicious golden-fried sturgeon, with potatoes and carrots nicely presented, and we take tea from a large, silver samovar resting on the bar. We're still in Finland, and we use most of our remaining finmarks to pay for the lunch. The bilingual menu, over which I struggle to sound out a few words in Russian while the waiter—in his fresh white shirt and large, purple velvet bow tie—waits patiently, that menu says that once we cross the border we can pay only in rubles.

Is this how it's going to be throughout the U.S.S.R., plenty of caviar and vodka and fresh fish and good service? Josh and I are more than half charmed by all this. How could anyone want to leave a country that provides for its diners in such fashion? How could my father have given it all up?

How indeed! I'm steeped in the vodka, worrying about my father's patriotism to his native nation, wondering what kind of forces could drive a man to take another country as his home. As if I knew nothing about his history, or about history itself. As if I could pass judgement on his loyalties in the way that I did habitually when he was alive. As if sitting back in the dining car with a stomach full of food and a head full of vodka gives a man license to forget.

Last night in the hotel in Helsinki, Josh and I talked about journals—he's going to keep one, too. I envy him his talent for art and design, for making photographs. I can't seem to do much else but write, at least not with any passion. I dream back to conversations at home while I was in high school, my mother saying things like, You should be a lawyer, You should be a doctor. I didn't know about that—cutting into all that bleeding tissue. I knew then that, if I could learn the technique, I'd rather cut with my words.

"Are you nervous?" Josh asked me as we turned out the lights. All summer long people had been asking the same thing, and I'd been replying, "No, it's just work, just this book

I'm doing about my father's life in the U.S.S.R. and mine with him in the U.S." But right now I'm as nervous as someone about to make his first parachute jump or kiss his first date!

Josh and I discussed some of this in the dark. I mentioned Edmund Wilson's great work on the Russian revolution, *To the Finland Station,* that had excited me in my high school days. That book along with *Ten Days That Shook the World,* John Reed's masterwork of reportage, pushed me into thought about politics and life in revolution, charged my imagination, really, like nothing else before them. My father's *own* account of his early days in the Soviet Union I had always disregarded. (And what could have been worse for a young artist type to have cut himself off for so long from so much of his family's past and from so much history? How stubborn I was! And how American!)

Lenin lingered in Helsinki a while before taking this very same train trip to Russia where he assumed control over the insurrection against the Czar. Jack Reed walked the Helsinki streets as well before taking this train to Leningrad and reporting such epochal events as the storming of the Winter Palace. And now, after reading so much about all these events, after writing my novel about Reed, I'm rolling toward the borders of the U.S.S.R.!

The train slows down. The same trees that we've been travelling through for several hours suddenly take on new significance. Signs in four languages announce the border zone where barbed wire fence runs along the track, and even as we see these growing signs of another country my heart fills with that deeply breathed awareness that comes in such moments as these, when we're about to find ourselves in the presence of something we've dreamed of for a long, long time. I believe that somehow I've inherited this . . . call it the tendency to *feel* toward the world, without compromise . . . from my father. There is a passage in *Doctor Zhivago,* which I'm reading, that dramatizes this sense quite beautifully: the ability to connect things and spirit, earth and heaven, in a feeling glance. The hero, Zhivago, is walking along on "a clear frosty autumn night. Thin sheets of ice crumble under his steps. The sky, shining with stars, throws a pale blue flicker like the flame of burning alcohol over the black earth with its clumps of frozen mud." Well, there you have it; it's nothing but physical description, but the life of things in themselves leaps out from such passages.

We're coming to a stop, lurching past some guard towers and more barbed wire fences.

I've got to hide the Pasternak book—been advised by a former student of mine, a Russian emigré, that Bibles and Pasternak are not allowed in. "You've got to be psychologically prepared for this trip," she told me. "You've got to have a story and stick to it." I laughed to myself when she said this, but I do have a story worked up in my mind, because I don't want to tell people in the U.S.S.R. that I've come to follow the trail of my late flier defector father. A friend joked: "They'll put you in the gulag until you've worked off the cost of that airplane he ditched in the Sea of Japan."

I've stuffed the Pasternak novel way down in the bottom of my suitcase. If they look hard enough they'll find it, of course. But the book by my father that I'm carrying in my head, the story of his life as Fishel Kaplan, before he arrived in the U.S. and began another as Philip Cheuse, having Americanized Fishel and adopted his mother's surname so that he would be hard for Soviet officials to find—that volume they can't confiscate. Not unless they want to take my brain. These are true stories, shaped not unlike fiction. Normally one makes a novel to give a semblance of life, but in this rare case we have a life that seems as rich and as exciting and determined and powerful as a novel. My father's life bridges continents, holds the old Russian theme of war and peace, visions, youth and old age, the American contest of old worlds and new, families here, families there, generations of sons and daughters, the universal comedy, the pathos of dying and mourning. To live a life like a novel, to make a book that stings of life, that dream is on my mind as our train comes to an abrupt, crashing halt and we hear shouts and dogs barking outside our compartment window.

At least it's still daylight. This border would seem quite ominous at night.

ONE

A young, blue-eyed soldier in greenish-brown uniform comes down the length of the car and takes up a position guarding the end door. We can hear the customs officer making his way along the corridor.

"Passport, please," someone calls out in deeply accented English. We listen to the voice of the customs man in the compartment next to ours, the one where some Harvard political science students are making jokes. Another young soldier with a machine gun strides past our compartment window. These troops are Josh's age, twenty, twenty-one. I try to picture my son in a uniform, armed with a machine gun. I see Phil, my father, as his young self, cadet uniform smartly taut across his chest and back. He was nineteen when he left home in the Ukraine, left his mother, to whom he was the baby, and went to the Air Force Academy.

"Passports, please," says the official stepping into our compartment. He asks me to make room so that he can sit on the stool opposite our bench—I've piled some of our bags there—and proceeds to question us about what money we're bringing in, what other materials.

"Any Bibles?"

"No."

"Any anti-Soviet materials?"

Pretty stupid question, but obviously he's like our customs guys, an expert psychologist, using the question time to see if we're at all nervous about anything. But what would we be smuggling in?

Ah, the Pasternak. A dangerous book. Oh, to live in a country where books are as dangerous as bombs!

He asks me to leave the compartment while he speaks to Josh alone. A minute or so later I'm invited back in. He returns our passports to us, and the train begins to move.

"What is your profession?" the official asks me.

"Writer and journalist," I say, and mention my novel about John Reed and Louise Bryant.

"Ah, Reed," he says curling his lip in a knowing smile. "So you are a *progressive writer*—and does your government persecute you for your activities?"

"I wish they did," I say. "I'd sell more books."

Josh smiles but the official does not.

I wonder what he'd do if I told him my real reason for coming here. And my next writing project.

Then with a curt "thanks" he leaves us alone in the compartment.

"He felt me up," Josh says. "Weird guy. He said that he was looking for money belts, but he was really feeling me up."

"Maybe he was doing both," I say.

"You are progressive writer?" Josh says in a lilting, mock-Russian accent. "You write books about dee vorkers' state? Dee vorkers control dee means of production." He puts on his Walkman headset and dives down into the world of his music as the train rolls past more trees, trees, but these are *Russian* trees now, stretching from here all the way to the Arctic. Russia! at last we're here! we've crossed the border! we've carried our living bones back to the place of origins!

Outside the train window there is a sea of birches, Russian birches!

Vyborg, our first Soviet town. It's still light, and as the train stops we step down onto the platform as if onto an incredible stage set.

This is another world! Dilapidated concrete buildings surround a small square beyond the station, where red banners with Lenin's picture proclaim some message to the people. The road is full of huge ruts, standing pools of water. Dogs bark in the distance. The inside of the station reeks of urine. Dozens of people sit listlessly on the benches or lean against the walls, all of them dressed as if by the costume department for a movie about World War II, in torn coats, the cheapest shoes ever seen, dour faces. A badly muffled voice announces something over the static-marred loudspeaker. Josh and I look at each other, stare at our surroundings. Incredible! Our first glimpse at Russia and neither of us can help feeling as though we've landed on the moon.

"They don't exactly put their best foot forward, do they?" I say to Josh.

"Dad," he says, "maybe this *is* their best foot."

TWO

THE RULE AT THE ORENBURG AIR FORCE Academy Postgraduate School for Fighter Pilots was that an air cadet officer taking instructions from the ground by radio was not permitted to switch over from receiving to transmitting unless the instructor gave him permission. This rule could be dispensed with in case of emergency only.

The last day I flew over Orenburg was also the day I unexpectedly graduated from my training course, weeks ahead of schedule. My flight that morning in the spring of 1928 was unusual because after an hour aloft an emergency of sorts had begun to develop. The trouble was not with the plane, but with me, and I was afraid I was going to have an accident.

"Listen, Kaplan." My instructor, Major Zakharev, sounded cold, calm, and impersonal as his voice trickled into my earphone. "Since I am not your regular instructor, you should have guessed by now that this is an examination flight! And up until a moment ago, I was going to give you a good mark in aerobatics! Why the devil did you just ruin a nearly perfect snap roll? Please answer me."

"Sorry, sir. But I did it on purpose to have you question my behavior, as you just have. I need to land and run for the men's room, sir. I think it's an emergency." I switched off my transmitter in order to receive the major again.

"Permission granted!" I heard the major chortle to himself as I plunged downward, shedding altitude in a hurry in order to enter the landing pattern of the field.

The wind sock on the hangar indicated a strong northwestern wind blowing in from the Urals. It was a boisterous wind at all levels, a weather front that was transforming the warm spring day back into one of winter. It would not have been a good day for performing aerobatics anyway.

There were patches of snow still glistening on the steppe. Water had collected in low places, and like giant mirrors these pools reflected the clusters of cumulus clouds the tops of which were ablaze with the light of the morning sun. Beneath my wings as I descended were uneven avenues and streets lined with ramshackle little houses, with their front fences, yards, outhouses, chicken coops, piles of wood, and now and then a goat or two indifferent to the roar of my engine. I touched down, taxied quickly to the hangar where I jumped to the ground, and on the run removed my leather coat, helmet, and goggles. In the ready room I nearly ran into Alexander Kadikoff.

"Hang these up for me, will you, Sasha?" I pleaded as I tossed the bundle at him.

"How did the flight go, Fishka?" Kadikoff called after me as I dashed toward the latrine. "Piatogorsky made me fly the gamut!"

"Wait and I'll tell you," I yelled back.

"In which of these stalls is Fishka Kaplan, fellows?" I heard him say a minute later, in an official tone of voice.

"He flushed himself down the drain," another voice said.

"Commander Kaplan calling Commander Kadikoff . . . *peredayou!*" I sang out from my seclusion.

"The devil take that Major Piatogorsky of yours, Fishka, after what he asked me to perform for him in the wind this morning!"

"Major Piatogorsky is turning into an old grouch at an early age!" another invisible speaker put in. "I was no sooner up, one, two, do this, do that, and won't you please come down! Comrade Commander, I say to him, send me up and try me again! One of my foot wrappings was bunched up causing my left boot to pinch, sir," I said.

"Hah! A bad dancer complains that his pants are tight," another fellow called out from one of the other privies.

I emerged and went to a basin to wash the burned oil off the part of my face that the goggles didn't cover.

"By now it's too windy at all levels for precision flying, fellows!" said Captain Nicholas Tyatin, a lanky boy who stood a head taller than most of the men in the room. He had graduated from Borisoglebsk one year ahead of me and had been flying De Havilland bombers in the operational air force.

"This morning, comrades, we were being examined," a lieutenant observed, buttoning his tunic. "This morning the instructors were sorting out the eagles from the hawks."

"And it could happen that besides eagles and hawks they might discover a rooster or two among us," Captain Tyatin said.

"Yes, Tyatin," Sasha Kadikoff laughed. "And if they do discover a rooster, don't you worry it might be you they send back to fly bombers!"

"It's not funny, Sasha!" Tyatin said, then softened. "After flying istrebitels, I could never be happy going up in those unwieldly two-seaters."

"Tyatin, how come they didn't send you straight here from Borisoglebsk?" The question was clearly intended to annoy Tyatin.

"How many were there in *your* graduating class at Borisoglebsk?" said Tyatin.

"Forty-seven."

"And out of the forty-seven, how many were sent here for postgraduate training as fighter pilots?"

"Eleven of us."

"There's your answer!" Tyatin said. "It only took me a year to correct the error in my case."

"You mean you pulled strings, Tyatin?"

"A year lost, and now you're too old to fly pursuit."

"It's back to flying bombers for some of us, I guess."

Everyone in the room seemed bent on teasing Tyatin.

"They'll never wash out Tyatin, fellows! Tyatin has too much pull! Look at him, an important captain in less than twelve months out of Borisoglebsk."

"Whom do you know, Tyatin?" Kadikoff kept up the wheedling. "With someone in Moscow looking out for you, you might wind up behind a desk at that, because there's nothing safer to fly. Hey, what, little brother?"

"I would shoot myself first!" Captain Tyatin exclaimed.

After lunch, that day of the unscheduled flight examination, we Senior Squadron bachelors were taking our afternoon nap when Captain Tyatin tiptoed into the darkened room.

"Have you eaten yet, Tyatin?" I raised myself up on one elbow.

"Not yet, Kaplanchik. I was busy looking for you two."

"Why?"

"You fellows know, of course, that my brother-in-law Kobelev is the school adjutant," Tyatin leaned over and whispered to us. "Well, Kobelev tipped me off a little while ago that the general asked for my file and the files of two other seniors in our squadron. Yours, Kadikoff, and yours, Kaplan."

"Why us three?" Sasha Kadikoff asked.

"Kobelev thinks it has something to do with today's flight tests." Tyatin said. "The general, Kobelev told me, requested the instructor's evaluation of our work as soon as they were handed in at the adjutant's office."

"Perhaps the three of us have broken some rule?" I wondered.

"Throttle it down there, little brothers!" someone requested.

"You two jokers are members of the Party, of course?" Tyatin whispered, scratching the back of his head and wrinkling his face.

Sasha Kadikoff and I shook our heads.

"Did you two at least file applications for membership?"

"No," I said.

"You should have at least shown an interest in becoming candidates for membership. Don't tell me you two are not even members of the Komsomol?"

We nodded yes to that.

"What has all this to do with the evaluation reports?" I inquired. "What does being a member of the Komsomol or the

Communist Party have to do with how well we perform aerobatics?" I asked. "How can Party membership help me execute a snap roll?"

"You think it doesn't help, hah? Think again."

"Cut the conversation!" someone called out from one of the beds in the darkened barracks.

"Go to the married men's quarters and bother your wife, Tyatin," another fellow shouted out.

Someone in the room started coughing. It was a convincing, raucous hacking which evoked sympathy from all of us in the room, and we were relieved when it was over, until the same cougher suddenly became a snorer. Everyone laughed, and feigning suffocation Tyatin fled from the room.

"You must be Kaplan!"

Major Kobelev, the adjutant, rose from behind his desk and hurried to the banister dividing the office to greet me.

"Follow me!"

He ushered me into an anteroom where the light and the Persian rug underfoot were soft and pleasing. The clatter of a pair of typewriters in the other office could be barely heard.

"Wait here!" the major said and knocked on a door. Alongside a wall, in wicker chairs with a table and lighted lamp between them, were seated Lieutenant Kadikoff and Captain Tyatin.

"What's up, little brothers?" I whispered to them after the major vanished into the general's office.

"A court-martial for the three of us!" Tyatin said with a straight face. "Many an innocent man has been shot on someone's say so."

"Could be," I said.

"It may be funny, fellows, but I'm not laughing!" Sasha said, shifting uneasily in his chair.

The adjutant appeared and held the door open for us. "The general will see the three of you now," he said.

The light in the general's office was bright and gold, flowing in from four French windows. True to his reputation as an ace from World War I, as well that of a man who made a number of kills in the Civil War, General Rzhevsky had his desk arranged so that callers had to face the intense light of the setting sun, and together we stopped, blinked, saluted, and clicked our heels. The general did not rise, nor did he return our salute, but after touching his bald head with his plumpish hand he waved us down with a casual, "At ease!" We tried to relax as the general studied the three files on his desk.

"Alexander Gerasimevich Kadikoff . . . you are 5½ feet tall." Though the general spoke softly, Sasha stiffened. His fawn-colored cap contrasted with his short-cropped sandy hair. He had light blue eyes, a small upturned nose, and a determined mouth and chin with lips eager to smile. In Sasha's stiff pose of attention, in his willingness to carry out any given order, was a boldness that went well with the keen aspect of his eyes, eyes nonetheless kindly and capable of seeing the best in others around him. A Siberian, he seemed a person evolved by nature to survive its rigors.

The general turned to me. "You are Fishel Isaakovich Kaplan?"

I nodded.

"It says here that your eyes are blue, whereas they appear green to me."

"The color of my eyes depends on the light, tovarich General."

"Who told you that, a mirror?"

"No. Some girls told me."

"It is well that Lieutenant Kadikoff and you are not married!" Now the general shifted his attention to Captain Tyatin. In Tyatin's lively, dark eyes twinkled the challenge to test his bravery. He did not stiffen to attention when his turn came to be scrutinized by the general. Indeed, he became even more relaxed, and he was smiling as he stole glances to see the effect his behavior had on Sasha and me.

"How are you feeling, Gregory Ipolitovich?" Tyatin asked the general. His speech had none of the soft pronunciation of boys like myself who had been born in the southwest, nor did he have the twang and intonation of one born in Siberia. Nicholas Tyatin's Russian was that spoken in Leningrad and Moscow, and was the Russian the general himself spoke. Like General Rzhevsky, Nicky's father was a member of the class which had ruled Russia under the czar, and like the general, had had the good sense to transfer his allegiance to the Soviet government after the Revolution.

"How are you today, Nicky?" the general asked. " And how is your wife Nina?"

"We're both fine, thank you. I must confess though, that I'm anxious to learn why you have summoned the three of us."

"You are here before me because this morning the Senior Squadron underwent an examination, or an evaluation test to be more precise." As the general spoke, he returned his eyes to his desk. "The reason for it will be clear to you in one moment, comrade commanders. Right now there is an operational fighter squadron being fitted with new istrebitels. They are shy three pilots. Three replacements were being flown in a Junker transport from the Crimea to Tashkent when their plane slammed into a mountain in the Kavkaz, and all were unfortunately lost. We have received orders to fill the vacancies at Tashkent with three qualified upperclassmen whom we are prepared to graduate forthwith. You have been selected. However, if any of you object to this unorthodox procedure, you are free to decline."

"Tashkent!" Tyatin exclaimed. "Tashkent sounds wonderful!"

The three of us stood blinking in the light and grinning, happy to a point of near ecstasy. For me it was a dream come true, for my mother was tubercular and I had long anticipated the day I would graduate from the Air Force Academy and be able to bring her to live with me—and had I been given a chance to choose my base of service, I would have chosen Turkestan where the year-round climate was best suited for her condition.

"I take it then that you have no objections?"

The general smiled at the effect the news had on us. He rose from his swivel chair, walked over to the huge windows and drew the drapes shut. He was as short as Sasha Kadikoff, but heavier in stature. I visualized Sasha some thirty years hence, imagining him like the general, a brigadier, with a rhombus on his collar lapels instead of a little square inlaid with red porcelain. The general must have been as lean as Sasha in his youth, but now he was pudgy, so much so that I doubted he could fit into the cockpit of the istrebitel fighter plane we were flying.

The general cleared his throat and reached for the telephone, tapped the cradle of it and spoke softly into the receiver. "Alloh, alloh! Alloh? Kobelev? Get the *troika* in my office rolling for Tashkent!"

THREE

CALL THIS CHILD ALAN. I REMEMBER HIM WELL—I can put him back together limb by limb, word by word, reinvent the boy and the body that he was at that time, son of a Russian immigrant pilot and a candy store owner's daughter, in Perth Amboy, New Jersey, in the days that made up the decade following the year 1940, in the days of the war in Europe and in the Pacific, and the early days of peace that followed.

Listen, the first thing the man who was that boy Alan believes he remembers might have happened even before he was born. He recalls flying in an airplane, one of those early passenger planes that at least in recollection takes the shape of a cigar as it roars forward into the air, and among the passengers he recognizes his father and mother, just recently married. They're taking a trip from New York to Washington, the capital, to see the monuments.

Look, there is the dashing young flier, having arrived in the eastern United States after a long journey by train from California, and a long sea voyage from China before that, with a stopover in Hawaii that he will rave about all the rest of his life, the mountains in lush flower, the intensity of the ocean's blue upon the cloudless dome above the islands, the roar of the surf, the juxtaposition of yellow blossoms pressed upon dark skin, dark hair, hips in motion in dance, with all this and more on his mind, in his as-yet-relatively-unclogged heart.

This dashing young flier has met Tillie, in her teenful youth, at a dance in Brooklyn, his short and slender frame in the dark suit, pipe in his teeth giving him the stance of the reflective adventurer. They have met, danced, and she has fallen for him like a stone in an ocean, all the rest of her possible futures having sunk at once out of sight, and he has waltzed with her and told her stories about the adventures he had suffered in order to come to his new country, to be standing there when she entered the dance hall with her cousin Thelma and looked around to see who was puffing out that sweet smelling smoke.

Who travelled further? Phil who traversed half the world to meet her? Or Tillie who took the train into the city from Perth Amboy, and then the subway to Brooklyn? She hardly ever travelled out of town so that the trip to her cousin's was a big deal. She loved to dance, the Charleston in particular, though now and then a waltz allowed a partner to get close, and when it was someone she liked she didn't mind, though she never, never gave away anything more than a quick peck-like kiss to some of these naughty boys who wanted more.

She enjoyed seeing her girlfriends at school, and after school she would come up to the little store on Smith Street where her parents sold candy and cigarettes and newspapers, and she would sit in the back and listen to the talk and watch the customers pass in and out of the front door. It fascinated her most of the time, but her mother was such a vamp sometimes with the customers, talking directly to the men who bought cigars or some licorice for their children, some of these men who had come directly out of the saloon next door and still reeked of the yeasty air within—oh, Tillie thought that she would never be as forthright with a man as her mother, or wear lipstick that bright, or sweaters that showed off her bosom, though she herself had a fine figure that she had inherited from her mother, Sarah, and she was not all that old herself when boys began asking her to dances.

But oh! that evening in Brooklyn, with pigeons scattering all about from the rooftops above, nasty little boys on the street outside making comments about the women as they passed. It was autumn, it was warm, it was cool, it was spring, it was—it seemed a mixture of all of those times, the moment that smooth-looking foreign fellow in the dark suit turned and looked at her.

He had arrived in the United States by way of San Francisco, having spent some years in the Orient after leaving the Soviet Union (which had itself happened in a most remarkable way), and which he began to describe to her almost as soon as he had his arms around her out on the dance floor—in Japan and China—and now he had found his brother, who had been living in Brooklyn for years, and his sister in the Bronx (he had a few brothers left in the Soviet Union, but his mother, whom he had worshipped, had died years before of tuberculosis, and he didn't mention anything at all about his father except obliquely, saying his name had been Kaplan, as was his brother's name, while he had himself taken Cheuse, his mother's name, as a precaution against being hounded by the Soviets—hounded, he explained, because he had a lot of military information in his head that he had taken with him when he had ditched his airplane in the Sea of Japan, an accident actually, he had been blown off course, but he never went back—and, yes, he was Jewish, though he had not been inside a synagogue since he was a small child back in the Ukraine, though he had prayed when he felt that typhoon take his airplane as though it were a toy and spin it around over the waters, oh, yes, he had prayed!).

And didn't they fly together? Yes! He took Tillie up in his little airplane that he used to show tourists around Manhattan Island, twenty-five cents a flight. It took her breath away, she never got used to it. But did they fly to Washington? Alan has that memory, what may be his first, he thinks, of that trip, filtered as if through a sepia lens, probably only his memory of seeing a photograph of that flight.

Recollections of early bedtimes. Alan's mother's face leaning over him, a witch kiss was how he thought of it, the unaccountable vision of his mother in pointed hat and elongated nose filling his eyes in the darkened room—such a sweet mama transformed into a witch? Sometimes you could be frightened and no one could help.

And he remembers lying in bed with the chicken pox and watching a creature all black with pointed ears, the very replica of Krazy Kat from the comic strip that Uncle Don read over the radio on Sunday mornings as the family was gathered around the kitchen table in the State Street house, this krazy kreature not saying a word but torturing him by bobbing in and out of the pantry, the entrance of which he could see by leaning way over on the right-hand side of his bed in the bedroom off the kitchen.

And he remembers waking in the middle of the night and crossing quickly the cool linoleum of the kitchen and stealing into his parents' room and lying between them until first light. On one of these occasions his father had a book with a cover made up of abstract designs in orange and brown and read to him in a language that sounded both rough and comfortable at the same time, and his father showed him the odd shapes on the page and nothing about the sounds were familiar and nothing about the shapes on the page looked anything like the shapes on the surface of the newspapers that lay about the living room floor on Sunday. One day this boy Alan sneaked into his parents' bedroom to look for that book, but it had disappeared. He remembered the feel and look of the cover, the color and texture, the sounds his father made when he flicked his eyes across the pages inside.

His father would disappear, too, on a Sunday, only to be found by the trail of sounds he made tap-tap-tapping away at the black machine with lettered keys, these shapes on the keys becoming more and more familiar as Sundays piled up through the years.

"Don't bother me, I'm vorking," said his dark-haired papa from his hunched position at that machine in the little alcove off the living room. *V*orking, *v*orking—that *W* turned to *V* was not the only sound from his lips that didn't fit in to the rest of the speech in the household, the family, the block.

"Git out of here!" the man spat at him and the boy danced back away and out of the alcove, out into the living room, through the house, down the back stairs, to play in the hard-packed dirt behind the house.

"Git out, git out, git out of here!" the boy spat at the only other living thing in the yard, a weed-tree that rose as big as the roof

of the garage and sometimes served as a shelter for the stray sparrow or, in early spring, robin that might have mistaken this concrete and worn-earth neighborhood near the beach as a haven for the weary creatures of the air. "I'm *vorking*," the boy cried, in imitation of the man at the typewriter. But no one else he knew, mother included, spoke in this fashion and so he let it drop and never picked it up again, but not without once using that phrase as a bludgeon on his younger brother who trailed down the steps after him, urged by Mother to play with Alan in the yard.

Father always seemed to be *vorking*. Perhaps before the children came he found time for pleasure, for taking Til to the movies or to a dance at the local synagogue (a place he never attended except for the High Holy Days in the autumn of the year), but now at home he was either telling them to be quiet at the table . . .

"Quiet, Oll-an, I'm listening to the noose!"

. . . or he was tap-tap-tapping at his dark little machine, or he was taking a nap, snoring like a walrus on the sofa.

Work took him away on weekday mornings even earlier than Alan had to leave for school. From his day-to-day employment as a pilot out of Teeterboro Airport in north Jersey he had moved to a job at the Copper Works in Perth Amboy, and then to the assembly line at Wright Aeronautical, and then to General Motors in Linden where he used his expert knowledge as a former pilot and engineer to help smooth out troubled moments on the automobile assembly line. By the time he made the drive home each afternoon he wanted nothing more than to eat quickly and lie down. Listening to the radio seemed more important than talking to his boys. He wanted to hear the *noose* of the world. He had what appeared to be a mystical link to the radio speaker, as if at any moment the voice of the announcer might address him directly, about his past, his present, his future.

Come up and get dressed, we're taking a ride."

That was the announcement Tillie sometimes delivered, and you could hear Phil groan all the way down in the yard. But of a Sunday, whether the sun were shining or the rain coming down, this family climbed into the black Plymouth and drove across town to where Tillie's parents lived in the very same house where she grew up, a small, one-family structure made of wood and brick and a kitchen that let out onto a weed-filled yard.

Sarah, Alan's maternal grandmother, was a dark-eyed, dark-haired woman whose mouth was always lustrous with red lipstick, the middle child of Great Grandma, the broad-beamed, white-haired woman who lived a few blocks away in a house that Alan would later pass four times each day to and from Number Seven School.

On these Sundays, when he was still quite small and retained such innocent recollections as believing that he had flown to Washington with his parents even before he was born, young Alan looked forward to these visits to the badly lighted house of his grandparents mainly because of their phonograph, a Victrola that you cranked up with a beautifully crooked handle that obtruded from the side of the machine.

His Master's Voice

That inscription beneath the picture of the dog with head cocked toward the spinning record on a turntable, a duplicate of the larger one above it, intrigued the boy. He cranked and cranked, and lifted the eccentric tone arm and needle up and then turned it half around so that it came down to slide along the grooves on the thick, wax discs, and a man's voice sang

my time
is your time
your time
is my time

although despite this music in his ears, or perhaps because of it, he could not figure out the mystery of the dog with the head inclined in question. Who was the master? What was the voice?

"I want to try," his brother would say, reaching for the tone arm.

"Git git git git out of here," Alan would shout in the same rough way as his father.

"What's this?" Phil asked, stepping out of the kitchen where he and Til and Sarah and slight, white-haired Isadore, her husband, Tillie's father, sat around the table drinking coffee. "You want me to get the strap?" By this he meant his belt which, from time to time when Alan the Big Mouth sometimes spoke back to him, as he was doing more and more, he would undo at the buckle and slip from his belt loops and wave wildly over his head as he chased his hysterically screaming son around the dining room table.

"No," cried Alan, "I'll be good, I'll be good!"

"You better be," Phil said on such occasions, a strange and distracted look in his eyes. "You're lucky to be growing up in this country, you know that?"

What did Alan know? but he nodded his head.

"In the old country," Phil sometimes went on, "we never had nothing. When I was your age we had nothing. And when I got older I had only a little more."

The old country! What place was that? Some aging place that had been born long ago and was now turning white in the head like the grandparents and Gramma? Could a country itself be born, grow up, and now be dying? What was a country after all? This town to him with its dilapidated wood and brick houses. What happened in the *old country?* Did the buildings sag and sink and bend over double and pass out, to die and disappear like old weed-trees?

"Phil?" mother called from the kitchen. "What are you doing out there?"

"Playing with the boys," he called back, staring with distraction at the Victrola, at the record spinning to a stop. "You want me to crank it for you?"

"I do it," Alan's brother said.

"*I'll* do it," Alan said, and grabbed the crank before his brother could make a move.

"You be good now," said Phil, and he pursed his lips as if in thought, but said nothing, and then walked back into the kitchen, leaving at least one of his sons looking at his father's disappearing back and thinking to himself consciously for the first time, *This* is not playing with his boys, this is *not* playing!

The truth was Phil never played with his boys, scarcely ever. He worked hard during the week, and on the weekends he was trying to teach himself to write, to write his own story. It was a rare occasion when he took the time out to spend even an hour or two a month with Alan and his brother.

Yet when he did it seemed like a time that could change your life—such as the Sunday he came out of the alcove where he had been typing, called for the boys, and told them that he was taking them to the movies. There was a motion picture he had heard about from someone at work, he explained, a movie about a giant ape from the South Seas, and it was fabulous, he had heard, and he wanted to see it. Did the boys want to go?

Yes, yes, they did!

So Tillie helped bundle them into their clothing—it was a late winter afternoon, all the trees bare, the air still with the cold, and few people on the street uptown when they arrived for the mid-afternoon showing.

"Look at dot! Look, look at dot!" Phil said loudly as the monster gorilla first appeared at the giant wall that divided Skull Island in two.

Alan looked, but his younger brother, Shel, hid his head, uncomforted by either of his companions.

And now and then there came a Sunday, usually in the spring, when Tillie would decide that she wanted to ride to some of the more affluent towns north, and Phil would grumble and Phil would growl and Phil would sulk with passion, but in the end the family of four would set out in the Plymouth for a trip to the Oranges or Teaneck, a full afternoon's drive.

In the back seat of the car, lying against the deeply piled upholstery where the air was redolent with dust, the brothers played a little game. Alan would pretend that his fingers were adventurers, pirates, soldiers, and walk them through the forest of his brother's hair. The younger boy's scalp become the forest floor.

"Uh-oh, here's the bad man!" Alan would cry out, matching the index finger of one hand against the thumb of the other, all the while leaning on his brother with his elbows to keep the field of play from moving.

"No, no!" he'd challenge himself, doing more voices.

"My turn, my turn!" his brother would yell.

"What are you doing?" Phil would ask with a glance in the rearview mirror. But what could he see? The boys were lying almost flat on the seat.

"Be good, boys," Tillie would say.

"Help, help!" Alan would cry out in a falsetto as one of his finger people encountered some new danger in the woods.

"Be good, your mother said," Phil put in.

"Ouch!" Shel cried out as his brother applied more pressure on his skull.

"Be good, I said."

"You heard your mother!"

"Owee-oww!"

"Boys!"

"Do you want the strap?"

"No, no!"

"Then shut up, do you understand? Then you better shut up!"

"Phil," Tillie put in, "you don't have to speak to them like that."

"That's all boys understand," he said.

"No, no! Stand back!"

"Owww!"

"Boys! The strap?"

"No, no!"

"Shut up or you'll get it!"

Sometimes after school Alan would stuff himself with sweets from his grandparents' candy store. Gramma Sarah, or Mama Sarah, as they called her, would be working behind the counter near the rear of the store, serving milk shakes or sodas to some customers, and Grandpa Isadore would be standing at the counter that fronted on the street, selling cigarettes and newspapers and numbers slips in exchange for the money that people dropped onto the sticky rubber mat that covered the surface of the rectangular tray between him and the people on the sidewalk. The store itself was a narrow affair, sandwiched between a dress shop on one side and a saloon on the other.

Alan loved to stand just outside the doorway eating a chocolate bar and watch the beer trucks pull up to the curb. The drivers rolled the yeasty-scented kegs down the tailgate with a sound like thunder before they ferried them across the pavement through the swinging doors of the saloon.

"You want some chewing gum, darling?" Mama Sarah would ask from her station behind the counter.

He took some chewing gum.

"You run out of chocolate, take more."

And he did.

"You want to read a comic, take a comic, take some home for your brother, too."

He did just that.

"You want a soda now?"

He would love one.

"How about a sandwich?"

He nodded.

"Take a newspaper home for your father, darling."

He would.

"More candy? Take a little more, but don't let it ruin your appetite."

He did.

"Mama," he'd hear Tillie say later on the telephone. "Mama, you are going to make the boy sick. He ate nothing for dinner."

Alan stared in a sugar-induced haze at the weed-tree growing past the kitchen window in the fading light.

"You want to ruin your teeth?" Phil said, looking up from his plate. "Let me tell you, you had better take good care of your teeth. In the old country we weren't so lucky. Our teeth got ruined at an early age. Look."

And he'd open his mouth to show the twisted incisors that Alan, out of morbid fascination, couldn't help but stare at in wonder every time.

His teeth decayed but his love for his grandparents increased in proportion. On those rare occasions when Phil gave in to Tillie's desires for a night out at the movies, Grandpa sometimes was the one who came over to babysit, and when he did he brought his violin, and before bedtime played such tunes for Alan and his brother as "Hatikvah," the melody that would become the national anthem of the as-yet-to-be-born state of Israel, and he swayed from side to side as he moved his bow, and sometimes he showed them how to fix tissue paper to their mother's combs and hum through the paper along with his violin.

On one of these nights he appeared with a patch over one eye—the doctors, since the boys had seen him last, had removed one of his eyeballs. How amazing! Alan begged him to pull aside the patch! Finally after a lot of pleading Isadore gave in, and Alan stared into the dark, empty socket and saw red and blue and greenish nerves and tissue and perhaps even something resembling the bones of his grandfather's skull—it all happened so quickly he could hardly name to himself everything he saw—and that night he dreamed of that cavity and woke up screaming.

"You see, Til," he heard his father say in the night, "you see what they're doing to him, giving him all that candy? When I was a boy we had nothing! Nothing, you understand! We had to live without any of these things, candy and movies, and I want my boys to have everything but I want them to appreciate it, too. Til, do you hear me? Are you asleep?"

"Listen, Oll-lan," he said the next evening at the supper table. "Listen, I want you to stop eating so much candy."

"Why should he stop?" Tillie asked. "It can't hurt him. He brushes his teeth."

"Me, too," said the brother.

"You keep out of this," said Phil.

"Shut up!" Alan said.

"What was that?"

"Nothing."

"Nothing? Nothing?" And Phil leaned across the table and gave Alan a flat-handed thwack across the head.

"He learns that from you, Phil," he heard his mother saying behind him as he ran screaming from the room.

"Oh, yeah?"

"Oh, yeah!" shouted Alan through his tears. And at the sound of his father leaping from his chair and racing after him, he dove into the closet in his room and pulled tightly on the door.

"Come out, you brat!" his father called from the other side.

"Never!"

"You don't come out, I break the door down and get you!"

"Phil!" came his mother's faint cry.

"Ma!" came his brother's even fainter wail.

After a long tug of war the boy gave up, and the door flew open, and his father dug for him among the pile of clothing on the floor and yanked him out and flung him against the bed.

"Don't you touch him!" Tillie screamed, placing herself between boy and man.

"What did I do?" cried Alan. "I didn't do nothing! I didn't do nothing!"

"You brat!" spat out his father, turning aside from his wife and older child. "You, too, Til," he said with contempt, and strode out of the room.

Later Alan sneaks out of his room to see his father sleeping on the living room sofa, the radio playing silly, sentimental popular music, "Come on-a my house, my house-a come on . . . " The boy stands there listening, watching, watching, hypnotized by his father's sleeping form. Who was this man who had such power over him? What did it mean that he was his father? Where had he come from—that strange country he often spoke of? He seemed so vulnerable now in sleep, faint sursurrus of snores giving the only sign that he had not stopped breathing.

Who was he? This man who showed his crooked teeth in snarls as much as he smiled, this man who made his mother weep, this man as hairy as an ape when he emerged from the bath, this man who told him *do dis, do dot,* this man who went and came each day and seemed on the days between work weeks to turn the sofa into a private domain, a boundary beyond which the son could not enter.

So vulnerable, sleeping now.

FOUR

THE MOSCOW–TASHKENT EXPRESS WAS HURTLED through a barren, uninhabited steppe where only an occasional camel or nomad's tent could be seen on the horizon.

At long last my training was finished. I was now ready to start my job in the operational air force, to start enjoying myself and begin living! Now, in addition to my lieutenant's pay, I would be getting bonuses for flying time, for perfect maintenance of my plane, for no crack-ups, and extra pay for uniforms, for living quarters, for meals out—there was an endless list, I heard, of bonuses and extras given to pilots.

And now my mother would be able to live as my dependent, on the air base perhaps. Or I might find her a nearby sanatorium for a rest cure. It hurt me to think that if it had not been for me, my mother might be living in the United States of America, with my father and my brother and sister. Why did mother not listen to Aunt Rachel and Uncle Yankel and leave me with them and go to America without me? A half dozen years had passed since that unfortunate business of my mother's decision, but now, rushing over the countryside, it was still vivid in my mind, how my mother had been handed our passport and then had it snatched away. We had waited years for that passport! We had waited through World War I, the Russian Revolution, and into the bloody Civil War of 1918.

At last, the peace we so longed for had come, and mother received from my father, who had long ago emigrated to America, two steamship tickets on the White Star Line. Now all we needed was a passport to emigrate out of the Soviet Union.

I remember days and weeks of an entire summer spent running from desk to desk, from office to office, department to department, in Zhitomir, in Kiev, until we were tipped off by other applicants that it would be wise to bribe our way along. Inflation was rampant and the clerks were corruptible. Mother parted with some American two-dollar bills she always found in our letters from my father in New York, and in a matter of days, this time, behold! we were being granted our passport! Oh, I remember that moment. My mother's beautiful blue eyes were wet, and she was speechless. Her hand shook as she held the passport.

"Don't cry, Mamochka," I said.

"Who's crying? These are happy tears, son. This is not crying."

Just then the door opened, and a pudgy official with a portfolio appeared in the office.

"Was that a passport you just handed that woman and her boy?" he demanded, raising a hand to halt the transaction even as he stood in the doorway. "Have you a spravka stating the young fellow's scholastic record?"

"Everything is in order, Alexsey Ivanovich," the clerk said.

"Let me just examine what you have here."

"What do you want from us now?" My mother's tears were suddenly no longer of joy.

"Just as I thought!" the bureaucrat exclaimed. "You will have to bring in your son's school marks, citizeness Kaplan! There is a new decree from Moscow. We cannot allow you to take your son abroad unless he is stupid—I mean unless he is a poor student!"

My mother seemed paralyzed for a moment, then she said, "So help me, my Fishel is not very bright sometimes. Yes, my son is stupid! Do not be ashamed, Fishel, tell the man! Tell him, aren't you stupid?"

"Yes, Mama. I am stupid," I readily admitted.

"See? He said he is stupid! Who but a stupid would admit such a stupid thing, tovarich commissar?" Mother pleaded.

"We will have to hold this passport until we see your son's school marks, citizeness Kaplan!"

"Idiot! Did you have to be such a good student in all subjects?" she said when we got outside the government buildings. "Did you have to get all fives and five pluses? Could you not get a failing mark, or a one, a two at least, or make just a passing mark, like a three? Idiot!"

"Mama, if I knew that this might keep us from going to America, I would have played hookey from school altogether."

"Well, with God's help, and after I press a few dollars into the commissar's fat hand, maybe he will still let us have the passport."

"Mama," I said, "better rely more on the money and less on God."

"Since when is money stronger than the Almighty?"

"The Almighty does not, as a rule, interfere in the lives of men."

"And where did you learn this kind of crazy philosophy? In school?"

"No, Mama. In school they teach us that there is no God."

"So you know better, Fishel. What else does the Almighty have to do but watch out for His children, the people in His world?"

"It is Uncle Yankel who is of the opinion that the Almighty has more important things to do, such as regulating the stars and planets in the firmaments, rather than mess around with the mixed-up affairs of men." I added that I had read a book on astronomy in which it positively stated that the earth is only one of thousands upon thousands of worlds like it in the universe.

"Your own father," Mother countered, her eyes flashing, "who happens to be the son of a wonder-working rabbi, quoted to me from the scriptures the fact that the Almighty watches over and knows even when a sparrow falls."

"Mama, Mama, you don't understand. God could not possibly find the time to watch over every creature."

"This is blasphemy you are saying. You hear? Blasphemy! Only a year or two after your bar mitzvah and already the godless ones have gotten to you. Oh, the sadness of it, the shame! And you the grandson and namesake of Rabbi Fishel Ben Isaak Kaplan, may he rest in peace."

"You don't understand, Mama," I protested, "I believe in God, but my interpretation of Him differs from yours. I have already read enough on the subject to form some opinion. I am of the opinion that the Almighty seldom chooses to interfere in the affairs of men. He gave men the Ten Commandments, which have been derived and interpreted in the Torah, from which in turn all the laws of the Western world have been derived. Uncle Yankel says that if some men choose to disregard God's laws, and if other men and nations condone transgressions of others by doing nothing about it, then the guilty and the innocent, men and nations alike, suffer the consequences. In other words, Mama, the Almighty has created our earth, set up the laws of nature on it, given us laws to live by, and it is up to us to evolve into better beings in His image."

"You know what, Fishel?" I saw my mother smile again, something I had not seen since our passport had been taken from her hands.

"What, Mama?"

"Maybe you're right. Perhaps it is meant to be. And if they are not going to give you a passport, Fishel, then I'm not going to America either!"

Thus my mother sacrificed with a smile her dream for a better future and remained in Russia with me.

The lobby of the hotel in Tashkent was full of tunics and khaki uniforms of officers of all ranks. There were more blue patches on the collars of the tunics of cavalrymen than there were red ones on those of the infantry, but not many blue patches on the lapels of the open-collared tunics such as we were wearing in the Red Army Air Force.

From among the fliers in the lobby we picked a lieutenant whose prop and daggers over the wings on his sleeve indicated that he was a fighter pilot. "Little brother," said Captain Tyatin, "can you guide us to the squadron commander of the Second Fighters, attached to the First Bombardment group?"

"I can, little brothers, but I should hate to lead you into a reprimand for being out of uniform. Your sidearms are missing. What happened? Did you jokers lose your revolvers in some game? Were you held up and disarmed? Did you forget them somewhere?"

"The devil take it!" Tyatin said. "We weren't issued any."

"For this oversight we can thank your boob of a brother-in-law!" Sasha Kadikoff smiled at Nicky.

"My name is Koshkin." The lieutenant extended his hand and introduced himself, shaking each of our hands in turn. "You fellows must be the replacements for Slavin, Chaikin, and Ostorozhny."

"Yes. Exactly what happened to them?"

"Don't ask!" Koshkin said. "I'm in the Second Fighter squadron myself. Our commander's name is Smirnov. You'll find him in room number four, up that balcony and down the corridor."

"Smirnov?" I repeated.

"Is the major a decent sort of fellow?" Kadikoff asked.

"We think so," Koshkin smiled. "Only you must not hold it against him if he chews up the three of you for being without sidearms."

"This Koshkin looks like a kidder to me," Tyatin said as we took the stairway steps two at a time. We dumped our bags in the hallway, and adjusted our ties and tunics.

Nicky Tyatin knocked on the major's door.

"Enter!" Tyatin in the lead, we marched in, saluted the major, clicked our heels, and remained at attention while Tyatin produced our orders.

"We are the three replacements for your squadron, tovarich commander." said Tyatin.

"At ease! And in the future you need not be so formal and stand as stiff as statues. This is not the academy. My name is Kiril Kirilovich Smirnov." Major Smirnov smiled as he examined our papers, and then without looking up said, "It is tragic what happened to those three replacement pilots who were on the way here from Sevastopol."

We all nodded.

"Which of you is who?" Major Smirnov said.

"I am Tyatin. Those two are Kadikoff and Kaplan. Kaplan is the taller one, sir."

"I do not want you to think there is no discipline in my squadron, Captain Tyatin, but I dislike talking as much as heel-clicking, if you know what I mean."

"Just so, tovarich commander!" Tyatin stiffened.

"Stand easy, all of you. I shall try to find some time to check out each of you and assign you to your istrebitels. The machines arrived on railway flatcars partially disassembled from the factory. Say, where are your sidearms?"

"None were issued to us, sir," Tyatin said.

"I will try to requisition revolvers for you to wear during our flight to Khiva."

"May I ask if we are not going to be stationed in Tashkent, sir?"

"I hope you won't be too disappointed, Captain. We're stationed at Khiva. We're here merely to pick up our aircraft."

"Are the civilian dependents' quarters suitable in Khiva, sir?" said Tyatin.

"There are some dependents there, but not many. If you have a wife and want to send for her I suggest you wait and see if we can requisition a room or two for you by order of military priority, in which case some civilian family will have to be evicted. Khiva, as you will find out, is very over-crowded. And you might as well learn here and now that Khiva is no place . . . I hope I will not shock you, fellows, but Khiva is full of prostitutes who were rounded up from the streets of Leningrad and Moscow and were exiled there."

"And I had hoped to have my mother live with me, wherever I was stationed!" I blurted out.

"It's ironic," the major continued, filing away our orders into a portfolio, "that these pleasure girls were exiled there to be isolated from men. At the time it was thought that Djunaid Khan's counterrevolutionary bastards had been beaten. There are hundreds upon hundreds of prostitutes in Khiva, and shortly after our squadron and the First Bombardment group arrived in Khiva a virtual epidemic of venereal diseases broke out. Civilian medical teams were rushed in to treat the diseased."

"Forgive me, Major," I said, "but it's not clear to me . . . this, Djunaid Khan . . . who is he or what . . . I do not understand."

"Good question, Kaplan. I will get around to him, or rather of what's left of his armies which had been assumed destroyed during the Civil War. But first I wish to explain to you that besides the Russians who had settled in the area during the Czar's times, and the playgirls who were sent there along with some criminal elements, there are also Russians in Khiva who are former nobility, families who did not escape abroad, titular families, if you know what is meant by that. In Khiva there may be grand dukes, and I think there's a princess or two, and some barons and counts, grand this and that or something or other, who formerly glorified the family of the Czar. What I'm getting at is that it's important for you to remember not to associate with these people."

"Yes, sir," Captain Tyatin said for all of us.

"Now then," said the major, "I would rather leave this to our political commissar, but since you know nothing of the attempted uprising against the Soviets in Turkestan, in the region of Khorezm around Khiva and Urgench, I should enlighten you. Here again, comrades, I do not wish to shock you, but there is a limited guerilla war going on in Khorezm right now. Actually, it is nothing like what it was when it first started, but still it flares up now and then. Whenever the enemy manages to build up his strength, he hits us. Incidentally, your mail will be censored, so don't mention a word about this little war we are engaged in. Not one word and that *is* an order!"

"We've read nothing about this, sir," said Tyatin.

"Naturally, because we're under orders not to discuss it. There's nothing about this unpleasant, bloody mess mentioned in the papers, but we're nevertheless fighting and dying in the countryside around Khiva. As a matter of fact, the men you are replacing were actually lost in action."

The major paused to look each of us in the face to observe our reaction. Startled by the revelation, my heart had jolted and now my blood raced with excitement. The prospect of an enemy who might be more experienced or braver than I frightened me for a moment, but then fear gave way to the rather delicious prospect of putting all my aerial combat training into practice. The major must have read this in my eyes.

"Sorry to disappoint you, Kaplan, but the enemy has no aircraft to fight us with. The pleasure is one-sided. However, they're the ones who're shooting us down. Too often, I regret to say. They're very skillful with machine guns, the Basmachi bastards are."

"Then we operate against ground targets," said Tyatin.

"Yes. Mostly we're on constant patrol, doing reconnaissance. By the way, while I'm at it, I wish to point out that when strafing, better results are achieved when we kick the rudder a little."

"It must be quite a battle if they're shooting our machines down," Sasha said almost to himself as he scratched the back of his head.

"This is no longer so. Right now it appears we've broken their back. As a matter of fact, it's been comparatively peaceful these past few weeks." The major was clearly making an attempt to lessen the shock. "Your reaction, comrades, is not any different than was mine when I first learned about these so-called 'maneuvers' we're conducting. Our job is to do the flying and the fighting," Major Smirnov concluded in a tone of voice indicating that the matter was closed. "Were you given your pay allowance?"

"Just so, tovarich commander!" Tyatin confirmed.

"I will telephone the hotel clerk to billet you here. You can take your meals with the garrison men at the aerodrome, but if I were you I would find some restaurant and eat something other than what's being served in the mess."

The hotel clerk was a middle-aged man, shortish and plump with a clean-shaven, healthy, sunburned face, and eyes which revealed that he was under constant harassment.

"Needless to say, you fellows are not afraid of heights," the clerk observed, looking the three of us over.

"Any floor will do, papasha!" Tyatin replied.

"Exactly," the clerk said. "We have reserved the top-most accommodations for you, comrades. We have cots with pillows and blankets on the roof."

"The roof?" the three of us exclaimed in a chorus.

"The roof is a fine and even healthy place to sleep," the clerk responded.

"What if it rains?"

"It hardly ever rains, comrades! And if it rains, you come down here into the lobby." The clerk shrugged, amiable and patient.

So up we climbed. At the top of the third floor there was a door which opened onto the roof. Swept clean, the baked clay surface of the roof was like the legendary flying carpet set against a backdrop of minarets and mosques, interspersed by avenues and parks, and streets with cottages, lined with palms and lush with flowers and gardens and thick with patches of verdure.

Some five cots formed an island around the dormer in the center of the roof. We deposited our bags in a perimeter as a boundary and wisecracked about who would be the first to sleepwalk off the edge.

"What if it rains tonight?" Sasha asked.

The western horizon was turning crimson. "It does appear that it's going to be windy tomorrow," I said, studying the sky. Then, from someplace in that sky, arrived the high-pitched voice of a muezzin calling the faithful to prayer. We were startled since it was the first time we heard a mullah's call.

The air was dry and pungent with the smell of cooking oil which drifted up to us on a slight breeze. The sidewalks and the dust on some of the streets was splashed over with water. The bluish evening held promise for a cooler night and relief from the heat of the day.

We dashed downstairs to the street and headed off in search of a restaurant. The braying of a donkey started us as we walked, and a man in a turban and flowing robe passed by followed by two women with faces concealed by veils. A cart with two huge wheels, pulled by a horse, rolled along squeaking for lack of axle grease.

We found ourselves hemmed in by high gates and earthen walls. Now the smell of cooking oil was intense and tingled our appetites and nostrils. Men in pajamas and skullcaps lurked along the way.

"We better double back, little brothers. I think I'm lost!" Sasha said.

"Fine navigator you are!" said Tyatin.

"This is not the way the crow flies," I threw in.

"I wish that I *did* have a sidearm," said Sasha.

"If they jump us, keep in mind that they all carry daggers."

Tyatin spoke up. "Relax, fellows! The Uzbeks are not likely to lay a hand on a Russian! It's when we get to Khiva, where the Turkomen bastards are, that's where we're likely to get stabbed in the back."

We retraced our way back to a boulevard, then, by following a hungry-looking local we soon detected shashlik roasting on a charcoal fire at a restaurant from which we were separated by a tall fence overgrown with grapevines.

Inside we discovered the waiter and part-owner of the place was an Armenian, a giant of a man named Yashka, with bulging biceps which filled the sleeves of his pink silk shirt. His clean-shaven head shone in the candlelight and his fleshy face was all smiles as he met us, bowed his welcome, and ushered us to a table.

We allowed him to seat us, and readied ourselves for an exotic feast. In all the world, we didn't know three young men who deserved it more!

FIVE

NIGHT FALLS AS WE ROLL INTO THE TRAIN YARD of Leningrad's Finland Station. We stare in fascination at the pastel colors of apartment houses seen hazily behind the screen of mist, which is either fog rising from the streets or a light rain falling, difficult at first to say which. And then we're sure it's rain. These vast outskirts of a city—I don't know what we expected to find, but to discover an enormous complex of houses and streets seems a wonder.

"This is where your grandfather went to school," I remind Josh. "The Air Force Academy used to be here, in the old days."

He's staring out at the buildings, orange and yellowish stucco, behind the dreamy veil of rain.

"That's cool," he says, not truly present. I don't know what he's dreaming about. I've got Fishel Kaplan, a.k.a. Philip Kaplan Cheuse, and a local author, Dostoyevsky, on my mind. The colors of the houses, the light, clinging rain, and, as we pull into the station with its broad expanse of columns and arches, an odd mixture of classical and art deco design all make me feel as if I am entering the set for an epic or opera.

I feel a rush of blood and electricity through my body. *Ah-ha, Oll-an, you finally got here!* my father says to me. *Velcome. Velcome, velcome to Leningrad!* His familiar voice is alive again in my mind.

The Finland Station! Lenin stepped off the train here and went out to address a meeting that changed the world. I want to linger here, stare through the drizzle at the milling mobs of travellers, some in Western dress, others in the drab, grey clothing that we saw first in the Vyborg waiting room, the cheap mass-produced clothes worn by down-and-outers on welfare in the United States.

Just as I'm wondering how and where and when the fabled Russian Intourist people will make contact with us, as they're supposed to, a young man in a zipper jacket and corduroys looking much like an American university teaching assistant comes up and asks for us by name in good English. We shake hands, and he hails a porter, a red-faced fellow with the look of a drunkard right out of Dostoyevsky. This man wrangles with our guide the entire time he is hoisting our few bags onto his dolly and pushing the load with us across the station to the street. The topmost bag seems about to fall and the man from Intourist points that out to the porter, who, with a grumble, thrusts out his hand to keep it from slipping off, cursing the guide under his breath, and this goes on all the way to the curb where a black Volga (the fanciest of the three Russian makes of automobile) is waiting, the driver in attendance. Our luggage disappears into the trunk, our guide fades away into the crowd at the station, and we drive off, leaving the porter standing alone in the rain.

"No tipping?" Josh asks.

"No," I say. "Not the style here."

"Different," he says, looking out at the rutted, unpaved streets, the houses that seem to be held up by a mixture of fading paint, and the rain, "really different."

We roar along the streets for what seems like thirty minutes until we cross one of the city's famous canals. Such wide avenues as these we've never seen before, though there's not a lot of traffic—crowds at street corners wait for buses, and once I glimpse a sign that has to be the entrance to the Leningrad metro. We pass high-rise apartment buildings under construction, drive around massive lakes in the roadway, then turn back onto smooth blocks of good road and old buildings. This city seems to emerge out of the mist like some scene in a bas-relief, some living metropolis etched in copper and paint.

FIVE

Our hotel stands out because of its sleek outward design—Finnish conceived and built, says our brochure. Glass and concrete, wide modern entrance, very up-to-date, a huge lobby, the vast entrance facing onto the massive monument to the dead of the Great Patriotic War—that's World War II.

But our first Russian hotel room is small, and I remember being warned by a returning traveller earlier in the summer that the beds would be tiny, too, and they are, but I can just manage to fit my six-foot length onto it without turning myself into a pretzel. The bathroom seems up to U.S. modern motel standard, though nothing fancy. However, this is Russian *deluxe*, so it's clear that everything they say about accommodations has to be taken down a grade in order to make it true.

Our room faces west, looks onto the apartment house across the way where clothes hang from lines on a number of balconies. Weeds glisten in puddles illuminated by street lamps, exaggerating the contrast between our neat room and the bedraggled outward facade of the apartment building. After we unpack, Josh and I ride the elevator down to the lobby in anticipation of our first real Russian meal.

The maître d' at first turns us away at the dining room. We remonstrate about our status as hotel guests and finally he grudgingly admits us to the room, a vast, high-ceilinged place with a stage and a large dance floor in the center of the space. The band is in the middle of a tune, an awful imitation of American disco, but the couples on the dance floor, in imitation of American disco dancers, don't seem to mind. All around us people are eating, drinking vodka and champagne. Our first evening in Russia, and it feels as though we've stumbled by mistake into a bad New Year's Eve party at the Kiwanis Club in Des Moines. It's so garish, the vulgarity of it so stupefying, that I have the sickening feeling which comes when you're a teenager and you catch your parents kissing.

The menu offers many choices, but only one kind of beef dish and another of chicken are actually available—and the meal I order turns out to be some kind of beef cutlet smothered in mushroom sauce with some carefully fried potatoes and carved radishes on the side.

"This music is making me sick," Josh says. A little later up in the room he appears to be already stricken with a slight case of dysentery and wants to go to sleep. I tell him goodnight and head down on the elevator to further explore the hotel.

I've heard about the so-called dollar bars or hard-currency bars, the only place where you can hear music and sit as if in a Western cafe. I follow the signs through the lobby and down the stairs. Loud disco music on cassette tape and cigarette smoke fill the room. The Russians seem not to have heard any warnings about smoking and lung cancer such as we've learned to take seriously in the U.S. There are many inebriated single men at the bar and many attractive single women at the tables. It doesn't take but a minute before one of the women is looking at me and wildly patting an empty seat at her table.

She's got medium length brown hair, a face out of a Renaissance painting, feathers and sequins on her black cotton sweater. In our country she could appear in an advertisement in the pages of *Vogue* or *Harper's Bazaar.* Up close I see that she wears no make-up, that all of her attractiveness is completely natural. No perfume either, though she has about her the odor of some foreign treatment for cleaning clothes, a slight tinge of gasoline mixed with the fumes of the cigarette she's puffing lightly every fifth second.

"Good evenings," she says in a husky, heavily accented English, inching over on the bench so that her thigh makes contact with mine.

"Hello," I say, suddenly remembering another warning given me earlier in the summer. "I haven't seen them," I was told, "but a man I met from the U.S. consulate told me that at the tourist hotels you can see some of the most beautiful whores in the world. He said that they come to meet the Finnish men who take weekends in Leningrad."

So, the beds are short, and the hookers are extraordinary.

"Drink champagne?" the woman says to me.

I nod and buy a bottle, as much to experiment with the taste as to make a party. Without the warning, I might have been stupid enough to think that the woman was actually motioning me to her table as someone other than just another potential customer. I realize as we talk a little – her English is terrible, and my Russian is virtually nonexistent, so "talk" might not be the correct word for it—that at first she thought that I was a Finn. When she realizes I'm an American her efforts at seduction only increase.

"You like Russian woman?" she asks.

I pretend that this is an abstract question. I nod.

"I am business girl, understand?"

I nod again.

"So you have American dollars? You come to my homes only fifty dollars. You come to my homes?"

Now I shake my head in the negative.

"Why you don't want to come to my homes?" A puzzled expression crosses her lovely face. "My homes is very nice. I make design of Japanese. You like this? Very nice homes."

Still I shake my head.

"You want sleeping? You come to my homes for sleeping, only fifty dollars. You want?"

I try to explain that I *don't* want, and add that my son is upstairs asleep and that I won't abandon him. I suppose I want to leave her with the impression that he's a child, but she's launching into an explanation about her own child, a seven-year-old boy named Vladimir. Her name, which she only then tells me, is Irina.

"So you come? How old your son?"

I tell her the truth.

"Twenty? You want to bring your son for sleeping too?"

"No, no," I protest.

"I am business girl," she says. Something flares in her eyes then flickers out. "Don't want to come to my homes? Buy me cigarettes."

I buy her a pack of Marlboros at the bar. When I return to her table she starts in again on me with a more intense pitch about coming to her homes, and she's working her full thigh against mine as if she's realized that she's had to turn up her approach by several degrees. All around us there is similar action at other tables, with just as many business girls as tourists. The alcohol, the cigarette smoke, the loud, awful music, the lovely women making their pitches, all conspire to give a picture of decadence quite unlike any I've ever seen outside of American gangster films. Here we are in the Soviet Union, and I'm a figure in a living tableau that seems to be the antithesis of everything Soviet life is supposed to stand for. I feel a wave of shame passing over me at my naiveté. We could be in Berlin in the twenties, the Copacabana in the thirties—and all of this is obviously approved, perhaps even encouraged by the authorities, because of the foreign currency it brings in? As a way of keeping foreign tourists amused and apart from ordinary Soviet citizens at night? A way of picking up useful bits of information that foreign tourists might let slip, from black market activities or minor smuggling to business strategies, whatever?

Or is it more loosely organized? Difficult to say. Difficult to think straight about much of anything with this lovely girl trying to entice me to her homes. But I recall myself to my purpose, excuse myself and stagger off to the room.

Sometime in the night my father begins talking to me.

You see, he says, *these Russian girls, how beautiful they are?*

Very tempting, I say. Were you ever tempted?

Don't be ridiculous. Of course I was. And I gave in. When I was Josh's age, I gave in all the time. Didn't I ever tell you about the girls in Khiva where I happened to be stationed? Not the prostitutes, but the others? I told you this, didn't I?

I suppose you did, but I don't remember.

So now you know.

So now I know.

The next morning we don't waste time getting to the street, a long avenue lined with shops that display mediocre consumer goods, bolts of cloth in one store, shabbily made suitcases in another, men's clothes in another, children's wear in another, and here and there a few people stare through the glass, and in some of the stores people are lined up at registers.

We reach the entrance to the Metro, and decide to chance it. Our destination is the Hermitage, the fabulous former residence of the czars in winter, now one of the world's great museums. So we descend, down, down, down the escalator, and the twenties design of the Russian underground gives the impression that one is going down into the pit in a film like Fritz Lang's *Metropolis.* Down, down—the subway here makes the London Underground look like a shallow trench. We come to a long passageway with doors every few feet, figure out our direction, and wait for the doors to open. Josh guesses that these are more elevators, but they turn out to be doors that coincide with the doors of the subway cars. In a few seconds a car roars in, stops, the doors open, we enter and we're off riding underground across the city toward the Neva River. We get a few stares, not many, as we hang on to the straps on a very smooth ride.

We leave the train and ride the escalator back up to the street and wander through a section of town that could, in rain and darkness, seem really drear. Adequately dressed (everyone seems to be adequately dressed here, but nothing more) crowds line up at street-corner vendors to buy bunches of grapes, and at the doors of vegetable shops where turnips or cabbages are piled into pyramids in the window. Here and there is a meat store, there a small department store with a window display of shoes. With the typical European notion of separation of goods, so that a shopper must go to a butcher shop, a vegetable and fruit vendor, a dairy store, and then a bakery in order to buy the stuffs for a balanced meal, and with the tripartite Russian process of choosing, paying, and picking up items within each variety of store, the Soviet shopper has a weary time ahead each and every day since this, as well as an inadequate distribution system of goods and frequent shortages, makes it necessary for a family either to hoard goods and watch them spoil or have someone make the rounds every day for every need. The sweet odor of burning tobacco mingles with the smells from the gutters where water pools at every other step.

After reaching Nevsky Prospect we get lost, but this main thoroughfare of shops is swarming with people and we enjoy the human parade. Now and then students approach us asking if we want to trade goods, and Josh arranges to meet one of them at our hotel later this evening. Soldiers, workers, bureaucrats—the streets are filled with all types and sizes of Russians, lean, squat, tall, small. We're losing something of that effect we felt last night at the first stop over the border, when it seemed as though we had stumbled onto a stage set to which central casting had sent up a couple of hundred extras dressed as Russian peasants in a movie.

The sun that warms us slightly also warms the sidewalks of Nevsky Prospect, and the hundreds, thousands of faces we pass—mothers with children dressed like little dolls; the militiamen in their khakis; the loungers in jeans; the pretty, slender girls dressed as though they're heading for a tea party. Josh wears his Fila cap turned sideways on his head, and using his camera every few minutes draws sly stares from the passersby. I try to picture my father in such a crowd . . .

In 1970, about a dozen years before his death, he and my mother took a tour to the Soviet Union, to Moscow, Leningrad, and Yalta. I know now—having filled out the visa forms myself—that he had to lie on the form since there is a question about previous Russian citizenship and how, if you were a Russian, you lost it or gave it up. Since he left the borders of the Soviet Union in an army airplane, in the mid-thirties, under circumstances that you would have to call a series of "misadventures," he would find it difficult to explain himself to any Soviet official on the question of his citizenship. He sometimes found it difficult, I think, to explain it to himself and so began some years before his death to write it all down. His manuscript is a sort of visa application in which he could set down the truth as he remembered it. On the actual application he lied. Otherwise he would not have been granted the visa. Born—American. That's how he put it. His passport declared him a naturalized citizen, not listing country of origin. He guessed that he'd simply fade into the large tour group they travelled with, and he was right. He and my mother had no trouble at all maintaining their anonymity as two American tourists, since the Soviets, or at least the Soviet bureaucrats, much prefer to deal with groups rather than individuals, as Josh and I have already learned. So they arrived in Leningrad, with Phil ready to show my mother where he had gone to school. And, they turned one of these corners and saw—a park. No Air Force Academy! The buildings had been razed by Nazi shellfire during the siege of the city. And when he saw the large, empty space where once his school had stood (the academy having moved elsewhere to be rebuilt) he burst into tears. In fact, he cried almost all the time during the weeks they were in the Soviet Union. He cried during the ballet, during the concerts, during the circus, sometimes during the bus tours.

That's right, Oll-an, he says in my head. *And wouldn't you have wept if you had been me? Returning to all these places of my young manhood? Who would not have wept?*

I'm almost weeping now, I say. Dad? I could weep because of the way I hear you in my mind.

Is that where I am? he says. *I'm just in your mind? Listen, you feel me in your chest, you know that, you feel me pressing on your heart, don't you? That's where I am, too.*

I feel that, I admit. I am this crazy, crazy, crazy man walking along the Nevsky Prospect talking to a ghost in my brain. And in my chest, yes, and in my heart.

We never talked like this before, I tell him.

No, no, we never did. I couldn't talk to you.

And I couldn't talk to you, I say. I couldn't talk. I didn't know who I was.

And I knew who I was? That's why we couldn't talk, we didn't know ourselves, so how could we know each other?

We reach the square before the Winter Palace, a vast space that seems to bleed off into the northern light where the land gives way to the Arctic Ocean, space that flows toward Moscow to the southeast, where the country rolls and rolls onward—how do I know this? I have my maps with me, I read the maps—toward the distant Urals. Jack Reed, hero of my first novel, barged his way past the Bolshevik guards who had just stormed the palace, and wandered about making notes just as I am now. This confluence of forces, my father, Reed, Josh: it staggers me to think how so many once apparently disparate elements in life all come together to create a pattern. One writes novels to make a pattern out of life, but what does one do when life seems to be making patterns of its own?

Reed, are *you* there too? I ask in my head, staring up into the afternoon sky, an off-white sheet of something like heavy silk or finely sliced shale stretching over us to the four horizons.

No answer.

Dad?

Nothing from him either.

"Dad?"

Josh elbows me in the side.

"What are you doing just standing there?" He's finished taking some pictures of the palace from the outside, and now he wants to hurry in. I prevail on him to take my photograph where Reed once stood. He does so, but grudgingly. I know the artist in him balks at taking mere pictures of people without an aesthetic incentive. I would be the same way. I am the same way.

We spend the next several hours in the Hermitage museum, this stately building with marble pillars thicker around than sequoias, gold inlay everywhere, rooms filled with—among other works—Impressionist paintings usually never shown in the West, before this year never even reproduced in the West. I shiver at the sight of some of them, that pleasurable shock of seeing great new art—it doesn't happen often these days—the tingling in the blood, the surge in the mind. It's like meeting an attractive new lover!

When we leave the museum we cross the street to the quai on the Neva where a tour boat is moored, and off we go on a river trip, several miles in one direction, then back in the other, gawking at old palaces and new government buildings, parks and piers. On these embankments my father once walked. Dostoyevsky also walked here, and here dreamed his dreamy hero of *White Nights,* here conjured up the bizarre figure familiar to all us all, the Underground Man. My father comes to mind again, and I picture him on one of these boating trips, perhaps in a party of cadets, or later, after he got to know the city, maybe like that fellow sitting up ahead near the bow, the young man in uniform with his arm around a slender blonde girl.

This complex life of thought and feeling, time and presence—here I am riding this boat with my son, watching the shore, the couple, the other parties, almost all of them Leningradites out for a Sunday ride, thinking about my father,

Dostoyevsky's heroes, my ex-wife, lost loves, past life, the present, the ache of solitude. All of it comes together–and I can't write fast enough in this journal to catch the impression of how it all feels in this singular complexity of everything at once. Some art forms give you the look of things, some give you noise of experience, some give you the feel of it, but no art form gives you everything–sight, sound, taste, smell, feel, the internal action and the outside world pressing in on you–except life itself. But life is inexpressible while you're living it. Perhaps death is the art of life, and when we die we do not go to some undiscovered country but to a place beyond life where we can recreate it in its plenitude of senses and thoughts.

But what a bunch of paradoxes to carry on board a river boat on the swiftly flowing Neva!

Now, when the boat stops, I see my father disembarking, see him helping the young girl back onto the pier, and then onto the pavement. They're crossing the road to the Winter Palace side, and he's discoursing about the paintings in the museum, about the tyrannical nature of the czars and the possibilities for life and unlimited freedom under the new government, and though she remains silent as he speaks he can tell by the way in which her body sways while walking and her hip gently bumps against his, that she feels sympathy for him and his ideals, and he puffs on his pipe and points up at the sky, the sweeping white clouds blowing in from the Baltic, the bluer horizon toward the north, the colder regions, the pole.

She's a city girl just out of school who still lives with her family–grandparents on her mother's side–mother and father, two younger brothers, and an uncle and his family–all in three rooms, near the Moscow station. Her father works for the railroad and now and then comes up with a pretty souvenir as a result, such as the bar of French soap that she's redolent with this afternoon while walking with her Red Army Air Force cadet, taking his arm now, steering him along the embankment–they both love to walk along the river, they discover–and after the boat ride they know what it feels like to be out there on the water, the clouds overhead catching the late afternoon sun, a respite from all these recent summer rains.

And where are you from? she asks him, and he begins his tale of Tikhorechka, the village where he was born, and life in Zhitomir where he grew up, the great love he feels toward his mother, who was so sorrowful when he left for the academy, but he does write her every week, not just out of duty but with the genuine love he hopes one day his own children will feel for him, of course he'll have children, with a woman whom he will honor like no other creature in the world—and he recites Pushkin to her on the subject of romance, and Tolstoy on the importance of a true loving marriage, and explains that he believes he can have both kinds of life, his adventures as a flier, which he is sure he will have once he graduates from the academy, and the family life, as well, because he is devoted to his mother, and any glory that he achieves in battle would only reflect on her, and on the woman he loves.

She seems to move closer to him at these words, though it's difficult to imagine how they can walk if they are pressed together any more than before, but they stroll slowly away along the embankment, toward the bridge, and if they walk along the other side they'll soon reach the park before the Peter and Paul fortress, with its high walls that offer shelter to lovers in the oncoming dark.

And then they're gone, faded away into the crowds on the bridge, and the water flows grey beneath the abutment as the sky turns strangely copper in the twilight that has crept upon the city.

We have a visitor at the hotel the next morning before we depart from Leningrad, a friend of a friend, a young foreign service officer from the U.S. consulate here, and when we tell him that we're leaving for Moscow on the day train he's amazed. No one that he's heard of before has been allowed to travel on the day train. They've always put American tourists on the sleeper that takes longer and travels through the night. Perhaps there's a bit of a thaw going on under

Gorbachev? he wonders aloud, and puts this bit of information into some file in his head for further consideration.

Our driver appears, and we load our luggage into the trunk of the black Volga and we're off, in the rain, to the station. The driver is playing American big band music of the forties on the radio. I ask about it, and he turns around and, with a broad smile that immediately dispells the coolness that he had maintained until now, says how much he likes the big bands.

"Gleen Mee-ler, Tahm-y Dor-say, you know them?"

"Sure," I say, "and how about Bunny Berrigan, do you know him?"

And this burly Intourist driver, the model of the American notion of what the KGB might send to keep watch on suspect tourists, launches into a chorus of Bunny Berrigan's most famous tune.

I've flown around
Dee vorld in a plane,
I've settled revolutions
In Spain,
But I'm broken hearted
'Cause I can't get started
Vith you . . .

Holding that smile, he delivers us to the Intourist functionary waiting at the Moscow station, and this fellow in turn leads us to the proper platform. In a few minutes we board the train and soon we're rolling southeast past rye fields, open farmland, a few stands of birch forest here and there, a village tucked away along a creekside, toward the heartland of this vast country.

Other passengers keep our attention more than the countryside, though: the family opposite us, each member with a book in hand, and now and then one or the other of the parents calls the rest of the family's attention to a particular passage and reads it aloud; the couple in front of us, both in jogging suits, the woman with her hair all frizzed up, the man with a mustache, slightly balding, the picture of an intellectual on an outing; across from them sit an elderly couple, the man in jeans and checkered shirt, the woman in a suit, who might be riding the el through a Chicago suburb.

I try to read, Josh puts on his Walkman. Before too long a young, dark-complected boy about ten or eleven comes down the aisle and studies Josh as he listens to the music. He says something in Russian and when I tell him that I don't understand he gets a funny look on his face. Who are we? he makes his meaning clear. I tell him that we're Americans, and his eyes light up. He points to the Walkman and Josh takes one earplug out and puts it against the boy's ear. His eyes turn wider still. His name is Aram, and when his parents look around they, too, reveal themselves by their faces as citizens from the Armenian Soviet Socialist Republic. Aram wants to borrow the Walkman to show his mother, and Josh accedes.

"Dee vorkers control dee means of dee Valkman," he says, squinting up at the roof of the car. "What's that horrible stuff on the loudspeaker?"

These trains have loudspeakers that broadcast music of several varieties throughout the trip, and this speaker has suddenly flared up much louder than during the first hour of the ride, spitting some bouncy synthetic rock and roll into the car:

Cheri, Cheri, Baby,
Let me be your lover . . .

"I don't know," I say to Josh, "but it's awful isn't it?"

Cheri, Cheri, Baby,
You know how much
I want you . . .

"Excuse me," I say, tapping the balding guy in the jogging suit on his broad shoulder. "Do you speak English?"

He nods, and I ask him who the singing group is.

"Oh," he says with a smile of recognition, "that's Modern Talking, very popular group in Soviet Union."

"Oh, of course," Josh says to me in a jaunty imitation of the man's accent once he has turned away, "Modern Talking, very popular—ughh!" And he steps past me and heads up the aisle to retrieve his Walkman from young Aram who has been listening to Josh's Big Audio Dynamite cassette.

While he is gone I learn that the couple in the jogging suits are East Germans. The woman is the conductor of a ballet orchestra and the man, her husband, is the pianist in the orchestra. They're on vacation, heading to Moscow to visit friends.

"Why aren't they defecting?" Josh asks when he's come back and I've explained who the people are. "They're going in the wrong direction."

He's joking, but the thought has already come to my mind. Here are these millions of Russians and Soviet bloc citizens and they're going about their business, struggling to get through their ordinary days, brushing their teeth, dressing their children, working, eating, kissing, singing, tapping their feet, worrying, suffering headache, heartache, pleasures, anxieties, having dreams and ideas and nightmares and birthdays and promotions and shortages and hesitations and making decisions right and wrong, getting caught at cheating or praised for conservation, taking the river boat ride, walking through the Impressionist rooms at the Hermitage, lining up for suitcases, riding the Metro, driving cabs and walking and swimming and sometimes stopping to stare into space, and occasionally suffering with a cold or a fever or a sore toe, or eating chicken or fish and drinking vodka or Pepsi or *kvass*, most of them rooted in their lives like trees in a forest, but never, never making a move toward the West . . .

We'd been prepared for a police state. Where's the KGB? Josh asks from time to time. But we haven't seen a single armed policeman, not one threatening incident, since the border.

Obviously, this is quite a different place than we've had pictured for us by emigrés and our own propagandists, quite another place all its own—another world right here on our own planet. Reading the great Russian works has prepared me a little for the Russian soul and for the Russian landscape, at least this western part, and my father's story has prepared me somewhat for the romantic side of things, and reading *Zhivago* should have prepared me for the yoking of great heart and imagination and cruelty that seems to characterize the current system, and yet, and yet . . . there is more here for me to learn, more than I could imagine from just reading and from living with (and without) my father—and I have this feeling that we're on the trail, hot on the trail.

But on the trail of what? Of a Russian ghost? We don't have the language and we're not historians and all we have is the deep emotions that we carry because of Phil, because of our lives with him, and his life here before us.

And that's not enough to satisfy you? comes his voice.

Dad?

What about your D. H. Lawrence you like so much? Didn't he just walk into an Indian village and think he knew everything he needed to know in a few minutes?

Thanks, I say to him, or to myself, whomever I'm conducting this conversation with. But that was Lawrence, he was a genius, and . . .

Look, Oll-an, he says, *he was just somebody riding a train just like you before he got to be that big writer you worship. Listen, haven't I been a hero? But you know what I was before I was a hero? I was a dreamy-headed boy, just like you.*

I'm hardly a boy anymore—dreamy-headed maybe, but I'm in my forties.

Darling, you'll always be a boy to me. I remember the first time I heard you cry out . . .

Moscow! We're approaching Moscow! In the dark of the early evening lights lights lights like stable fires fill up the space around the train. Moscow! Capital of all this strange alternative world on our common planet. Moscow! Moscow! Who wouldn't be diverted from even the most serious of conversations at the prospect of rolling into the station of one of the world's great capitals! *Moskva! Moskva!* Even my father's spirit in my head joins in the chant.

SIX

ONCE WE PASSED OVER SAMARKAND, THE SUN overtook our squadron. The blazing ball of light hung above us in the cloudless sky, while we sat—as if motionless—in our open cockpits. The glare grew more annoying when the sun passed us and grew larger as it neared the western horizon.

Major Smirnov altered our course slightly, north by northwest. We were approaching Chardzhou. The dark grey waters of the Amu-Darya divided the lush landscape beneath us. The river resembled a boa constrictor which had stretched itself north, slightly coiled and reaching from horizon to horizon. Nestled on the banks were hamlets and fields laid out in checkered squares and a spiderlike railroad line with a toy train speeding along the western side of the river toward a larger settlement.

So this was Chardzhou! Delicate lines of cottages were strung through green tree-lined streets.

"Calling Aerodrome Chardzhou," I heard Major Smirnov say in my helmet through the dull roar of my plane's engine. "My squadron approaches. Acknowledge. Peredayou!"

"Operational post, Aerodrome Chardzhou. Identify your flight! Peredayou!"

"Twenty-one eagles in flight to their nesting place."

"Turf area clear for landing. Wind zero to five kilometers, southwest." A pause filled with the crackling of static followed. "Alloh, alloh! Tovarich major and your twenty-one eagles. You will notice that the oil storage area is blackened and in ruins. This is the result of a fire which was started when hand grenades were tossed into our benzine tanks by guerillas who infiltrated the field during the night."

"Can we expect to be fired upon when we descend?"

"No, no, no! The band was dispersed after the attack, and the area around the aerodrome is now secured by a regiment of Red Army infantry. It has never happened before and you may rest assured it will never happen again. We can see your machines now as well as hear them. The sun is reflecting off your wings and makes you appear as if on fire."

"God forbid!" I involuntarily said to myself, visualizing the plight of a pilot without a parachute in the cockpit of a burning plane.

Sasha Kadikoff and I were the last ships of the seven echelons consisting of three istrebitels each to circle the Chardzhou aerodrome prior to landing. As we neared the ground, I saw bivouacs close to the barbed wire fence around the landing field. On the fringes were black smudges of burned grass, and ruptured drums scattered around the skeleton of a burned-out building. The charred remains of a hangarful of De Havilland bombers lay in a caved-in pile, mute testimony to what must have transpired during the predawn attach by the Basmachi.

We taxied over to an intact tent hangar, cut our engines, and climbed out.

"My tail is dragging," I said when we were out of our samolets, beating Sasha to his favorite expression.

"Nu, Fishka? What did you expect?" Sasha wrinkled his face as he pulled up his goggles and focused his gaze on the ruins of the hangar.

"Looks like our work is cut out for us," I said. "Looks to me like there's a war on around here."

"I guess it's not for nothing that we were taught the trade we were taught, Fishka." Sasha shrugged his shoulder and made a wry face. "I never would have believed this if I weren't seeing it with my own eyes."

"And not a solitary word about this in our papers! Pinch me, Sasha. Could all this be a nightmare! Is it possible to keep a mess like this a secret?" A ground crew sergeant hurried over ahead of his men to take charge of our ships.

"You are being lodged in that unfinished, tar paper-roof barrack," said the sergeant, pointing. "You can wash up there, and a hot meal is being readied for you in the mess hall. Pilaff with raisins. That's rice with lamb meat." The sergeant saluted us and turned his attention to our planes. "Right from the factory!"

The barrack was one of a row just inside a barbed wire fence on the boundary of the field. Inside the building were two dozen cast-iron beds with night stands and shelves for our belongings. There were windows, some with blown-out frames and glass shattered by some kind of explosion. Besides the odor of fresh pine of which the barracks were built, there was a strong smell of carbolic acid in the air.

We filed in, washed up, tossed chunks of soap at each other, and plopped down to relax luxuriously on our beds. Most of the men of our squadron were feeling playful, despite the evidence of destruction we had seen.

"The last man to reach the mess hall is a dodo bird!" someone poked a head through the door and shouted. "Supper is served!"

Those among us who were more hungry than tired leapt up and raced for the door, others rose and proceeded with somewhat more dignity. Followed by Lieutenant Kadikoff, I stepped out of the barracks and met Major Belomirov, our political commissar. "Kaplan? And you must be Lieutenant Kadikoff. Where is what's-his-name?"

"Tyatin? He must be close behind."

"I did not have time to become acquainted with you three in Tashkent. You will sit at a table with me so we can talk."

"Over here, Nicky!"

"I am Battalion Commander Belomirov, your squadron's commissar." The major shook hands and introduced himself to Captain Tyatin. "Did you find the flight tiring, comrades? No doubt there are questions you wish to ask me." He glanced at the charred tent, then lowered his eyes and looked at his boots as we proceeded to the mess hall.

"We understand the situation, tovarich Commander," Tyatin said. The major was an unmistakingly friendly man, probably nearing forty, and he impressed us with his fatherly manner. "Bit by bit, from the boys, we've gotten the picture."

"Then this did not shock you?" he said as we entered the mess hall, nodding in the direction of the ruined hangar full of burnt planes.

Tyatin continued to act as our spokesman. "Actually, up until a couple of days ago, we had no idea. Why all the secrecy? Why not rally . . . ?"

"This is like trying to talk to my son about sex," the major mumbled to himself. "The situation here is quite illicit." The air in the dining room was heavy with the day's heat and thick with the odor of cottonseed oil, fried onions, bacon, and boiled lamb. "There's good reason for keeping this trouble secret. Word of it would only serve to encourage our enemies. It is no secret *here* that this harassment against us is being financed and encouraged from abroad. We believe that without publicity of what is being accomplished with the munitions, the source of money will dry up in due time. Let those who contribute think that they are being swindled! It's therefore imperative that we fight our enemies with all the energy and weapons we have, and at the same time keep silent about what we are accomplishing. Understood?"

"Just so, tovarich Commander."

"Understood!" I said, nodding.

"From a political point of view, it makes sense." Tyatin smiled.

"This is the reason Major Smirnov had given you an order not to write or talk about it," Major Belomirov went on. "Not your girl friends, not even your wife, Tyatin, must hear of what or whom we are fighting. I can tell you, confidentially of course, about some Red Army men who had been discharged from the service and who learned too late that they should not have blabbed about their exploits in Khorezm. You must not repeat this, but there was one ex-army man, a simpleton who had been wounded in action and discharged. He could not keep quiet whenever he got drunk. This simpleton was warned that if he could not hold his tongue they would have to cut it out of him, and so they did. The argument is that they should not have gone this far when he could have been shot in the first place."

I suddenly saw the pieces of lamb meat in my plate as pieces of human tongue, torn out to keep one from talking.

"This is lamb, not ham, Fishka," joked Tyatin, noticing my reaction.

"Are you not listening to me, Kaplan?"

"I beg your pardon, Major."

"Kaplan is not partial to ham," explained Tyatin sheepishly.

"In your case, Kaplan, your people are more cosmopolitan, as Comrade Stalin has so correctly stated, and more literate, and therefore writing . . ."

"I shall refrain from writing or talking about our business here, Major. As for 'my people,' " the words boiled out from inside me, "can you please tell me who we are, how we are different? What are 'my people'? Am I not as Russian as any of you? Do I not love my motherland the same as you do? And what does 'cosmopolitan' mean, by the way?"

"By cosmopolitan we must presume Comrade Stalin meant that the Jewish people are residing in cities all over the world," the political commissar said between forkfuls of food.

"The same can be said about the Christian people, Major."

"In your case, this discussion is academic, Kaplan. I saw the resumé of your political activities before we took off from Tashkent. You were born in a small town in the Ukraine. What is it's name?"

"Tikhorechka. It's a town on the northwestern boundaries of the province of Volynsk."

"That would make it now a town in the district of Zhitomir."

"That is correct, Major."

"Are your parents still living there?"

"We were forced to run away from Tikhorechka soon after the Civil War started. The countryside was at the mercy of marauding bands who robbed and killed indiscriminately, but

Jews in particular. It wasn't much better in the larger towns and cities, but somehow we felt the need to flee. We fled to Zhitomir."

"Is that where your family is living now, in Zhitomir?"

"My mother is living there. She's being cared for by an aunt and uncle of mine. My mother, I'm afraid, is ill with tuberculosis."

"Isn't your father living, Kaplan?"

"He is among the living, Major."

"If your father is among the living, why then is he not the one caring for your ailing mother."

"My parents had become separated."

"If your parents are separated, Kaplan, where then is your father presently living? Also in Zhitomir?"

I had dreaded the day this question would be asked of me. Lieutenant Kadikoff was the only person who knew that my father was in America, and we had decided that if ever I were asked officially where my family was living, I would tell the truth without hesitation lest this question lead to accusations of subterfuge.

"My father is living in America, Major," I said.

"Oh? And when did your father emigrate to America, before or after the October Revolution?" The major was so overcome with surprise he held his forkful of rice in midair while all the time he looked at me as if seeing me for the first time.

"My father left for America before the Revolution to escape the conditions we all suffered under the czar."

"How is it that he left your mother and you behind?"

"I also have a brother and a sister. My father sent for them as soon as he had earned their passage money. By the time the three of them had saved up enough to send for my mother and me, the World War had erupted, then the Revolution and then the Civil War. When next my father sent for us, I was refused an exit visa to travel to America and my mother refused to leave me behind." Sasha Kadikoff stole a glance at me when I was done explaining. His look was pathetic. He was clearly upset that the secret he and I had harbored for years was now out in the open, since, among other negative possibilities, it no longer served us as proof of our abiding friendship.

However, the ease and the unhesitating manner with which I answered the questions apparently allayed the major's suspicions, if he had any, because now his lips were forming into an indulgent smile that clearly suggested he had prompted my story out of interest, not suspicion, and now he had heard enough.

"Just think of it, Fishka!" Captain Tyatin said with great sincerity in his voice. "But for a tiny twist of fate, you could be an American right now!"

We slept late the following morning. I arose happy that I had not been awakened by a whistle. A pair of Red Army men doing orderly duty informed those of us who were awake that breakfast was being served in the mess hall until eleven. I got up and pulled the blanket off Sasha Kadikoff who jumped out of bed, winked at me, then delivered a swift kick into the protruding posterior of Nicholas Tyatin. Then Nicky joined us as we next hurled a barrage of our straw-filled pillows at the sleeping lieutenants Baranin and Koshkin.

"There are straight razors in the washroom," one of the orderlies told us.

"These boys are so young," Koshkin said, "that they've never even heard of shaving."

"We shave at least once a week," said Kadikoff. "How often do you shave? In the spring and in the fall?"

"Hurry, hurry, kiddies!" Tyatin was shouting from the washroom, "I'm hungry as a bear!"

"There are so few of us here," I said. "Where is everybody?"

"Probably in the mess hall, eating our breakfast."

"I hope it's as good as dinner was last night."

"It's tea and bread, comrades," an orderly informed us.

"I'll have none of that!" Lieutenant Koshkin yelled, summoning the orderly with the crook of his finger. "I want you to go and tell the cook to make me an onion omelet and that I want hot tea."

"Are you our squadron's officer for the day?" I asked.

"I am."

"Then will you please see that instead of water my thermos is filled with cold milk? I detest drinking lukewarm water on a prolonged flight. It makes me seasick," I said with a straight face as we left the barracks. "And if you could find me a soft pillow for my bucket seat. It doesn't have to be stuffed with down, but I do want it to be soft."

"While you're at it, comrade, make mine cold tea instead of cold milk," Nicky joined in without cracking a smile.

"You boobs are joking with me, of course!" said the officer of the day.

"Do you think it's safe to eat the ham with the eggs we're about to order for breakfast?" I asked Sasha.

"Make mine wheat cakes with honey and eggs," Sasha said and stopped abruptly. The shudder of a Liberty motor in a De Havilland bomber sounded over the field, and the drone of its propeller sounded erratic to our trained ears.

"It's not the engine, it's the pilot," Sasha said after looking up and pausing.

The bomber straddled the tops of the tents as it came in, much too fast for a normal landing.

"Not that much, not that much," I heard our O.D. mumble.

"Nose up! Nose up, little brother!" I cried.

"He's heading in too fast and too low," Sasha shouted.

The De Havilland swooshed over our heads. "Nose up, nose up," I whispered.

There were involuntary cries from all of us. The De Havilland plowed into the dirt with a force that tore away its undercarriage. We saw the propeller splinter as the nose dug into the earth, and watched as its tail rose, then stopped in the air.

"Switch off! Switch off," all of us cried out, fearful that the airplane might burst into fire as we ran to help the hapless men. We found the commander of the plane, and his lieutenant, hanging upside down, each strapped in his cockpit.

The engine was sizzling, spewing coolant, oil, and gasoline. The commander, in this case a major, was already dead. I could see where a stitch of machine gun bullets had entered his coat and exited through the top side of the fuselage. The lieutenant was alive in the front cockpit, and we cut him free from his harness, lifted him gently, and carried him some distance from the ship for fear that it would catch fire.

"Give him air, fellows! Hah! Look at his left hand! No wonder he couldn't operate the throttles!"

"A bullet did this to him?"

"No, you idiot, a bow and arrow!"

"Shrapnel?"

"The bastards don't have artillery, nothing more than machine guns, unless they captured one of our three-inchers."

Over the archway in the aerodrome's reading room was a sign which said, "Little Corner of Lenin." Lenin's bust in bronze sat prominently in the center of one of the walls. Between bookshelves there was also a large portrait of Stalin, and beneath a slogan printed on red bunting: "Glory to our great leader, Comrade Stalin!"

I had never before seen such a huge portrait. Beside it was one of Klimenty Voroshilov, the commander in chief of the Red Army. A slight breeze blew in through open windows and disturbed the newspapers strewn across a table: *Pravda* and *Izvestia,* and the army's *Red Star,* all several days old. There were no headlines in any of them, and the titles told of the approaching planting season which would in turn produce an abundant harvest, the coming plenary session of the Party, and of meetings and speeches regarding the Five Year Plan. It was all so dull it made one feel sorry for the typesetter whose job was to put all the dreary words together into print.

Lieutenant Koshkin came looking for us. "Commander Smirnov wants you, Kaplan, Tyatin, and you, Kadikoff. He has three Mauser pistols for you."

"I will swap my revolver for a Mauser," Lieutenant Baranin said, "if any of you wishes to swap."

"Mausers are too bulky to carry around!" Gorokhov said.

"If you're brought down, a Mauser is a better weapon to have!" Baranin argued.

"If you're brought down, little brother, all you will need is a bullet for yourself," Gorokhov said.

Sasha looked shocked. "They kill their prisoners?"

Things continued to look and sound more grim as the days went on. We heard reports of more and more attacks in the region. But our daily reconnaissance flights were largely uneventful. A week went by. We were flying in formation over the silvery grey waters of the Amu-Darya, which divided the Kyzyl Kum and the Kara Kum deserts when we heard the distressing broadcast over our radio.

". . . like a fortress . . ."

The fragmented words broke through with a burst of static and dissolved in my ears.

". . . it cannot be taken . . ."

Then: ". . . the devil take it! . . ." The voice was weak, but the man cursed with a hearty urgency.

Finally, and more clearly, I heard, "We need assistance, comrade, whoever you are, and we need it soon," the man pleaded, and I tried to imagine speaking those words myself.

"Berezhkov! Berezhkov!" It was Major Belomirov now, coming in loud and clear. "Move alongside Major Smirnov and signal for him to switch over to listen! Peredayou!"

"Just so, Major! I hear it also. Peredayou."

". . . a three-incher would do nicely! Send us a three-incher and we will pulverize their machine guns in the aperture of the minaret."

"We could use some kind of a hand grenade that would stick to the surface of these damned minarets. Our hand grenades bounce off and explode harmlessly! We need to blow in the minaret door so we can run in and rush them up the stairway. We need something! I've lost half my men already, without results!"

"I will try and raise the aerodrome at Khiva! Where exactly are you? Please give me the coordinates."

"Village Gorgan Teh. Coordinate thirty-seven."

"This is Major Smirnov speaking. How can my fighters be of assistance to you? And who is speaking, please?"

"This is Battalion Commander Gregorovich. Do you carry bombs on your samolets, Major Smirnov?"

"No. No bombs. But we each carry two fifty-caliber machine guns. We're only a few minutes flying time from

Gorgan Teh. Do you wish for us to come and help you silence those machine guns in the minaret? It will not take us much out of our way. Peredayou."

"I not only wish it, tovarich Major, I beg of you to do so! Thank you! I shall move my men back a little to avoid ricocheting bullets from your samolets. Thank you, Major, and thanks to your pilots."

We followed Major Smirnov as he banked to the left and led us westward into the Kara Kum side of the Amu-Darya.

"Squadron ready—form into one echelon of two!" Our formation lost shape, stretched out, and formed again into two lengths of ten planes each.

"We will come out of the sun and hit the top of the minaret first. Planes to the right break away to the right. Left to the left. Follow Berezhkov's ship and mine and reform. After the first strafing we will decide if we hammer the machine guns on top again or concentrate on knocking down the minaret's door."

Major Smirnov's orders were executed and the enemy machine gun on the minaret was smashed inside of ten minutes. On a second run the minaret's door was smashed down also. But, alas, inside those ten minutes, during the first seconds of the beginning of our strafing, one of our planes went down.

Whose was it? Whose guns had ceased firing? Whose plane failed to clear the minaret? Which of us had burst into flames and fallen from the sky? There could have been no survival, that was clear.

I did not know until we had finished with the minaret and our job was over. Major Smirnov took roll call as we roared back to Khiva. God, how the tears choked me! We had lost Captain Tyatin. Nicky was lost!

S E V E N

LIGHT LEAPED UP OVER THE WOODED ISLAND just across the mile-wide water to the east. Light seeped up toward the highest part of the eastern sky, as though the world had been momentarily turned upside down and the colors from the bottom of the waters had begun to spill out before things righted themselves. Light spread up out of the broad bay to the southeast, where the western river met the ocean.

Where the woods grew to the water's edge, deer stood in this first glow nibbling on leaves, dipping their oversize heads toward the water. But at the sound of men walking quietly among the trees they raced away, disappearing into the stand of dappled maples and oaks as though they had never existed.

The men, short in stature but moving as carefully as the deer, wore shirts and leggings made of leather. One squinted up at the sky, the others kept their eyes on the trail as they carried a long wooden boat down toward the beach just south of the point of woods. At the water they set the boat in the gently lapping surf and paddled out toward the rising dawn. Behind them other men and a few women stepped out of the woods and set to work digging in the sand. They spoke quietly among themselves, though now and then a voice raised a directive, or a laugh, which broke over the constant shush of the wind in the trees behind them, the splashing surf at their feet. When they looked out over the bay, their cousins in the long canoe had disappeared around the southern tip of the island, where the tide came from, pulled by the season's silver moon.

This was how young Alan pictured the Ompoge, the native tribe that first inhabited the wooded site that became the town of factories and refineries where he discovered at some early age he was living.

The Ompoge had lived here for hundreds, who knew? perhaps thousands of years before the Dutch sailed their boats into New York harbor and in a southerly direction down the Arthur Kill, the stretch of water that separated the western shore of the large island, Staten Island, from the wooded line of New Jersey. The Dutch sailed to the very point where the deer fed and the Indians dug for clams and set their rough boats into the bay to fish. The southern beach was washed by the river later called the Raritan, which came down from the wooded hills west of New Brunswick and plowed sluggishly through marshes that seemed as reedy as any flats of Egypt, before surging eastward toward the bay and the Atlantic.

Behind the Dutch came the English, the agents of the Lords Perth and Berkeley and Carteret. It was Perth who made claims on this woods and beach and encouraged the settlement that drove the Ompoge west into the fresher woods. In the mouths of the British, Ompoge became "Amboy" and the town became known as Perth's Amboy, or Perth Amboy.

Although the factories and oil refineries had sullied the waters of the bay so that long ago the clams on the bottom were ruined as food, still the water all around made the days into adventures for local boys—such as those summer afternoons when young Alan and his friends rented a rowboat down at the local yacht harbor and rowed out among the many tankers anchored where the Kill flowed into the bay.

But these boys knew little of tides, and one afternoon, no matter how hard they rowed—and they rowed until their hands turned raw and bleeding—the pull of the ocean hauled them past the tip of Staten Island and they began to panic, staring back at the receding land and up at the darkening canopy of sky, while feeling their hearts race and their legs tremble, until a large local motor yacht approached from the east and its owner towed them back to the docks.

Call it a sense of wonder. While most of the adults he knew lived their lives as they might have in any other town in America, whether near mountains or on the plains, the boy somehow saw things differently. Perhaps it *was* the proximity of kill and bay and sea, the tidal pull of the waters, and the special way the light appeared to him each morning at the edge of the land. Even as he became more and more entangled in the events and twisted wrangles of his family, his links to the water and island points seemed to enlarge his ability to feel.

His family wanted only the best for him. That's what they said. On Smith Street he had free run of the candy store, the chocolate, the comic books, the chewing gum, the sodas. Mama Sarah and Grandpa Isadore continued to lavish their special gifts upon him, and when Isadore died of the same cancer that had first eaten away his eye and then spread to his liver, Sarah moved in with Ed, the dour, white-haired candy man whom she had, apparently, been spending time with on the sly for years before her husband's illness and decline. Ed was no less generous with the stuff of the store than Isadore, though a lot less demonstrative in his affection.

"Sure, take," he'd say to the boy, handing him the newest copies of *Plastic Man* and *The Heap* and then disappearing behind the curtain that separated the little back kitchen from the rest of the shop. There he'd slurp the good soup that Sarah had prepared for him as sustenance for the long hours he would put in up front selling cigarettes and cigars and pipe tobacco and candy and sodas and magazines and newspapers and numbers. And the beer trucks pulled up at the curb and the drivers rolled the thundering barrels down the ramp and onto the pavement and into the sweet-yeasty saloon as though nothing had changed at all.

Other members of Tillie's family loomed large in the boy's life, Mama Sarah's sister Bess, Great Aunt Bess, a widow for many years, who lived with Great Grandma and her only child, Alan's cousin Marv, while commuting every day by train to Newark where she served as an executive secretary at a large federal agency. Bess worked hard outside the home while Great Grandma cooked and cleaned. But Bess played hard too, especially at the old piano on Sunday nights when Tillie and Phil and the boys and Marv and Great Gram would gather for Bess to lead everyone in singing the old songs, "My Gal Sal" and "Moonlight on the Wabash," "Pennies from Heaven," and "Paper Moon."

But it wouldn't be
Make believe if you
Believed in me . . .

Bess's forceful contralto cut through the long, difficult week like a knife, making everyone around the piano sing all the harder themselves, so joyful was the noise this woman made when she threw herself into song. Tillie's soprano voice surprised the boy with its delicacy. Who of those who knew his mother as a steady laborer who cooked and cleaned and washed and sewed would not have been surprised when she suddenly spit out sound like a bird at play? Marv, nine years older than Alan, sang too, and the younger cousins tried to follow along, but only just having been initiated into such matters as music, they faltered, and sometimes they stopped.

But Phil, it seemed, never joined in. This family of secretaries and shopkeepers, students and children, workers and singers, seemed to drag Phil down, down into dark regions of foreign moods.

"Phil, Phil!" Bess would call out to him from the piano as she raced gaily through the bridge to one of the tunes, "Come on and sing! You think you're better than us? Come on, come on!"

On one of these occasions Phil leaned down and touched his son Alan's shoulder and said, "You think this music is pretty? You should hear the songs we sang where I came from. Now that was real music, this is garbage." And he showed his incisors in a little half-snarl of contempt.

He scarcely did anything but show that face to life, or so it seemed to Alan. Up early and out to the Plymouth to drive from Perth Amboy to Linden and the General Motors plant—

out all day at work—and then returning after work to eat quickly and lie down on the sofa and listen to the radio, though the radio had been speaking its woes and advertisements throughout the meal itself.

"Hush, Oll-an," he'd say in that old refrain whenever the boy would try to talk about some event at school, or sports activity, or movie that he cared about. "Hush, Oll-an, I'm listening to the noose."

Or if the mother tried to arrange an outing for the weekend to come, an afternoon at her mother's, or a drive toward the Oranges, or an evening at Bess's, he would gather himself up and show those teeth his childhood had ruined, and say her name in such a way as to make her step back and consider retreat before trying to convince him again:

"Oh, Teel, Teelie, you know what I think of all that!"

The little tenderness he showed his boys came out only at bedtime, when he would kiss both brothers and stroke their hair, and tell them that he loved them more than life itself, and melodramatically roll his eyes upward in his head and declaim that he would gladly sacrifice himself if need be in order to keep them well and safe.

"I would stand between you and bullets," he said once. "I would go to the firing squad instead of you."

But he wouldn't go to a baseball game—not, as he put it, "for all the tea in China, and I've *been* to China!" And he would launch into a long diatribe on the stupidity of the game, the one sport that his older boy showed any aptitude for. "Those jerks running around the bases," he'd complain. "And the pitcher, how long does he have to take? And the batters, they just stand there waiting, waiting, and by the time they hit the ball I am bored."

Other fathers held other views. Even when the boys were as young as five and six, Ron Berkowitz's old man would take Ron and Alan out to the nearest park and toss around a softball with them. Better yet, he took them to a Yankee game where the vast, green field, the beautiful symmetry of the base paths, and the crowds in the stands, all conspired to make the boy believe for the first time that his father knew absolutely *nothing* about what he espoused. Cousin Marv treated him to another game soon after, and that became a ritual, leaving the moody and unaccountably angry-faced Phil behind on a weekend and taking the train into New York City and riding the subway uptown until it emerged out of the tunnels and roared above the tenement roofs and came to a stop at the subway platform in the Bronx, where they hurried out amidst pushing, shoving mobs to the stadium.

And from Ron's father he learned other things. There were early Sunday morning expeditions when Ron and his dad would pick him up at his house on State Street and head for the beach, where under gathering thunderheads the three of them would scour the sand for driftwood and collect enough to make a fire and bury potatoes in the sand and ignite the fire above the pit, then spend an hour or so digging for tiny sand crabs which they would collect in old tin cans to watch them wriggle and squirm in the sandy bay water. Without fail they would find a horseshoe crab shell or two and Ron's father would say that he heard that these crabs were among the oldest living creatures in the sea, which meant in the world, and that they had been around in this shape for, what did he say? something like a thousand million years? And they would eventually return to their fire and figure that it was time and take a stick and brush aside the smouldering wood and dig out the potatoes and cut them open with a kitchen knife and spread the spuds out on an old tablecloth Ron's father brought along and sprinkle a little salt on them and blow on them to cool them off a bit, and the taste was better than anything the boy had ever known.

Something changed in Phil's face the moment he came into the company of his own family, of which there was some in New York City and its environs. First and foremost among these people was his brother Joe—Uncle Joe, who had, as the boy Alan pieced the story together from conversations overheard during these family encounters, first left their home region in the Ukraine, left the town of Tikhorechka and then Korastan and then Zhitomir, where they had lived a while, and gone to Paris, where he had worked and tasted the good life among the French, particularly French women who during World War I found a young Russian Jewish boy a treat to have around while most of the local men were at the front. Joe came to America in the twenties and established his own interior decorating business in the New York City borough of Queens. With his wife, Sadie, he had produced a large family, three boys and two girls, most of whom were present when Phil and Tillie and their two sons visited.

Before he had met Tillie, Joe and his family had been Phil's only comfort in New York City. He had his own room but he went over to their house often. He even left an extra flying suit in a closet there, and his young nephews loved to play with it, and Phil would occasionally take out the helmet and let them put it on their heads.

Sometimes he worked alone in the basement, the odor of chemicals boiling up the back staircase. What was he up to? Inventing some salve that was going to revolutionize the way that metal worked against metal and keep engine parts from wearing out, or was it a special oil that cleaned radio tubes and gave them extra long life? One of these things or another. But they never came to anything. He didn't enjoy the basement anyway, since he would rather be out in the sun, up in the air in the little two-seater that he flew out of Teeterboro, and he took the boys up sometimes and he took Tillie up a lot, before they were married—and when on the ground the two of them were quite a pair of love birds! that's what he overheard his sister-in-law saying once to his brother as he was coming up the stairs from the basement—and once he even flew over the house and tipped his wings, and his nephews cheered.

So he still really enjoyed seeing Joe's family, and now in summer he loved to take his own new, young family to the house that Joe had bought at Greenwood Lake, a pike-shaped body of water that straddled the line between New Jersey and New York in the northernmost section of the former state.

The drive up there could have been pleasant. Once you left the industrial pocket of the state behind and headed toward the greener sections of Jersey, you could have been anywhere but the state that called Perth Amboy its own. But Phil and Tillie usually argued during these long drives. Tillie and Sadie did not get along. The Jersey girl liked to look her best, and that Sadie was always commenting on her clothes. You must have spent a lot on that blouse, Tillie, so how much did it cost? Since they had to work together to prepare meals on weekend visits Tillie did not look forward to them.

Tillie was a sweet family girl, shy and somewhat confused when out of her immediate circle, a circle which in fact was dominated by women rather than men, so that while she could survive a meal with Phil's close relatives the thought of a weekend with the two brothers, who became rather (and, at least for Phil, uncharacteristically) raucous together, *and* Sadie, did a lot to unnerve her on these drives.

Usually they'd quarrel, sometimes she'd cry, often there was both. And in the back seat the two young brothers would play the hair game, transform the younger boy's scalp into a forest, Alan walking his fingers through more adventures, until as usual the entire game fell apart into a pushing match and Phil would turn around and threaten them.

"You're going to see my brother Joe and his family and I want you to show some respect," he'd say.

And more often than not Tillie would add,

"And to my family they never show respect?"

"Oh, Teel," Phil would say, "don't start in with me."

"Then don't tell the boys that your family is better than mine."

"Did I say that? Boys?" And here he'd try to catch Alan's eye in the rearview mirror. "Did I say that, Oll-an?"

Alan would duck his head, not wanting to take sides. But sometimes the younger boy, Shel, would dutifully pipe up,

"No, Daddy, no, you didn't."

And Phil would pick up on this, saying, "You see, Til, they didn't hear such a thing."

And Tillie would suddenly betray them both.

"What do they know, Phil? What do they know?"

Up in the family cabin later that afternoon the malty tang of beer lingers in the air, mingling with the odor of freshly caught fish that lie on the nearby sink top ready for scaling. Alan and his cousin have just caught the fish. One of Joe's boys first showed him how to attach a worm to a hook, and how to sit quietly attentive to the slightest motion of the weighted line in the water, how to turn fishing time into time outside of normal time (and so he came to love fishing as much as baseball because of the special feel of the time involved), and how to take a small, wriggling, silvery bass off the hook, and later how to toss it into a butter-smeared pan and fry it up, and how to separate its tiny bones from the meat.

The sun slants into the cabin and is still hours away from slipping down behind the low mountains to the west. Alan, his face a little flushed from a few hours in the sun, slinks off to a corner of the large common room ready to settle in with a new comic book and stretch with Plastic Man or fly with Superman or watch in awe as Wonder Woman deploys her magic bracelets that send bullets ricocheting back at the very criminals who've fired them.

In through the door comes the dark-haired, slender woman with his younger brother and other cousins. They've walked up from the bottom of the hill from the woods around the lake. Sadie hangs dripping bathing suits on the line while humming a little foreign tune. Soon she'll come in and prepare the fish for supper. Someone turns on a radio in the far corner of one of the bedrooms in the rear of the cottage, and *Bei mir bis du schön* . . . , the voices of the Andrews Sisters enliven the mote-laden air.

"Means what is your name," the dark-haired woman sings to herself in a flighty soprano, smiling benignly at her oldest son, who from his vantage point in the far corner looks up for a second and then buries his gaze back in his comic.

"Oh, Teel," her husband says in a complaining voice from where he sits at the table with his brother, "what is that singing?" Then he looks back at his jovial, chunky, balding brother and continues talking, sometimes in a strange, mixed-up language only they can understand, rough-sounding speech full of foreign words and special looks. They've been sitting like this for hours, talking about family, about the old days in the old country.

Tillie asks Sadie if she is ready for some help with the meal, but the older woman shakes her head no as she serves more tea to her husband and brother-in-law.

"You want some tea, Alan?" she says to the boy as she passes his corner. Sadie has a broad, pleasant face and a squat, stocky comfort to the way she is built.

"He's too young to drink tea," Tillie says, looking up from a copy of *Life*.

"Oh, don't be silly," Sadie says, "he's part Russian, isn't he? A little tea can't hurt him."

"I want some beer," Alan says, making most of them laugh, all but Tillie that is.

"Alan," she says, a cautionary tone in her voice.

"Just joking," says the boy.

"It's all right, a little beer couldn't hurt him either," says Sadie, heaving herself across the room toward the small icebox next to the sink.

"You've got a big mouth," Tillie says to her son.

Lowering his head, he buries his eyes once again in the cartoon strip in his lap.

Meanwhile the men at the table fall deeply back into their often hard-to-understand conversation, talking of docks and "dachas," of war and peace and villages and rivers, the weather, the destruction wrought by the Nazis, motors, sky, airplanes, Jews, gypsies, Roosevelt, taxes, one of their boys doing this, one of their boys doing that, the New Deal, New York, farmland, sister Pearl, their mother, their other brothers.

There had been one brother more before the war, but when the Nazis rolled into the Ukraine, burning houses and flattening entire sections of the small towns among the fecund fields, they had found him and hitched him to a wagon and whipped him and whipped him as he hauled the wagon around the town square. At last his heart gave out. Another brother, who had witnessed this incident, Zalman was his name, became a sergeant in the Red Army late in the war and found himself among the first units to enter Berlin, where he took his revenge. He had recently written to Joe about this, and the two brothers now talked about such matters in the humid damp of a late summer Saturday afternoon—and cursed the Germans and cursed Stalin and wondered how they could get other members of their family over here. And they drank tea and tea and more tea, sipping it with two lumps of sugar at least, Russian style.

It has been now more than a dozen years since Phil left the Soviet Union, and he doesn't speak Russian much at all anymore, and Yiddish hardly at all, and so he enjoys this conversation because using these tongues conjures up his years of best memory, he tells his brother, including the years when he was the baby of the family, and their mother, Sonya, was healthy and attentive to all their needs.

Joe laughs his lusty best and slaps his younger brother on the arm. "You're not a baby no more!"

But as Joe is laughing the boy looks up and sees Phil's face darkening at the thought, reflecting his own deep sorrow at the loss of his mother. The boy can see the man's eyes narrowing, can somehow feel his father's chest tightening, and Alan wanders with him in his mind as he casts back over all his childhood, not just his own life but the hard, long, lonely years his mother spent without her husband, and the boy can almost ride the hot wind of his anger rising at the mention of that other man about whom he has never heard a word until today.

"I saw him once when I came to New York," Joe is saying, and Phil nods, both in recognition of the story that he has heard before and the seriousness of the telling.

"I did, too."

And Joe tells his part of it; and then Phil tells his, the account of how after his long trip from San Francisco, you remember? he arrived in New York and got in touch with Joe and among other things got their father's address from him, and without Joe telling him more than a few words about what he knew would happen when Philip went there, the youngest brother set off on the subway for that address on the other side of Brooklyn.

He had put on his best suit that morning, he is telling Joe, the same suit he would in fact be wearing when he went to that dance at the Jewish Club that one Saturday night when Tillie would come from Perth Amboy to visit Thelma. And he put on his best tie. And he wore his wings pinned to his lapel, and the Air Force Academy ring he always wore (but on the train trip over he found himself rubbing it and rubbing it against his trouser leg as if he could polish it more than it already was).

What crazy things were going through his head? Thoughts of his mother, of course, and his comrades in arms, and some of the places he had seen and passed through, flown over, roared into, images of the sea and the clouds when flying in formation, and sounds in his ears too, the roar of the samolet and the pata-patap of the guns mounted on the wings, the rush of traffic in Shanghai, the calm sky above the old villages in the Ukraine—it was as if he was about to drown, *his entire life was passing before his eyes,* except that he wasn't drowning, he was riding in a subway car beneath the streets of Brooklyn, part of this new city where he had migrated, after long travail and journeying over mountains, seas, oceans, continents, half way around the world, and he was about to meet the father he had not seen since he was six years old!

How does a man behave at a time like this? He is asking Joe (and from the corner Alan is listening). He had reached the age when he was ready to become a father on his own, and he was feeling those years rapidly falling away from his life the closer and closer he got to the correct station, and he was a war hero and a world traveller, a man who dared to fly and fight and work with his hands and stand up to bigots and put everything behind him when the time seemed right and plunge ahead into a new world, a new life—and he could see himself now as a young boy, younger than his oldest was now, and he could see himself *seeing himself* as a young boy, and his knees trembled as the train slowed down, and he carefully read the English of the sign outside the train to be sure that he was leaving at the right stop, and he left the subway tunnel and climbed up out into the air of a warm, sunny Brooklyn autumn afternoon, thinking, I could be standing right now on a street in Zhitomir waiting for my uncle to accompany me downtown.

I wish I were, he thought. And tears brimmed up in his eyes so quickly it caught him unawares.

He missed his home, his homeland, though he had been travelling now all these years away from it—and missed it all the more as he was telling the story again to Joe, missed it so much that he not only knew tears were coming but he actually wanted the tears to come.

People passed him on the street and stared at the young man weeping. He glanced back at a woman in feathered hat and sleek green skirt. The woman tugged him momentarily out of his mood—women did that to you, they had a certain power, or elicited a certain power in yourself. So he pulled at his lapels and took out his handkerchief and dabbed at his eyes and strode off along the street in search of the number Joe had given him. And apparently he had delayed long enough, had taken all the time he needed to hesitate, because when he found the building he fairly well leaped up the stoop and pushed the bell and bounded up the stairs to the second floor. When the woman opened the door and asked what it was he wanted and he asked for his father by name he already felt as though he were a train car moving along a rail, an airship in full flight.

Was this the one, the woman who . . . ? His heart pumped hard, his breath raced, and pictures of Mama came with each breath, too. Mama, Mama . . .

"Shto?" said the stooped, grey-haired man in the blue dressing gown who came to the door.

Phil looked at him, looked at him and looked at him, then tried to spit in his face. He cursed him instead and with his own tears returning, fled from the building.

EIGHT

CAPTAIN BEREZHKOV WAS THE NEXT OF OUR group to perish.

Since the morning our squadron had destroyed the enemy in the minaret, and we lost our friend and comrade Nicholas Tyatin, there had been skirmishes by cavalry detachments operating far from Khiva about which we heard, but our own daily patrols were uneventful. Then Captain Berezhkov's luck ran out. The captain's teammate was Lieutenant Koshkin, and it was he who arrived within radio voice range of our base with the news that Captain Berezhkov had been forced down by a malfunction in the engine and had made a landing on a level stretch of clay on a dried-up lake on the edge of the Kara Kum. The captain, Koshkin said, had ordered him to return to Khiva and relay a request to fly in a mechanic with a distributor, a rotor, a set of ignition wires, and most of all, a high-voltage coil, because the one on the captain's istrebitel appeared to be shorted out.

Major Smirnov himself, in a two-seater, picked up one of our best troubleshooters, an aviation mechanic named Arkhipoff, and they took off to fly to Berezhkov long before Lieutenant Koshkin even landed in Khiva. Major Smirnov and Sergeant Arkhipoff had little trouble spotting Berezhkov's plane. It was on fire. Seeing the smoke, the major abandoned all caution himself and came in low for a closer look. According to Arkhipoff, it was then that the bandits materialized as if from the clay itself.

"At first we saw not a soul. Then, as we dove down past a column of smoke," Arkhipoff illustrated to us, using his hands to describe the maneuver, "ooh . . . ooh. Then it was that I saw it!" He shielded his eyes with a sleeve. "It was . . . he was . . . it had to be Captain Berezhkov, who else, who? . . . he was in flames, standing on what was left of the wing over his cockpit . . . ooh . . . and as we flew through the smoke, I got a whiff. And the bullets! Zzzing . . . zzzing. Finished, I thought we were. Finished!"

There was no telling how many times Sergeant Arkhipoff described in vivid detail how Captain Berezhkov had met his end. At mealtime that evening, Arkhipoff barely touched the lamb in his pilaff and kept muttering, "I would not be a pilot for all the raisins in Turkestan!"

We buried the charred remains of Captain Berezhkov in the garden of an agricultural experimental station, a lush and lovely acre surrounded by a high fence and situated at the edge of the Khiva aerodrome. Berezhkov had once said in jest that he would like to be interred there, close to the field, so he could watch take-offs and landings.

"If we cannot give our comrade this resting place, what *can* we grant him in return for his life that he has laid down for his motherland?" our Major Smirnov said in his speech over Berezhkov's grave. Privately, to the local authorities, the major said he realized that the agricultural station was no cemetery, and that after our squadron was moved elsewhere the body of Captain Berezhkov could be shipped out.

The complement of the Second Squadron of Fighters in Khiva was housed in the Khanate House. It was said that Djunaid Khan had lived in this many-winged structure whose facade was of colorful ceramic, which stood in a small park like some apparition from past Islamic splendor. The poplar, acacia, and oak in the garden were thriving despite the absence of care, but the many flower beds had succumbed to weeds.

Like the ancient city of Khiva, the Khanate House was also surrounded by walls, but unlike the massive clay fortifications of the city, these garden walls were only ten feet tall, without battlements, and rather recent compared with a thousand years for the city walls of Khiva. These walls were a mere century or two old and topped with broken bottles. The only entrance to the house was its garden gate on the main street, and save for some native men on the staff, and the Red Army personnel, no one was permitted to enter without a pass, and females were forbidden entirely—at least officially.

When we returned from Berezhkov's funeral, our cook, Ali Khassan, had prepared a bowl of grape punch for us in the courtyard. To add some tingle to the taste he had poured into the punch bowl two bottles of vodka, three bottles of cognac, and assorted bottles of champagne, which improved it considerably and in very little time altered the mood of the men from being sad and morose to sentimental drunk.

A mechanic who hardly ever uttered a word when sober turned talkative, scampered up the balcony of the former harem's dormitory and began making a speech, saying how tough it is for a young fellow with normal feelings to sleep in a room where funny business had formerly transpired day and night, and that he personally was unable to sleep because the rooms upstairs were haunted by the ghosts of such delicate creatures.

Before we realized it, all of us were drunk and life had assumed an exaggerated slow-motion pace in which all was right and time was syrupy and languid—where laughter mingled with the sound of the water from the splashing fountain and blended with the sunlight which streamed through the lofty branches and lazy leaves.

Arkhipoff staggered onto the balcony, but was shouted down by the voices of some who thought he was going to tell us again about Berezhkov. He was replaced by a sub-lieutenant named Androtieff, who bowed to us from the balcony and said that he, as representative of the ground crews, wished to thank us pilots and might, if we desired, make a speech.

"Speech, speech! Go ahead, boy!" Voices encouraged him and some bleary-eyed applause was offered in advance.

"Comrades, shall I let it roll off my tongue?"

"Lie on, boy, the devil take you."

"We of the ground crews have thought of you pilots as showoffs, and some of you as great complainers, but comrades, we love you all as friends! What else did I want to tell you? Ah, da! For you it is sometimes possible to smuggle girls into this Khanate House to spend the night, and many of you have your own rooms. What I was trying to say, comrades, is that one of the purposes of life is to obtain female companionship, correct?"

"Correct!"

"Blab on, Androtieff."

"As spokesman for all of us who sleep in these rooms of the former khan's harem, I am reporting herewith that we suffer from insomnia! And the kind of insomnia we suffer requires a cure! What *kind* of a cure is required? I will tell you! We require females who would massage us and make other adjustments to our masculine machinery! Let us then drink a toast to female masseurs! Hurrah!"

Lieutenant Pirozhkin, in charge of the armored division, came with his accordion and struck up a pleasant tune, and it was so lively that it sent Sasha Kadikoff and Lieutenant Baranin off dancing together on the patio. The merrymaking was gaining momentum. Most of us were unaccustomed to the concoction we were drinking, but we imbibed it anyway, if only to keep up the magic mood and to help us forget, or at least put to rest, what had happened to Berezhkov.

Soldiers under the rank of sergeant felt too shy to join the party on the patio, but they were also too curious to ignore it, and too amused to stay away, so that many of them climbed up on the roof and sat there and were having a great time watching officers make fools of themselves, splashing water at each other in the fountain, dancing the hopak, arm wrestling and laughing at each other's funny stories.

Some of us pulled the cots from our rooms and sat on them, and others were sprawled out on the ground in the sun—having removed our ties, shirts, and tunics—and caring little whose hat it was floating in the fountain.

The punch we were drinking and the party we were having was growing louder and louder when the major showed up and someone shouted, "Smirnov!" causing those not too drunk to jump up and come to attention.

"Volno . . . as you were," the major ordered, surveying all with disbelief.

"Kiril Kirilovich, little father," someone with an unwieldly tongue greeted him, "let me get you a drink."

". . . So, as I was saying, Kaplan, it's not so much the girl one marries . . . the question is, what kind a mother does she have? My witch of a mother-in-law lives in Pskov, but nevertheless manages to poison my life by writing letters."

Another brother officer was waving his hands and saying how he admired his in-laws, who were the most refined and most cultured family residing in Khiva, and really belonged either in Leningrad, Moscow, or perhaps even Paris. Taking his cue from this topic of conversation, still another buddy was saying that at least wives and sweethearts, as the case may be, should be permitted into the garden of the Khanate House, at least to picnic on the grass and eat grapes and other fruit of the garden and listen to the bullfrogs in the ponds and feel free to run around barefoot and fancy free, be they married or not.

But the good time crashed to a halt the moment Major Belomirov showed up. Unlike our good major, the political commissar absolutely declined to take even one drink.

"I am most disappointed with you, comrades!" he shouted, looking at each of us severely, including Major Smirnov. "You there!" he ordered a junior engineering officer, "dump that bowl of vodka into the fountain!"

"It is not vodka, tovarich Commissar."

"Whatever it is, pour it out!" It was enough to sober one to see the anger on the commissar's face, the amazement on the major's face, and the disappointment in all others.

"Just so," the junior officer said, saluting.

"There goes our benzine," said Captain Solontzev who kept me from sagging as we witnessed the sad event. "I have just enough fuel in me to make for Lyola's place. Would you care to come along?"

"Who is Lyola?"

"You want her pedigree, Kaplan? Lyola is a sweet girl! And I would not be asking you to come along if Lyola hadn't ordered me to bring you, what's your name, Fishel, Fishka?"

Solontzev had put on his tie and was looking for his tunic.

"I will never begin to know why, but of all the men here in Khiva, Lyola wants *you* to meet her sister, Tamara. She ordered me to bring you at the first opportunity, Kaplanchik, so if you have no objection why don't you tag along. Lyola is my girl. Tamara, on the other hand, is technically speaking still a teenager and she is not forcibly residing in Khiva. In other words, Tamara, technically speaking, according to my Lyola, is not even yet a woman."

"Strange, indeed," I said, a bit dazed. "Why would your Lyola, whom I had never met, want me to meet her sister?"

"Come to think of it, Kaplan," Solontzev smiled, "now that my brain is beginning to function again, clearing up that is, I recall that I was the one who told Lyola about you. I had merely mentioned that we have one Jewish pilot among the men of our squadron, and since Lyola happens to be a Jew herself, she naturally would like you to meet her sister, who, by the way, is quite an attractive young thing."

A bit later, Lyola Kaminskaya was swearing to me that she had been framed, that although she had never practiced the oldest profession, she had nonetheless been sent off to Khiva to remain in exile for fifteen years. She and Tamara were born in Bobruysk, where the family had lived up until they fled because of the Civil War. Following this move, their parents died during the typhus epidemic of 1919 and the girls were once again forced to move. They found an aunt in Leningrad where they attended school, after which Lyola had worked for a debauched Soviet official, a Party bureaucrat, who had abused his female subordinates. Her story coincided with one I had heard when I was at the Academy in Leningrad myself, and this convinced me that she was telling the truth and had been sent into exile unjustly.

Lyola had large, hazel eyes, chestnut hair, and a very good figure. Add to this that she was good-natured, treated me like a brother, and had a lovely sister who would be coming home from town at any moment. But still there was something wrong, and I did not want to get things started that could not be easily stopped.

"Look, Lyolinka," I said to her, "it will take Tamara at least six more years before she could possibly become as attractive as you are, and I can't wait that long. I would ask for you, Lyolinka, but you are Solontzev's girl."

"And don't forget that, Fishka!" said Vladimir Solontzev.

"Tamara would like you," said Lyola. "She would be very good for you, Fishka, if you were willing to register with her."

"I'm not ready for marriage," I said.

"No man ever is," Lyola smiled. "But there is something so nice about you as a person, Fishka. What I mean to say is that I want to help you out. There is no need to deprive yourself of something so natural to both sexes. Don't blush, silly! So, if Tamara is not to be the girl for you then we must find another, and I know exactly who it must be. Her name is Antonina, and we must introduce you immediately."

"Just so," I said with some relief. "Tell me more."

"She was Berezhkov's girl. She is far from bright, but she is pretty, and absolutely healthy, that I can assure you. She would be right for you, Fishka. And Antonina is familiar with the 'flying carpet.' She used to visit Berezhkov's room in the Khanate House almost every other night."

"Flying carpet?" It was then that I learned that the cook, Ali Khassan, had a smuggling service by that name. It consisted of a ladder and a carpet used to throw over the wall as protection from the splinters of glass imbedded in it. The ladder and the carpet were kept in the back yard of Khassan's adobe house, which happened to be on the other side of the wall of the Khanate House garden. For his flying carpet service Ali charged nothing to Red Army men whom he knew personally, and five rubles to each of the girls he smuggled in for them.

I told Lyola that I could not agree to meet with this Antonina until I had discussed it with my friend, Sasha Kadikoff. After all, this was Captain Berezhkov's girl and we had only that day heard words spoken over his grave. But Sasha, when we talked later that night, thought that Berezhkov would not want his girl forgotten, and so the next day things were arranged with Lyola, and the night after that Antonina Edmundovna Illyashova used the flying carpet to come to our room.

Sasha and I were both there when she arrived, since we had also agreed that each of us should meet her.

Antonina was about twenty, and she was "thrilled," she told us in a slightly quavering voice that made us think that perhaps she had had a drink or two before she came, to scale the walls once more, though she would certainly miss Captain Berezhkov. Our quarters were a bit different than his, she said, and she could not get over the Persian rug that filled our floor. "Oh, my—how wonderfully cozy it is here."

In her hand Antonina held, of all things, a salami. "A present for you both," she said. "My father manufactures them."

She was indeed a beauty, a trim redhead who wore a low-cut blouse of Chinese silk, riding breeches of English wool, and custom-made soft red leather boots. And if she was not too bright, she was certainly cheerful, and Sasha and I were both immediately in love with her.

However, Sasha had arranged to go to the movies in town for the evening if all looked well with Antonina and me, and soon enough—after we had made a sad toast to Captain Berezhkov with the Three Star Hennessy cognac we had on hand—he made his excuses to leave.

"No, you mustn't go," Antonina said.

"Pour yourself another drink, Lieutenant Sasha Kadikoff. And please pour me a drink, Lieutenant Fishel Isaakovich. Permit me to call you Fishka. No, I will call you Fishenka. You are both so good-looking. I love you both. Do not go to the movies this time, Sasha, Sashenka. I love you both. Let me take care of both of you. Do not let your friend go looking for a good time elsewhere, Fishenka, the town is full of diseased whores. Have a drink with me!"

Sasha and I looked at each other in amazement but not really with embarrassment—we had shared so much of our private lives with one another already that this too now seemed natural—and with our eyes we reaffirmed our friendship.

"We will do anything with you you want us to, except have too much to drink," I said. "We have to remain sober in case we are roused to go up at dawn."

"And I will go to the movies for a few hours, as I said I would," Sasha maintained, "but I promise to be back soon enough."

"No! You are not running away to the movies, not even for a short time. Right, Fishenka?"

"Right!" I said this time, dawn patrol or not, thinking it through perhaps too quickly. "And let us all have a drink!"

And we poured ourselves general portions of the Hennessy and we drank it as we sang:

Pour another drink into the tall glass
Since only God knows what'll happen to us
When we've risen through tomorrow morning's haze . . .

But we did not have to fly the next morning, and I was still in a dreamy state of mind, wondering about this young woman, and women in general, when without bothering to knock, Ali Khassan poked his close-cropped head, with its skullcap, through the door. "For Lieutenant Kaplan, a letter. It came on an airplane, I was told."

"From my mother!" I leaped up and took the envelope. It was postmarked Zhitomir, addressed to the academy in Orenburg, from which it had been forwarded to Tashkent to our squadron and then found its way to Khiva. What alarmed me was that none of the writing on the envelope resembled my mother's hand.

Khassan had let himself into the room and stood blocking the light from the door. I tore open the envelope and started to read.

"My dear Fishele," my Uncle Yankel began. "The Almighty, in His infinite mercy, has chosen to relieve your mother of all earthly pain . . ."

"No, my God!" I said aloud. "Oh, Mama . . . Mamochka." I stopped reading and shouted at Ali Khassan who had been hovering over me. "Get out! Get out!"

Lieutenant Kadikoff jumped up from his bed. "Don't you understand Russian? He said get out!" Sasha swept Ali out, as he left himself, slowly closing the door to leave me to my grief.

"Oh, Mama, Mama, Mama," I shouted through my tears, and threw myself back on my cot.

Much later that day, after the sun had gone down, I was still lying there, listening to the plaintive notes of an Uzbek flute. The sad and endlessly repetitive sounds of the native dance tune drew out of me more misery than I had ever imagined any human being could contain. Our life together, my mother's and mine, danced before my eyes. I had survived true hardship, but now I felt that I was alive for no purpose except to somehow make a fitting memorial to her still utterly vivid memory.

NINE

MOSKVA.

I've visited some great cities, lived in others—New York, Los Angeles, Washington, Paris, London, Santiago, Bogotá, Montevideo, Belgrade—but I think only Mexico City, with its system of government modeled, consciously or unconsciously, on the Aztec notion of centralization, has prepared me for Moscow. These avenues that lead toward the center of the city from the train station must be the broadest streets in the world—city streets as many-laned and as wide as the New Jersey Turnpike! And this is real traffic, not like the sporadic rush of cars in Leningrad. Here flows a continual double and sometimes triple stream of automobiles in each direction, with people making some of the wildest left turns and U-turns in creation! The combination of multitudes of cars and these vast avenues and the high speed at which everyone travels and the antic methods of changing lanes and directions all at once makes Moscow just about the craziest driving city I've ever seen.

The Intourist limo greets us at the station and so we're off like dignitaries rather than frenzied tourists. Some people warned us before we left that Intourist would keep constant track of us, and that this was like being watched by the FBI. That really hasn't seemed the case. So far what their attention has done is make our travelling very simple—since we don't have the language it's a lot easier for us to have someone point us to the train we're supposed to take and pick us up at the other end and drive us to our designated hotels than for us to fend for ourselves.

Our driver makes an insane U-turn in the middle of the vast traffic flow of Gorky Street and we glide in under the marquee of the Hotel Intourist. The lobby is huge, and the number of people milling about at this early evening hour suggests that some tours have just come in or are about to leave. We turn in our voucher for the hotel—our entire itinerary is stapled together in a book of vouchers, for hotels, trains, airplanes, cars to and from airports and hotels and train stations, for special guided tours of the sites on our pilgrimage, for just about everything except lunches and sleep—and head up to our room.

We're on the twentieth floor, overlooking Gorky Street, facing apartment buildings that could fit, at first glance, right into the Upper West Side of New York City. Here are large, impassive buildings lined with windows which glow with lights, other buildings as tall stretching away into the darkness, a tower glowing to the north, a few neon signs flashing here and there before us, cars rushing back and forth along the broad roadway, thousands of people hurrying along the broad sidewalks.

We check out the room, unpack. This is considered deluxe, but it's really one of hundreds of rooms in a beehive for tourists—and though there's the "floor lady" who seems to be ubiquitous in all Russian accommodations sitting behind her desk in the middle of the hall, the place seems quite anonymous—a hotel vast enough for this immense city, and it seems clear to us that it's going to take everything the Russians have to make the beds and keep the sinks clean in a hotel such as this, let alone bug our conversations. The halls echo with voices in a number of languages—I make out Finnish, French, Russian, and some stranger tongues. We shut the door behind us and take the elevator down into the Moscow night.

It's definitely not the Upper West Side down here. There's a crowd of people at the door, but it is much more quiet than you would ever find in the West. First, there are the doormen who keep out the ordinary Russians who might want to wander through the lobby. *No way, Sergei!* You can't get in without some special permission or authorized purpose. Guests must show their hotel cards, little cardboard markers stamped with your date of arrival. Muscovites need not apply! On the other side of the door stand a number of drivers, some working for Intourist, others taxi drivers who have parked in front of the building.

Then there are a number of "business girls," easily recognizable to us now after Leningrad. These women are beautiful, and beautifully dressed, and if we don't see them in the lobby but only in the foyer, and outside the hotel door, does that mean Moscow is a straighter town than Leningrad? In Leningrad the women clearly appeared to be working with the maître d' and the waiters in the tourist hotels. Here they seem to be merely tolerated, a service to foreign businessmen in Moscow for trade purposes. They must wait outside. Or is it that the bribes are higher here than elsewhere in the Soviet Union, so your ordinary business girl must wait outside for economy's sake?

We walk the gauntlet of women and taxi drivers and join the stream of passersby, Muscovites on their way home from shops that are just closing, and head toward the corner where a number of young men dressed in army surplus jackets and blue jeans are loitering.

"You are American?" one of them says as he steps out of the crowd. "You vant to trade?" He and Josh begin a conversation about comparative goods–T-shirts and cassette tapes and American cigarettes on our side, and army hats and belts and lacquer boxes and icons on his–which continues as we descend the steps into the underpass that takes us beneath Karl Marx Place and over to the Red Square side of the wide avenue roaring with traffic. Josh and the young Russian arrange to meet later, and the fellow disappears.

"You vant lacquer box?" Josh says to me. "Dee vorkers control dee means of dee trading."

We emerge on the little street alongside the G.U.M. department store and the police fortress at the foot of Red Square, and follow the crowd across the dark, ancient cobblestones into the square proper. We expect this place to be one of the largest in the world, this square where the Red Army marches and the missiles roll by on flatcars during the obligatory holiday parades. But we can see that those flatcars have to make some very sharp turns in order to get through. We're boxed in, and with the Kremlin wall to our right and the history museum and the G.U.M. department store to our left, the square *seems* large, but hardly large enough to contain all of the illusions we've acquired about it over a lifetime.

Another of those illusions is that Moscow is ruled by an omnipresent police force, but what we see in Red Square at eleven thirty at night is something unusual for Americans to lay eyes upon: thousands of strollers, including families with small children (and what are those kids doing up this late?), taking in the sights, the red flags flying in the breeze above the Kremlin towers, the eye-catching futuristic-looking mass of stone slabs that comprises Lenin's tomb right in the center of the wall that lies along the square, or the gingerbread castle of cupolas that is St. Basil's Cathedral at the far end.

So many idle wanderers out in a city at this hour! Where in our country can you see such a thing? In our own capitol? Where? In New York City? Never! By this time of night people pick up their pace, never dawdle as these couples, these families, do. Where in Los Angeles? This must be something like the famous "law and order" that certain regimes have achieved in their streets for a time at least in the past, and it seems tranquil and innocent enough, a vision to be yearned for, the chance to stroll arm in arm with someone you love, or those half-steps you take with young children on a walk—look, there's a girl with a little pup, and her parents don't seem to be anywhere in sight—at any hour of the day or night. I'd hate to think that the price of such pleasures comes at the cost of individual freedom, but that's what this picture before us seems to imply. These visions amble through my head as Josh and I walk across the square toward the doors of Lenin's tomb.

A crowd has gathered to watch the changing of the guard at the doors of the mausoleum. Two young soldiers in dress uniform face each other, rifles at post, their only visible movement the occasional blinking of their eyes. A murmur passes through the crowd as out of the Kremlin gate comes a high-stepping twosome, led by an officer, who will replace this pair, and as the clock in another tower chimes the hour the new guards take the place of the old, who are led back into the tower by the officer in charge. This apparently happens every hour on the hour every day of the year. In the winter it must be fierce duty. Tonight, with summer weather still holding, it seems merely arduous. Now the crowd raises its voice, and its satisfaction at the precision of these moves becomes audible throughout the square.

Josh tugs at my sleeve. "Dee vorkers control dee means of replacement."

He steps back to take a photograph, and for the first time this evening people stare at us, but only for the briefest moment, and then turn their attention once again to the business of being with each other.

In the midst of all this touristy stuff I've momentarily lost track of my father. But here he is now, stepping across the cobblestones, with yet another young city girl on his arm, walking slowly, gesturing with his pipe in his free hand. His uniform, with its special air force designation, draws attention from those in the know. He is not a Muscovite, of course, just passing through here on military business as is many a young man in uniform, but he does have a knowledge of the history of the various monuments around the square, the Tower of Ivan the Great built in 1505, with its fifty-two bells, and the Czar Bell standing at the base weighing in at two hundred tons—at twenty feet tall and twenty-two feet in diameter it is the largest bell in the world.

And as they stroll he points with his pipe to other towers, the Nikolskaya Tower, the Sobakina Tower, and they descend the steps into the Alexandrovsky Garden, the park that stretches along the western wall of the Kremlin where he shows her the Middle Arsenal Tower, the Troitskaya Tower, the Kutafya Tower—he has learned all this in his class in high school, the history of Moscow, and in particular the Kremlin, being almost synonymous with the history of the nation.

There's a bench and like a true gentleman he suggests that the girl might like to rest here and discuss for a while such matters as the turbulent past of their native land, and tells her how he, as a new officer, flies in the service of a revolution bound to take the country forward and become the first nation to base itself on the universal principles of liberty, equality, and fraternity, everything France tried to do but could not because it was bound to the nature of the capitalist system.

I find that I'm staring at Josh, studying his features for a glimpse of both my father and myself. No kid should have to bear that burden, I know, but this trip is shrinking time for me in a way I never thought possible—and expanding years for both of us in ways that we never imagined.

Back at the hotel, Josh takes a leisurely bath while I read a little, then we turn out the lights and watch the end of a war movie on one of the two TV channels still broadcasting at this hour. Then it's over and we climb into these short, narrow beds. I get up a few times and stare out at the Gorky Street traffic, the business girls milling in front of the hotel, late walkers, a taxi driver or three also wandering back and forth, and I stare at the red star above the Kremlin, proving to me beyond a doubt that I have arrived somewhere I have never been before.

Josh breathes in counterpoint to the faint noise of traffic on the wide avenues below as I return to bed.

The next morning at the American Embassy, I talk to Tony Kasanof, a bearded, scholarly man in his mid-fifties, a career officer with an interest in Middle Eastern and Turkish history. We discuss the small war in Russian Turkestan where my father flew, and he gives me the name of some scholars and histories to check facts against when I return to the U.S. Then we talk about Chernobyl, since I have a double purpose in talking to him. Josh is worried about our upcoming trip to the Ukraine. "I want to have children some day, you know, Dad, and I don't want them to have two heads."

"Weird," I say to Kasanof. "I can't tell you how gratified I was to hear about this particular concern. He is a very cool and sophisticated boy just about to turn twenty-one, and I had figured that the last thing on his mind was one day having a family. Not that it's the first thing, but it seems to be when the subject of our trip to Kiev comes up."

Kasanof gives me a run-down on the current situation with respect to radiation. He says that he himself wouldn't go out of his way to be there, but since we have our mission his best advice is to continue with the trip. The school year begins next week, and he's curious as to whether or not the children, who were whisked away for the summer after the accident, are going to return in time for the opening of classes.

Peace is on my mind, Alan," says translator Frieda Lurie that afternoon.

We're sitting in her cramped office at the Writers Union on Vorovsky Ulitsa, a number of English-language books piled around us, on the desk in front of us, at our feet, and stacks and stacks of Russian books. Lurie, an auburn-haired Russian woman in her sixties is slightly on the chubby side, and has already complained about her weight, about the need to go on a diet. Dieting is a luxury for women of her generation who lived through the war years. Free talk with foreign writers must also be considered a luxury for someone like Lurie who lived through the Stalin years as well.

There is a large public relations campaign going on, she tells me (propaganda campaign is how I suppose our government would technically classify it), on behalf of implementing a policy of reducing the military budget. Gorbachev appears ready to negotiate away Soviet missiles in order to eliminate the necessity of manufacturing new weapons. A reduction of the large military budget is the only way the Soviet people are going to see more consumer goods in the stores. The government has to prepare the people for budget cuts since it has spent decades telling them that the reason they haven't had it so good in necessities and luxuries has been that the military budget, in a world of American warmongers, has to take precedence over consumer goods.

Some talk about books creeps in. Lurie pats one of the Russian stacks. She has just finished a translation of Ann Tyler's *Dinner at the Homesick Restaurant.* She's known several generations of visiting American writers, beginning with John

Steinbeck, on through the other Johns, Cheever and Updike. She tells me a few tales out of school, but talks mostly about their work, and how much she admires it. And how much she wants more writer exchanges between the U.S. and the U.S.S.R. She asks about our mutual friend, poet and playwright Jim Ragan, and tells me the story of the visit of Jim, Robert Bly, and Bob Dylan, which she translated for, describing a paranoid Dylan, worried ever since the John Lennon murder that he might be next, besieged by Soviet teenagers who want him to autograph their bootleg albums and diving onto the floor of the car to get away from them. I feel bad that I can't talk to Frieda about the real reasons behind our trip, this crazy, ephemeral family quest, tourists in search of ruins and a ghost. But I don't. It's better to say too little than too much in this country of suspicions.

I hail a cab back to the hotel. After an hour Josh returns to our room with a military fur cap and an army belt and a lacquer box that he's acquired from the Russian kids, in exchange for a few T-shirts and an old denim jacket. Oh, and an extra pair of jeans. He'll give the lacquer box to his mother.

He's down to one jacket and one pair of jeans for the rest of the trip. This generation is travelling light, lighter than mine, it seems.

Tomorrow is Josh's birthday, and for the evening we have decided to take another walk through Red Square. At midnight the chimes ring out, and by the time they strike twelve the sentries have changed posts at the doors to Lenin's tomb—and Josh, the infant I used to carry on my shoulder through long lost starry Mexican nights, has turned twenty-one!

We each toss a kopeck into the fountain in front of St. Basil's gingerbread towers.

"I wish Phil were here to see you. To see us," I say.

"Dad, you're so sentimental," Josh says.

"And you're not? Don't you feel these things?"

"I do," he says, "but I don't *show* it."

NINE

One more day of sightseeing. Having been outside Lenin's tomb, we must now make the obligatory visit inside. On Red Square long lines have been gathering since early morning and the double rank stretches back now all the way into Alexandrovsky Park. We've heard a rumor that foreign passport holders are given preferential treatment, and we discover it's true—after only thirty minutes in the line a militiaman motions for our group—a dozen or so English and Australians and Jamaicans and some Orientals—to show our passports and move forward to cut back in to the line only about a quarter of a mile from the entrance to the mausoleum. Fantastic progress!

Josh has dutifully left his camera behind. Others must rush into a building nearby and check theirs. No cameras allowed! And twice along the way a guard motions for men to button their coats—out of respect, so goes the word down the line. But it might also prevent you from reaching in and taking out a brick to break the glass case in the tomb we've heard so much about. We move along quickly now, halting to get patted down by young sentries just at the entrance of the tomb.

After not much more than an hour—and some of the Russian tourists from outlying republics will wait in this line half a day!—we are ushered into the tomb, down several levels of stairs, and into the hushed and darkened heart of the mausoleum where under the spotlights above the glass case rests what appears to be a perfectly preserved body in a brown suit. We're given half a twitch of time to stare, then motioned by hushed guards to move along and we're past the body up more stairs and in a moment out into the air again.

"That body . . . ?"

"Yeah, I know, Dad."

"I thought I was in Madame Tussaud's."

"Dee vorkers control dee means of dee mummies."

"I don't think it was a mummy. I think it was a wax figure."

"You trying to get us arrested, Dad? You vant to go to the Gulag? If they think that's Lenin, that's their business."

"But imagine if we had George Washington or Abraham Lincoln under glass like that."

"We do things just as strange."

We're moving toward the Kremlin wall now, where all the Soviet leaders are buried, and where I hope to catch a glimpse of the plaque denoting the burial place of the ashes of Jack Reed.

"What do you mean, Josh? What do we do that's *that* weird?"

"I don't know, but we do."

"Yeah, okay," I say to Josh, "we're just as weird."

I scan the Kremlin wall for a sight of the Reed plaque, but we're moving along quickly, urged on by bored militiamen. I unbutton my coat, take a deep breath, and get whizzed past the last monuments on the wall without seeing his name. After all these years of reading about him, after writing a novel about him, and now given the one chance to get close to him—if seeing someone's grave is getting close—I miss it.

I vow then and there not to let the opportunity to visit with my father get away from me.

But how can it? He's with me, suddenly I sense it, his voice in my inner ear and on my lips, his face superimposed on my face, on Josh's, and we're walking off across Red Square where he walked, where he is walking now.

"I'm taking you out for your birthday dinner tonight to one of the best restaurants in town," I hear myself saying to Josh.

And he nods, pleased at the prospect.

And in my head I hear Phil's voice: *Do dot, Oll-an. Do dot.*

Dinner at the Homesick Restaurant? No, at the Hotel Berlin, where I've reserved a table for the two of us so that we can celebrate.

Seven courses, capped with what appears to be the greatest luxury of all, a bowl of fresh apples in the center of the table. We're surrounded by, judging from some of the languages we hear snippets of, Greek financiers and French shipping captains on tour, along with what appears to be Communist Party sleazeballs, drunk men in fine suits with wives as big as the Ritz.

A band starts up in the dining room of this prerevolutionary hotel, with its gilded ceilings and ornate arches. Music *so* rinky-dink that this time Josh finds it fascinating. Fat cats bob up and down doing what they must think of as the Communist Funky Chicken. I've never seen such pathetic dancing in my life! And I think they're actually having fun! Here is the height of consumption, garish clothes and a bucket of apples, music out of a Sinclair Lewis novel, the hep cats of Communism jiggling it around and shaking it up, *bay-bee!*

And a little later on the streets, nothing. We walk for hours, and never see a cafe or an ordinary restaurant where some strolling lovers or an elderly couple on a lark might duck in for a cappuccino.

Back in the room after our heavy celebratory meal, I lie awake for what seems like hours, dreaming of Emma, Sonya, and me riding on a train—and somehow there are tens of thousands of crows flying outside the train window. A man, a porter, bearlike in form, comes over to tell us that he's surprised that I'm so big a man and yet so gentle. The porter?

My old man! He's still with us, despite the rush and hurly-burly of this big city, *Moskva,* this huge place that's such a mixture of fervor and boredom . . . will he fly with us tomorrow to Kiev?

TEN

I COULD TELL BY THE WAY MY HORSE THREW ITS head back that it had picked up the sound of the engines being revved at the Khiva aerodrome. The wind brought these sounds, sometimes as a faint, dull throb and sometimes as virtual thunder. And then just as unexpectedly the wind changed direction and the noise of the istrebitel engines would be cancelled out by the distance.

As we galloped through Khiva's northern gate, the noise and the wind blended into a single turbulence of sound and blinding sunlight. My mount reared when I forced him to a sudden stop at the sentry booth before the aerodrome. Sasha Kadikoff and others had arrived ahead of me, while some of our squadron were still galloping behind me.

The aerodrome was full of activity. All the ground personnel seemed to have been summoned to the field as well as all the pilots. De Havilland bombers were taxiing for their take-off runs in tandem. Our istrebitels were being warmed up, refueled, and armed by swarms of men.

"You are familiar with the area around Badir Tazh," said Major Smirnov, standing on a platform before a map of Khorezm, "but let me review our mission for the benefit of you men who are just coming in. Here is the triangle you have often patrolled. We have long suspected that the enemy hides out on camouflaged islands in this swamp, in this tangled forest, and in these dunes close to the Amu-Darya where it sweeps into the Kara Kum. The enemy sustains himself by the produce from this triangle. Up until now we have not been able to identify specific camps in the area, and thus been unable to rout the Basmachi. But after months of watching we have finally figured out how the bandits manage to muster their units to strike at us! They move either at night or with the population, pretending to be villagers, travelling with them, particularly on market days and holidays. Based on our intelligence, we are now prepared to counteract a probable enemy attack on Tashauz. Our mission today is to support some of our forces which have surrounded and trapped a company of the enemy in the village of Badir Tazh. If the enemy is not destroyed before sunset, he will slip away as soon as it is dark."

Minutes later we were flying low in a triangle formation, taking advantage of a slight tail wind. The shadows of our ships moved swiftly beneath us over fields of ripening cotton and acres of rippling summer wheat ready for harvest. Irrigation canals, like arteries, carried the life-giving waters from the Amu-Darya to the fields. Here and there in the lush acres divided by the canals, ancient water wheels turned in their endless circles driven by camels and donkeys walking unhurriedly in the circular paths etched forever in the earth. Here and there we could make out clusters of trees as well as grapevines climbing the walls of adobe farm houses.

A hamlet of clay huts which was marked on my map as Zan Gorgan moved under my port wing. Fields of cotton gave way to an incursion of sand dunes of the Kara Kum, and in formation the squadron rose on the hot air of the desert. Suspended in a noisy, shimmering, furnacelike wind, we looked down on swamplands, and then some small lakes, like chunks of broken mirrors.

"Badir Tazh is ahead," Major Smirnov announced calmly over the radio. Then, with matter-of-fact resolution he said, "Add quarter power and climb. Squaddddronnnn . . . execute!"

Soon we could see that the minaret of Badir Tazh was missing, and saw smoke billowing up from a cluster of clay barns and huts just outside the village.

"Squadddronnnn . . . quarter turn to the right! Bank! Quarter turn to the left! Bank!"

From a different point in the sky above Badir Tazh we noticed that its mosque was also smashed. The dome was crushed in like the shell of a half-eaten egg. Only a few of the adobe houses in the village were intact, the rest were in ruins. We were too high to observe much more. "Alloh, alloh . . . Battalion Commander Davidov here! Alloh . . . Eaglets Squadron? Peredayou!"

"Major Smirnov of the Eaglets Squadron here. How can we help you, tovarich Commander? Peredayou."

"The bastards are entrenched in the ruins and our bayonet charges are proving too costly. Bomb craters are providing shelter for their snipers! They have three machine gun nests to the west of what is left of the mosque, and there are riflemen strung out on all sides inside the ruins. The machine guns must be eliminated before I can order another ground attack. Note their locations, tovarich Major! One is on the roof of the barn opposite the cemetery where my men are entrenched. The second gun is in what is left of the minaret. The third is on the roof of the only barn left on the west side of the village. Peredayou!"

"Smirnov to all pilots, attention! We will divide into three segments of five. Nikolayev, your segment will attack the gun on the west side. Solontzev, you take the machine gun in the stump of the minaret. I will take on the barn next to the cemetery. Assume positions to come in from the sun and hit all three guns simultaneously! Separate into your segments! Segment leaders repeat orders!"

"Nikolayev speaking. I am to attack gun on the west wall."

"Solontzev speaking. I am to take out gun in stump of minaret."

"Attention, squadron! No sloppy shooting! Our men are dug in just outside the ruins! This position and altitude is just about perfect. Complete your turn and climb. Get in closer on each other's tails when you begin the dive. Squaddddronnn . . . execute!"

I was flying with Major Smirnov's segment. When his plane peeled off into the dive, Major Belomirov followed him, and I stayed on Belomirov's tail. Following me was Sasha

Kadikoff and he was followed by Lieutenant Baranin. "This should be easy," I reflected when my turn came to peel away. "Nothing more than an exercise." The earth came up at me like a wall. Buildings loomed up and grew larger and larger with each passing second. The tail of the ship ahead of me kept moving its elevator part as if in slow motion, then lifted away. The roof of the barn appeared in my gun sight, then I saw the gun and men in a large nest of grain bags, many of them split open. I kept pressing the button on my control stick. Through the dust on that flat roof, figurines of men continued to fire back at me. Then I gently pulled up on my stick and lifted away, back into the silent blue sky. A moment later we could see that we had not succeeded in taking out the gun. I found the tail of Belomirov's ship and I stuck to it, and we formed up into an echelon.

"Calling Major Smirnov . . . calling Major Smirnov . . ."

"Just a moment, Commander Davidov. I must attend to my command. Squaddddronnnn . . . segments two and three join segment one! Maintain altitude of segment one and follow same through its maneuvers. Now, calling comrade Commander Davidov! Can your company commanders please ascertain the condition of the two other enemy guns?"

"Company Commander Nikitin here. Good work! This gun is knocked out and it will be no trouble to mop up the remaining crew."

"Gavrilovsky reporting the same. There is still rifle fire, but the machine gun is silent."

"Right. We will now finish up the job for you, Commander Davidov. Give us five minutes. Peredayou." Major Smirnov's voice trailed off and weakened for an instant as he turned, leading the entire squadron back into an orbit around Badir Tazh. Then, in an attack assured to be devastating, he led all fifteen of us down at the one remaining gun. Each of us gave the poor devils in the crew a deadly salute, and five minutes later, as promised, we were winging our way back to Khiva.

Villages like Badir Tazh, with its adobe houses and barns levelled by our bombers, were soon buried by sand dunes from the Kara Kum. One deserted, but not yet buried village was called Kum Taszhis. Irrigated by ditches from the Amu-Darya, the fields of Kum Taszhis had been a source of food for the Uzbek people since time immemorial.

But this year there were no fields because nothing had been planted. The summer before, as a punishment for cooperating with the Soviets, a band of Turkomen guerillas had killed all the Uzbek inhabitants except for the mullah. So with no farmers left, the cotton had been harvested by the winter winds and was piled in snowlike drifts against the village walls. Grapevines grew out of the adobe ruins. Donkeys wandered in the unharvested orchards, feeding on the fallen, dehydrated fruit.

This was what Sasha Kadikoff and I knew about the village from flying frequent patrol over the western bank of the Amu-Darya. But this time we were told before we were sent off once again that a riverboat had been fired upon from the shore at Kum Taszhis, and our orders were to take careful reconnaissance, and to respond to any activity we might discover.

Following the Khiva canal, Kadikoff and I reached the river and continued south. The only sign of life we saw was a small barge carrying passengers. Towed by a tractor, the boat was struggling south against the current. Soon we spotted the half-demolished minaret of Kum Taszhis.

If there were enemy soldiers there they wouldn't be taken by surprise. With the warning noise of our engines, they would have ample time to take cover. When we arrived the village appeared deserted. We kept searching the village at a safe height, but the remaining homes and courtyards facing the village streets seemed completely uninhabited.

"I'll keep searching on the outer perimeter, Sasha!" I said into my radio as I looked to my left at his ship, expecting him to acknowledge me by nodding. But instead of nodding, Kadikoff pointed at his earphone which meant that he wanted me to switch over and listen.

"Look down there, at the base of the minaret, Fishka! Women!" Kadikoff kept pointing downward, beyond his starboard wing. The pair of figures wore veils and they waved at us as they shielded their eyes from the rays of the morning sun. "I'm going down to take a closer look, Fishka!"

TEN

"Wait, Sasha! Hold it!" I shouted into my microphone, hoping that he had switched over to listen. The two women suddenly seemed to me to be moving more like men. "Wait Sasha," I shouted. "Don't go down!" I waved frantically, signaling for him to stay up, but his istrebitel was already plummeting in the direction of the figures. I dove down but before I could overtake his ship we came astride the minaret, with his plane to the left of it and mine on the right. Kadikoff kept staring groundward, keeping his eyes on the two veiled figures while I kept waving him up and cursing.

Sasha must have heard the dull thumping of the machine gun bullets as they splashed into his ship, for I saw his goggles flash in the sunlight as he turned and spotted the gun in one of the apertures on top of the minaret. His istrebitel streaked upward and away as he gave it full throttle. This time it was Sasha waving me upward.

". . . in the minaret!" I caught his frantic cry as I, too, gunned my engine to get out of there in a hurry.

"Let's take it out!" I shouted when I had caught up with him—but just then I noticed the disk of light reflected by his propeller change, quiver, skip and slow.

"Oy, oy! Fishka! My engine is dying, little brother." Over the radio Sasha's voice seemed to gasp, and he was clearly panting. The "peredayou" which followed sounded more like desperate resignation than a sign off. Then Sasha put the nose of his ship down into a glide. Next he dove the plane, attempting to restart the engine.

"Do not waste altitude, Sasha!" I shouted into my mike. "Glide for the other side of the river!"

"Altitude insufficient to reach other shore! Peredayou!"

"Do not land on this side!"

"I cannot stay up in this coffin and I am a poor swimmer, droog Fishka." Sasha spoke calmly now and seemed fully resigned to his fate as he glided in the direction of the river, fighting for every inch of altitude. "I will drown like a kitten, Fishka. My fuel line has been severed . . . carburetor must be dry . . . she won't start . . . peredayou."

The empty cotton fields beneath us seemed flat enough to be a likely place for a dead-stick landing, and I encouraged him to try it.

"Set her down parallel to the shore of the river, Sasha! Watch out for that irrigation ditch! See it? Land anywhere and in any way you care to come in! I'll duplicate your glide and land alongside. I want you to jump out and climb onto my left wing! Lie down and wedge yourself between the struts just as we rehearsed it once in fun. Remember?" As I, too, went down, gliding alongside Sasha's ship, out of the corner of my eyes I caught a glimpse of a rising cloud of dust, horsemen racing out of the village and heading in our direction.

"Don't do it, Fishka!" Kadikoff shouted when I switched over to get a confirmation from him. "Don't land! You might not be able to get back into the air with the both of us. There's no need for the both of us to die, Fishka!"

"No more talking, droog," I said as calmly as I could. I was scared, but I didn't want him to know just how scared I was. For the next few seconds neither of us said anything—we were too busy coming down to meet the earth. Sasha brought his ship to a dead-stick landing, and ground-looped it to a stop just short of the irrigation ditch. Since I was under power, I did the same with less effort. Sasha jumped from his cockpit and ran toward my plane.

Climbing onto my port wing, he pointed behind us and shouted something which was drowned out by the noise of the engine. The mounted mob was still far away, emerging from the trees lining the road from the village, but some horsemen were already galloping through the cotton field. To one side of me was the river, and ahead of me was the deep ditch. To attempt a take-off along the shore would have been foolhardy, for the distance along the bluffs before the river bent was far too short, especially with two of us on board. There remained only the field we had just flown over, and that meant turning around and taking off into the galloping enemy horsemen. I glanced at Sasha. He was wedged into the wing struts and ready, lying there in his leather coat, helmet and goggles, holding on with gloved hands.

I taxied the plane around, into the blinding light reflected off the surface of the river. There was no wind to hamper my take-off, but there wasn't any to aid me, either. Sighting on the village minaret I rolled forward until I gained enough momentum to lift my ship's tail. The horsemen screamed and fired their rifles as they galloped toward me, closing fast, most of them directly in my path.

I had my right thumb on the button of my control stick, ready to fire my machine guns, but I hesitated, not wanting a dead horse in my path until I was in the air. We were bouncing forward over the rough terrain and fortunately the horses were frightened by the roar of my engine and gave my ship a wide berth. The riders kept firing their rifles at us but without taking time to really aim, as I gave my engine the best mixture of air and fuel and it, in turn, gave me all the power it could possibly deliver.

At last my ship's wings bit into the air. The horsemen were behind us now as I continued flying low over the cotton field. I needed speed and power and momentum to pull up sharply before the clumps of trees ahead, and even more to clear the village walls and turn away from the minaret and away from the machine gun that had caused all the trouble to begin with.

I lifted the ship, cleared the clump of trees, and was banking my plane over the village itself, away from the minaret, when I became frightened that I may have carried out this maneuver too sharply and that I might have dumped Kadikoff! I leaned out of the cockpit and saw him grinning back at me. And it was then that I looked past my port wing and saw one of the rebels, a large man in a tall fur hat, standing some fifty feet below. In the crook of his arm he cradled a Lewis machine gun which—as I watched—he raised and aimed. From the barrel appeared small white puffs of smoke. The scene did not seem real until I felt a jarring inside my bucket, and simultaneously a searing pain in my seat and a terrible burning in both my thighs.

The bandit and his machine gun fell away beneath me as my ship gained altitude, but the pain did not leave. Red hot pokers jammed into my flesh. I wondered if Sasha had also been hit. He was no longer smiling and seemed to be trying to point with his chin toward something on the fuselage with great effort. I leaned out and saw rivulets of blood spreading over the surface of the plane. It was my blood and I felt it soaking my seat and felt more of it running down my legs and saturating the inside of my boots. A coldness moved upward from my legs into my torso, to my arms, my fingertips, and also into my head where it converted into heat and blurred my vision.

A few versts across the river, in friendly territory, lay the village of Turt Kul. I wanted to try to make an emergency landing there, but I could barely see the compass. The river was to my rear, and the sun to the right. I should soon see the tent hangars of the Turt Kul landing strip on the western horizon. Somehow I forced myself to function as I clenched my teeth and summoned all that was still alive in me to fight the drowsy feeling, and my strangely indifferent attitude: I was dying but so what?

Somehow, I reached Turt Kul and put the ship down. From that moment on Sasha Kadikoff took charge. Fortunately there was a doctor and a medical clinic at Turt Kul, and still more fortunately, Sasha's blood matched mine and the young woman doctor at that clinic knew how to perform a transfusion. The lady doctor also extracted two bullets, each of which had lodged near my hip sockets. A third had lodged inside my groin. To extract this one, she said, was far beyond her skill, and so she only bandaged the wound. I heard her say to Sasha that only the most skillful of surgeons should be entrusted with extracting the bullet from my groin. It would be a matter of luck, touch and go, whether my masculinity could be saved, and whether I would retain the ability to . . .

"Hey, hey!" I called out to Sasha and the lady doctor. "What good is life without that!"

"Here, chew on this onion, young man," the doctor ordered. "Raw onions restore your blood."

ELEVEN

THE COLD: EARLY ON A BITING, WINDY NOVEMBER morning filled with sunlight that lay on the skin like ice, the family piled into the old Plymouth and drove into the city and parked on a side street down which the wind rushed like water in a Western flash flood. Off they marched to find the Macy's Thanksgiving Day Parade. Within a few minutes the two young brothers had spotted the giant helium balloons, bears and moose and rabbits four stories high! Between the legs and thighs of other onlookers they heard the marching bands and watched the baton twirlers. Then Phil hoisted one and then the other onto his shoulders—until he complained about their weight.

"Are you cold? Are you cold?" Tillie asked the boys over and over again, but they did not tell her the truth since they were waiting for the fabled Santa to appear on his sled.

"Are you cold?" Phil asked. "Listen to your mother. Tell the truth."

"They're cold," Tillie said over the raucous, blaring blast and wails of the marching bands.

"They say no," Phil said for them.

"N–n-no!" said Alan.

"N–n-nooo," said the younger boy, echoing the older.

"You're cold," said their mother, but by that time the sled with the white-bearded elf-man in red satin with white fringe came heaving into view over the street-corner horizon.

"Santa!" shouted the older boy.

"S-s-s-anta!" echoed the younger.

"It's just a myth," said Phil. "I don't know why we waited in the cold so long just to see a man in a costume."

"Don't tell them that," Tillie said.

"I just told them," Phil said, rubbing his hands against the icy air. "They're smart boys, anyway. They know, they know," he said, his breath coming out in great puffs of steam that rose up toward the streetlamps decked with green and wreaths. "Don't you, boys?"

"It's a myth," said Alan, watching the sled pass by and then turning his face to the nickel-cold coin of the sun.

"You're ruining it for them, Phil," Tillie said.

"Oh, Teel, ruining what?" The boy could see those incisors catching the light from that icelike orb up above. "They're Jews, what do they want to know from Santa Claus?" His voice brimmed over with derisiveness and disgust.

"I just wanted them to have a good time," said Tillie, her eyes turning liquid—which made at least one of the boys suddenly afraid that her eyes might freeze. But with a power he hadn't seen her use before she turned suddenly to his father and said, "Some Jew you are anyway."

With a few quick movements of her hands she turned and herded her boys away from the now rapidly disbanding crowd.

"Come on," she said. "Let's get out of the cold."

"Now what did you mean by that remark?" Phil asked as they walked along behind the children.

"Which remark?" Tillie asked.

"About my being a Jew."

"Well, you're not much of a Jew," she said.

"So, it's all a myth, anyway," he said. "Santa Claus, the Jews, everything. Science shows that. This is the modern age. Teel. This . . ."

"Oh, Phil, please leave me alone."

They drove for a while around the city, the parents silent, the boys gawking at the buildings, at the decorations that decked the streets full of shops. Around four o'clock Tillie began to ask if they were hungry. Yes, they were. Phil parked the car and they wandered through the midtown streets in search of a restaurant—only to find, everywhere they stopped, that all the tables had been reserved for the holiday meal.

Dark collapsed over them as though it were a balloon from which someone had pulled the plug.

"Let's go home, Phil," Tillie said.

"We're going to find a restaurant."

"I can fix something at home."

"Can we have turkey and stuffing at home?"

"You know we can't. You know that you told me you wanted to go to the parade and then eat out."

"You said the parade and the restaurant and I went along with it. That's what happened." He caught Alan's eye and made a movement with his head, something the boy had never seen before but the meaning of it was clear: the two of them against the mother.

"You agreed."

"Because I thought we could find a restaurant and now we can't."

"Let's go home," Tillie repeated.

"You have no turkey and the boys want turkey, don't you, boys?"

The boys nodded vigorously, they wanted turkey. They walked along together, Alan admiring his father's stubbornness and determination while at the same time wanting his mother to feel happier about the decision, as his brother clung to Tillie's coat sleeve and was buffeted by the argument like one of those balloons in high wind.

"I can fix something at home," Tillie said again.

"It's Thanksgiving," Phil said, "an American holiday, and we'll eat turkey."

"If it kills us," Tillie said.

It didn't, and it did. They wandered through the freezing streets for at least another half-hour, the sliver of sky between the high buildings above them turning dark blue, their fingers feeling like little stalks of icicles even within the confines of their mittens. Alan's stomach rumbled. Shel began to whimper.

"Shut that up," Phil said, "we'll find a place soon."

"Phil . . ."

"Teel . . ."

And just then they rounded yet another windy corner, the streetlights winked on, and they saw the festive, brightly illuminated storefront in the middle of the block. A restaurant! But what if it too was already filled to capacity with holiday diners? They rushed forward and entered the place. Success! There was a table waiting for them!

"Phil?"

"I can see, I have eyes," Phil said as he stared at the menu: vegetarian fare only. "Soybean turkey roast," he read from the listings. "That sounds interesting."

"What is it?" the boy asked.

"You'll find out," his father said.

"I don't want to," the boy said.

"You don't? Let me tell you a story. A man goes to a doctor and says, Doc, my upstairs neighbor keeps playing his radio day and night and it's driving me crazy. I want to go up there and throw it out the window. *Do dot,* the doctor tells him, *Do dot.*"

Alan wasn't sure whether he was supposed to laugh at this story or listen carefully to hear more of it.

"What?" he said.

"Do dot," Phil said. *"Do dot."*

"Do what, Phil?" Tillie said.

"Oh, Teel," he said, "order the soybean turkey."

"But I don't want that," Tillie said, nearly in tears again.

"Order it," Phil said.

"Order it, Mommy," Shel said.

"You heard him," Phil said.

"Be quiet," Tillie said.

"Are you saying that to me?" Phil said.

"I'm saying that to all of you," Tillie said.

"I wasn't talking," Alan said.

"Be quiet," Tillie repeated.

"No, Teel, you be quiet," Phil said, slapping aside the menu.

"I want to go home," Shel said.

"Be quiet," Phil said.

"Don't talk to him like that," Tillie said.

"I'll talk to him," Phil said. "I'll talk to him any way I like."

"Not to them," Tillie said. "Maybe you talk that way to me but not to them."

"Who are they?" Phil said. "Are they a pair of princes? I want you to look at me. Teel? Teel?" He raised his hand in the air. "I want you to look at me," he said and brought his fist down on the plate before him with a crash, sending the other dishes and glasses and silverware flying across the table. Alan stared at the overturned water pitcher spilling liquid into his brother's lap, his brother the first one to cry.

T W E L V E

THE TIME AND DISTANCE FROM TURT KUL TO Khiva and Khiva to Chardzhou, then Tashkent, was stretched into a burning, agonizing pain, aggravated by my having to remain face down, resting on my elbows with my posterior extending upward. My midriff and the rest of me was supported by a partially inflated inner tube to isolate my groin from anything that might touch it. The only other patient in the air-ambulance was a gravely wounded Red Army soldier with a bullet in his larynx.

The pilot was a former classmate of mine, a lad named Zaitzeff, whose nickname was "Trussik." Trussik tried to cheer me up by cracking jokes about how much fun it would be for me when the nurses had to unbandage my unmentionable in order for me to perform my natural needs. It was funny at first, even to me, but not by the time we reached Tashkent.

"Forgive me for the jokes, Fishka!" Trussik said, turning around in his seat and reaching out to affectionately ruffle my hair when I looked up a him. "I hope the operation turns out right for you. The best of luck to you, droog!"

But the wisecracking and winking only continued when I had to be shaved around the wound and the area had to be prepared by a doctor and nurses.

"Ahhhemm," one of the doctors snickered into his surgical mask. "I see you were pretty near circumcised twice."

The voice of the same man but without a mask greeted me when I came to. "Lieutenant Kaplan? How are you feeling?"

"I would feel even better if I knew the operation turned out right," I replied, realizing that I was no longer in the operating room but in a room by myself, in a bed.

"Everything is fine, Lieutenant Kaplan! It all turned out fine!"

"Will I be able to function normally?" I inquired bluntly.

"I do not think you need worry about that," the doctor smiled. He was a man twice my age and his attitude toward me was paternal, leaving me with the impression that he had children my age, grandchildren perhaps.

"What worries me, sir, is that, I keep wondering whether I'll be able to have offspring some day, sir."

"All I can say to you, Lieutenant, is that when you verify the first and it turns out affirmative, then you can be assured of a similar finding in the second." The doctor turned away and cleared his throat. "Tell me, young man, how does it look in Khorezm? Do you think the fighting there will be over before long?" To assure me of his military status, the doctor lifted a corner of the collar of his white jacket and revealed the two bars of a lieutenant colonel of the medical corps, but his question only served to remind me of my orders to keep mum about this matter.

"What fighting sir? There is no fighting in Khorezm. There are merely maneuvers that we are conducting. Military maneuvers with live ammunition often result in wounds such as mine, sir."

A week after my operation I was able to gingerly sit in a canvas chair. Later I strolled the paths of the garden and paced the balcony of my room. Anything was better than sitting and lying on my stomach. After another week, I began asking my doctor to please return me to my squadron in Khiva.

"Not yet, not yet. We must make sure you are fully recovered, Lieutenant, before we expose you to danger again."

He did not realize, perhaps, that I was being exposed to a different kind of danger right here in the hospital. Her name was Dunya Duntzova and she was my nurse. Dunya made me sense that my masculinity was still as good as it ever was. Whenever she found me in my bed she would insist I remain in it while she changed the linen. She would deftly lean over me when it was time to tuck in the linen on the other side and in so doing press her firm bosom into my face. Dunya also had a way of setting me on fire when she washed me with soap and water and then helped me into a basin full of potassium permanganate in which I soaked my wounds.

Her teasing tormented me. I loved it and I could hardly stand it–and once, when it seemed too much, I grabbed her and held her. But I was still weak–she easily freed herself and smacked me in the face. My left cheek burned as she said, "If you want something, Lieutenant, do not grab . . . ask."

"Why Dunyechka . . . need I ask? You know what I want."

"Yes? But do you also want marriage?"

"Oh . . ." I said no more.

From that time on Dunya said nothing either. Deliberately she would press me with her breast, smooth the bed sheets in sensitive places, and smile at me in a sweet yet sullen way.

"Please stop it, Dunyechka," I pleaded with her. "You're making it very difficult for me."

"It could be the other way around, if you promised me we would go to . . . to . . ."

"Where, Dunya?"

"To register, that's where."

"That's out of the question," I said firmly.

"And why is that? Are you married already?"

It occurred to me that it was not a bad alibi to get her to stop tormenting me, but I could not bring myself to lie. Dunya in the meantime interpreted my silence as an affirmative reply.

"What's her name?" she asked.

"Whose name?"

"The girl you already married."

"Oh, her name is Aviation," I replied.

"She must be very nice."

"*Very* nice," I said, "and I love her very much."

"Then you should be ashamed of yourself for trying to entice me, Lieutenant!" Dunya exploded with anger and ran out of my room. After that she came to make my bed when I was in the garden, and by then I was able to take my own showers and bathe in potassium permanganate after waiting in line with other wounded in the Red Army men's ward.

It seemed they wanted to keep me in the hospital forever. Slow days turned into long weeks with little to do.

One day I at last received a letter from Sasha Kadikoff. Things had taken a turn for the better about "you know what," and things were "almost peaceful now." And Antonina sent her best wishes, he wrote, and kept asking about when I am coming back to Khiva. But best of all, Sasha said that it appeared that there was a wonderful surprise in store for me, underlining the words *wonderful* and *surprise.*

"Fishka, Commissar Belomirov says you can buy another little square insignia to have ready to attach to your lapels, because you are definitely being promoted to the rank of captain!"

And if that were not exhilarating enough, Sasha also wrote that he had learned from Major Smirnov himself that I was to be awarded the Order of the Red Banner.

"Just think what this means! You are being given the highest medal for valor in battle that our country awards, and with it comes a pension, and immunity from arrest and jail, save for treason, I believe, and murder. Major Smirnov said that according to information he has received from Moscow, General Budenny himself, if he comes to Tashkent as scheduled for the May Day parade review, will pin the medal on you in person. Fishka, I cannot begin to tell you how happy all of us here are for you! And needless to say, I am not only happy for you but grateful to you for saving my life at such great risk to yours. I cannot wait to see you when you rejoin the squadron! Hearty humble congratulations!"

And in a postscript he added: "Please write a letter to Antonina so that she will stop bothering me with questions about how you are getting along with all those pretty army nurses."

Days before the first of May, a list of the hospital patients who were to present themselves for review at the holiday celebration was posted on the bulletin board. My name appeared on the list. We had to be in uniform and on our feet, if possible.

And I was sitting around in my hospital robe, wondering what I would wear for the occasion, since I had arrived in Tashkent in sheets, when an orderly brought me my own duffel bag which had finally arrived from Khiva. Inside the bag were my custom-made boots, my changes of uniform all folded neatly and pressed. All my other clothing and personal items were also there, and just as I had left them, save that my Mauser had been replaced with a regulation revolver, the side arm I now preferred.

"Does this mean that I am to be discharged, sir?" I asked of my doctor when I was given permission to don the uniform in place of my pajamas and robe.

"It means just that, Lieutenant," the doctor said. "I might as well tell you that your discharge from this hospital was delayed because your orders are being forwarded to you by way of General Budenny's office."

On the morning of the first of May, an oddly-matched collection of cavalry, infantry and air force men, some in wheelchairs, some supported on crutches, and the rest in pressed and polished uniforms, lined up in the hospital garden ready for review. Those of us who were not in wheelchairs stood at ease, blinking in the sunshine of that bright morning. In the windows of wards, and on the verandas, patients and nurses and doctors waited for General Budenny to arrive.

The hospital's political commissar, a captain, was running back and forth, making sure that all the men lined up in the garden were in proper attire. "Do not forget," the captain cautioned us from time to time. "Speak only when spoken to! If the general asks you a question, comrades, it better be the right answer that you give him. All gripes are out! Hear me? No complaints! Save your bellyaching for the doctors!"

"General Budenny in person?" some asked.

"I've only ever seen his portrait."

"Mother of God! Budenny himself? I served in his cavalry when we chased the Poles to the gates of Warsaw."

"There he is!"

Everyone came to the best state of attention possible. The general and his retinue arrived on prancing, lathered horses.

They dismounted before an arch in the garden and marched the rest of the way, bowlegged all, their spurs jingling and their sabers swaying.

"At ease!" ordered General Budenny, twisting one end of his handlebar mustache. "At ease, comrades." He waved his hand at us to illustrate how he wished for us to relax. For a man whose business it was to wage a bloody war against a savage enemy, the general had a rather good-natured air about him.

Smiling benevolently, General Budenny came forward to shake the hand of a cavalry major in a wheelchair at the head of our motley formation. Then the general proceeded to distribute citations and shake hands in turn with all in the line until he reached me.

"This is the lad, General," I heard an aide whisper.

General Budenny looked me straight into the eyes, smiled, and with a friendly twinkle in his eyes shook my hand with both of his.

"This is the lad who is getting the Order, comrade General."

"Oh . . . you're so young, Lieutenant. Or should I say Captain, since your rank is herewith being elevated. I see we have an extra quadrate for each of your lapels. Ah, you fliers are all so young! But then I suppose one has to be young and foolish to do the things you perform in samolets high in the sky."

The general spoke softly and amiably, as he pinned on my captain's insignia. "So I see you have earned the Order of the Red Banner, young man. Most commendable! Now you only have two more to earn to have as many as I have on my chest. Ahemm . . . is this Captain Kaplan's citation? Very well, then I will read it."

General Budenny cleared his throat, twisted his mustache, and read, "For bravery beyond the call of duty, for an act of devotion to a comrade at arms during combat, to wit: Captain Kaplan risked his own life by landing his samolet alongside a similar machine flown by his comrade to snatch the latter from being taken by the enemy, flew his comrade out of the enemy encampment on the wing of his own samolet during which action Captain Kaplan sustained wounds. In consideration of the above, and for the bravery with which Captain Kaplan, for his display of heroism, for his devotion to his comrades and faithfulness to the oath of allegiance he has taken to the Soviet Socialist Federated Republics, the Communist Party and its glorious leader, Joseph Vissarionovich Stalin, Commander Fishel Isaakovich Kaplan is herewith awarded the Order of the Red Banner and all the privileges, pensions, and honors that the bearer of the above order is entitled to by law. Signed by Minister of Defense, Commander and Chief Red Army Klimenty Voroshilov and signed, so forth, by Deputy Commanding Red Army Air Force General Jacob Smushkevich, and signed, and so forth."

General Budenny broke off and turned to his aide: "I will need a penknife, Egorov, something to puncture the tunic to insert the stem of the order. Does this one fasten with a screw? Give me the velvet box, Egorov. And what is this bulky envelope?"

"His orders and his back pay, tovarich General."

I remained rigid, standing at attention, feeling a bit dazed, overwhelmed by the living, breathing presence of the legendary General Budenny, and afraid that I would awaken and find it all a dream. But it did not end before General Budenny smothered me with his mustache and planted a hearty kiss upon my mouth.

General Budenny and his entourage rode away and the onlookers rushed into the garden. Doctors, nurses, orderlies, patients and their visiting relatives, all hurried to congratulate and shake hands with those whom General Budenny had shaken hands. The first to grab my hand was a wild-eyed cavalry man who had hobbled over quickly on crutches. "So, you are immune from arrest, sir. Think of it! Furthermore, with all the wings and insignia on you, comrade sir, it is obligatory that an ordinary Red Army man like myself kiss your hand."

"Oh, ho," an infantry major standing next to me said, and smiled.

Then many others came forward with congratulations, so many that I found it embarrassing, and as soon as possible I escaped from the garden, only to come face to face with a pretty nurse whom I had noticed previously, but who had paid no attention to me. Now she looked at me as though we knew each other.

"Ach, how are you getting by, tovarich Captain?" she extended a dainty hand toward me.

"Captain?" I repeated, rather surprised by the term. "You are the first to address me by my new rank, comrade Sister of Mercy."

"Forgive my bold manner," she said, "but I must get to know you better." Bubbling on, she noted that only minutes before she had noticed me standing in formation as a lonely lieutenant and now I was already a captain, not to mention the owner of the very highest decoration adorning my chest. It was imperative that we become better acquainted.

"Well," I said, "permit me to introduce myself." I clicked my heels and saluted her. "My name is Fishel Isaakovich Kaplan."

"And I am Elizaveta Efimovna, but you may call me Liza."

While we were exchanging names and going through the formalities of hand shaking, Liza and I were looking each other over, and judging by the way she held onto my hand and blinked her eyes, it was plain to see that she now liked what she saw.

"Well Liza," I said. "I have just been handed my back pay plus bonuses. Would you allow me to take you to lunch?"

"Excellent idea, Captain! I'd love to have you take me to some secluded place."

It seemed that in no time we were sitting at a table being waited on by the giant Armenian, Yashka. We ordered wine and fireman's cutlets, but before the food ever arrived we had finished the bottle. Yashka apologized, explaining that it was May Day and he was alone in the kitchen because of the holiday. Would we mind sipping some more wine while he was chopping the cutlets? Liza did not mind, and by this time her wish was my command. We sat and sloshed wine into our empty stomachs. Brass bands were blaring away, it seemed, all over Tashkent, and there were columns marching to drums and burping tubas. Red banners waved from every building, and speakers were shouting themselves hoarse, one after another, to a crowd in the park across the way. Liza and I kept drinking wine and she kept on talking, saying how wonderful it felt to be alive, even if only on holidays such as May Day, and the first of every other month, meaning paydays.

"Ach," she said. "Captain, you know what? I think I love you. What's your name again?"

"We mustn't be hasty, Elizaveta Efimovna," said I, sobered by her babbling. "After all, we only met an hour ago."

"Your cutlets, sizzling hot!" Yashka said, placing the plates on the table.

"Who can eat? I am in love," Liza whimpered, her mouth in a pout.

We ate slowly, and Liza kept saying complimentary things between bites of meat and bread, and kept looking at me like a lovesick heifer, and I was doing the same.

"No more formalities, Captain! Please do not address me as Elizaveta Efimovna any more. Please! And if you displease me I may be compelled to toss my drink into your face! Please, Captain, address me as Elizaveta . . . no, as Liza . . . No, call me Lizechka, you hear? To you I am Lizechka! Call me that because I love you!"

Following this I must have asked Lizechka to marry me, because this time it was she who was sobered somewhat. "Ach," Lizechka exclaimed. "We mustn't be too hasty, Captain . . . what's your name?"

"Kaplan, Fishel Isaakovich."

"Ahmm, I happen to know . . . that is, I have heard and I even saw on the hospital records that there is no way of knowing whether or not the surgeon's hand might not have . . . slipped . . . or snipped something that may have deprived you of your . . . manhood," Lizechka stammered out. "At this very moment, Captain, you may be unwittingly proposing marriage to me under false pretense."

"Nonsense!" I said vehemently, sobering and coming to my defense.

Enlivened and pleased by my denial, Lizechka smiled and said that if I was so sure of myself would I care to prove it.

"Certainly!" I said, becoming intoxicated with the very idea. "I accept the challenge!"

"Ohhh," Lizechka cooed. "Then, afterwards, you will not be cross with me should I decline your proposal to marry you?" She blinked and blushed and beamed at me and was, I think, trying to let me know she was not being coy.

"Certainly not, Elizaveta Efimovna!" I assured her.

"Ach, please Captain, call me Lizechka."

We left the restaurant and strolled hand in hand toward a hotel, Liza and I, with but one thought in our minds.

"Ach, Fishel . . . Fishka," Lizechka sighed, gazing into my eyes as we staggered on, "may I dispense with formalities and address you as Fishenka?"

"Listen Lizechka," I said to her. "We are about to dispense with more than mere formalities. Do you know what I mean?"

"Ach," exclaimed Lizechka, "I do! I do! What do you think, I'm just drunk or something? I am in love!"

Liza's hand and mine were entwined as I maneuvered her as speedily as I could to our destination and she talked, carrying on about how love had eluded her until now.

"Ach," I exclaimed, having caught the expression from her, but actually saying little, since what I felt about Liza was that she was a dainty dish and that I thought I loved her, but that it could have been the wine that made me think that way. And so I said nothing but "ach, ach" and gazed back into her eyes the way she gazed into mine.

As we approached the hotel though, Lizechka hesitated. She had sobered up a little and so had I. "Ooh . . . ach," Lizechka stammered at the door of the lobby, "I had meant to ask you, Fishenka, is it true what the other sisters were saying about you . . . are you Jewish, Fishenka?"

"Yes, I am."

Lizechka's lovesick look turned to a nervous blinking.

"Well? Do we take a room, or do we cancel the proposed experiment right now?"

"Ach, no, Fishenka, darling. I was only asking." Now Lizechka dragged me on into the hotel lobby. It happened that the hotel was the same one where Lieutenant Kadikoff, Captain Tyatin, and I had stayed the previous spring. The hotel clerk was even the same. I recognized him by the way he kept sweeping at his mop of hair when he said "nyet." He would say it sometimes three times in a row. "Nyet, nyet, nyet! No rooms available because of the holiday! Nyet, nyet, nyet!" He reminded me of a cockatoo, since he sounded like one, and looked like one too with his hair which resembled ruffled feathers.

"I will take the roof," I suggested.

"Nyet! The roof has been shut."

"Too much rain in the windows?" I asked.

"No. I mean yes and no. Some clown ventured too close and fell off!"

"Look, old man, I will give you a bank note of a hundred for a room that rents for ten." I whispered this, but apparently not quietly enough, because a nosey civilian who had moved up close suddenly looked like he had caught the smell of something rotten.

"Nyet, nyet, nyet!" the clerk clicked off.

"What's the matter, darling?"

Lizechka had threaded her way through the crowd and stood at my side. I explained to her that there was no room to be had for love or money.

"Ach!" Lizechka cried, visibly disappointed and sobering up at last. Her happiness was wilting, but she refused to give up hope.

"Papashenka, little uncle, if you please, isn't there *anything?"*

"Nyet, nyet, nyet."

Lizechka smiled sweetly and persisted. If he was young once himself, she cooed to the clerk, then he could comprehend what love is. Was there not a room he might have overlooked? A broom closet perhaps? anything? But the cockatoo clerk could only say nyet, nyet, nyet, whereupon Lizechka became a faucet of tears which fell on the register.

The clerk jerked the book toward him and began blotting up the stains, glaring at Liza and shouting curses which were drowned out by the music of a brass band which was passing the hotel at the moment.

In fact, almost everyone had gone outside to watch the passing parade, all but a few people, one of whom now came forward to where we stood with the hysterical clerk.

"Forgive the intrusion, Captain," the cavalry major said, saluting Liza and me. He was a witness to our predicament, he said, and had a room which he had no need of that night. It would be a shame to let his room go to waste, he said turning to the clerk, and he would be pleased to let Liza and me make use of it.

Unhesitantly I accepted the major's offer. I saluted him, thanked him, shook his hand, and smiled in gratitude. Liza also brightened and broke out in smiles as she thanked the tall, young major with clinking spurs. He was older than I, with a little blonde mustache, a typical Russian face, and a nose shorter than mine, all of which I suddenly realized pleased my Lizechka. And he also outranked me.

"Ach, comrade Major," Lizechka commenced. "I adore horses, and horses must simply adore you!"

"You two are on your honeymoon, I presume?" asked the major. I was about to nod positively when Liza blurted out, "No, Major. The room is for the captain. We're not married. The captain has been discharged from the military hospital where I am a nurse, but he is planning to stay in Tashkent a little longer. I am accompanying him . . . to instruct him how to care for his healing wounds."

"Forgive me for jumping to conclusions, comrades!" said the major, making it sound like a profound apology. "But naturally I must take back my offer of my room."

I succumbed to silence and listened to Liza. Now she turned her full charm on, saying how embarrassing it was for an innocent girl like herself to be mistaken for a bride, in a hotel yet, but that she was ready to forgive the major.

Well, the encounter was a tactical error on his part, he said. And it was probably due to the fact that he was a married man himself with memories of his own honeymoon still vivid in his mind. He said that when he had sighted a young couple attempting to secure a room, his thoughts had galloped in the wrong direction, so to speak.

Upon hearing that the Major was married, Liza bit her lip and promptly turned from the major to face the clerk. "Are you certain there is no room, with a divan or bed or anything, for the captain?" she asked.

"Nyet, nyet, nyet!" the clerk recited and promptly yanked the register from Liza, in case she again start shedding tears.

"I will reserve a padded cell for you in our psychotherapeutic ward," Lizechka called back to the clerk as, a moment later, we found ourselves at the hotel's door.

Out on the street I sighed.

"Can you forgive me?" she smiled, shyly shielding her eyes from the sunlight.

"Nyet, nyet, nyet!" I said.

"Does this mean you have withdrawn your marriage proposal?"

"Da, da, da!" I said.

"Oh, oohh, ach . . . I was such a fool!" Lizechka almost sounded repentant.

We walked together back to the hospital where, sobered up by all of our antics, we managed to part in good humor and as friends.

Just as Lizechka walked away, nurse Dunya Duntzova came over to me, meeting me as I walked up the stairway.

"I saw you stroll off with that flirt Elizaveta Efimovna," Dunya said.

"Why should you care with whom I go off, Dunya?" I asked her, trying to treat her kindly.

"I don't know why, but I do," she replied in a low, hurt tone of voice. I could not have imagined her behaving so meekly. "It might just be that I'm in love with you, comrade Kaplan. But I thought you were married, to the woman you called Aviation!"

I explained the joke to her and she laughed, but I felt suddenly weary and said, "I don't know what you want with me, Dunya, but I've had a hard day and I simply must go to my room and rest."

"You're due for discharge tomorrow," Dunya blurted out, and her words served to remind me that I had neglected to open the envelope and read my orders! Now was as good a time as any, and standing on the steps I got them out, and oh, how surprised and disappointed I was.

"I'm not being sent back to my squadron," I cried out, wounded, to Dunya, to anyone who would listen. I was under orders to take thirty days leave and report on 1 June 1929, to the town of Volsk on the Volga River, where I was to serve as an instructor at the Volsk Military Aviation School for Pilots and Mechanics. "No, this won't do. All the friends I have are in Khiva!"

"Girlfriends also?" asked Dunya.

"Girlfriends also. Of course!"

"Listen, unless you like that flirt Elizaveta better, I would like to be your girl, Captain," Dunya said, looking shyly down at the ground, "if only for this evening."

"You have waited too long to make up your mind, Dunya. As you said, I leave Tashkent tomorrow."

"At least there is what there is left of today, Fishel Isaakovich," she said, still without looking up.

"Am I then to assume, Dunya, that . . . ?" I didn't quite know how to finish the question, but it was clear she understood it.

"I might, but not if you are also interested in that Elizaveta!"

"Could you meet me here at seven sharp, Dunyechka?"

"I might."

"I will take you to dinner."

Dunya was not at all like Elizaveta. To begin with, she disliked wine. She liked mineral water or milk with her meal, and she detested vodka, and even champagne. It was too hot to drink tea that evening, so in the end we drank milk to finish off our meal.

After we had eaten I left it to Dunya where we would go next. She had two choices, actually three: there was a concert being given by a Red Army band, there was the theater where the Uzbekistan national dance troop was performing, and there was the public park where we could go promenading.

"I prefer the park to some crowded theater or club room," said Dunya, sighing and sounding dreamy. There was an abundance of unbottled oxygen in the park, she said, stretching her long, pale arms and yawning. It was also, she acknowledged, the least expensive.

"Isn't this romantic?" Dunya said once we had reached the greenery and she had pointed to the moon which half hid itself behind stratus clouds.

"Yes, very romantic," I said, my thoughts lifting into the skies where, with or without my friends, I would soon once again fly.

"Only couples in love come here," Dunya said. "Hundreds of couples come here nightly, maybe even thousands."

"They couldn't all be in love," I said.

"They thin out by ten or eleven o'clock. Only the ones truly in love remain in the park after that hour," she said, falling in step with me and hanging onto my arm and squeezing. I took this to mean we were staying.

We strolled along the paths in the midst of laughter and voices exchanging trivialities and nonsense, past benches occupied by couples, until about ten, when indeed the crowd began thinning out.

"The moon playing hide-and-seek among the clouds is so beautiful," Dunya said, "like lovers playing cat and mouse."

"Lovers? Ah, yes!" I said. Romance was all around us. I suggested we sit down on a bench. And truly, all around us in the bushes there were sounds of romantic whispering, giggling, and groaning too, going on. We could clearly hear a couple whispering vows of fidelity to the end of time, of love beyond the grave. But the bench was too hard for my tender, bullet-punctured posterior. So we rose to promenade some more and see what place we could find that might be more suitable.

Now it was near eleven, and there were plenty of benches available. The couples who had occupied them before had graduated from the mumbling of their infatuations to an ardor where mere words no longer sufficed.

"Let's find some spot on the grass where you can be comfortable," suggested Dunya, dragging me by the arm toward some bushes. We sat down in a secluded, cozy place—or rather Dunya did, for I could not. I had to lie down—but soon got up in order to loosen the buckle on my Sam Browne belt when she complained that my side arm was banging her and that I should be careful lest, God forbid, my revolver go off.

Afterwards we listened to various sounds in the darkness. *"No! Nyet! Nyet! Nyet!"* some girl's voice implored her partner. The words reminded me of how I might have had a room at the hotel had it not been for that silly Elizaveta—but then I wouldn't have had Dunya in this love nest of a park, a woman who was clearly so much more correct for me, a sympathetic nurse for a wounded bird.

THIRTEEN

WE'RE SOARING THROUGH RUSSIAN AIRSPACE, heading toward Kiev on an aircraft something like our Western 727, six seats across, though cramped for space, with a passenger load something like a bus on its way from, say, Oklahoma City to Chicago—soldiers, housewives with children, old grandmothers, and a clutch of French tourists with thick faces and rough hands. (No one seems to be worried about visiting Kiev in the wake of Chernobyl.)

We're flying much higher than my father ever went, some thirty thousand feet plus above the eastern borders of the Ukraine, but I'm thinking about my poet friend Robert Pinsky's metaphor about soul-trails in the sky—that wherever people fly they leave invisible vapor trails, markers of their passage, and we cross and recross these wakes in the heavens. Robert was making a metaphor about poetry, I think. But I ponder its application to life as I stare out the window at the hazy clouds to the north, beyond the edge of the Baltic where shadowy Leningrad lies. I think that I see lakes where none exist, and I panic for a moment, thinking that, although I'm sure I read the sign correctly and heard the announcement correctly, we're on the wrong airplane, and we're flying off in some other direction to some other destination—who knows where?—in the heart of the Russian nation where we will spend days trying to get back on our correct itinerary, if ever.

I want to ask the young soldier sitting next to me about this, daring to try a sentence in Russian, but he has his eyes closed, and I decide not to disturb him. I don't say anything to Josh—he'll tell me I'm behaving like an old fart. He'd be right. I don't want to fight with him. I remember all too well the battles with my father. I don't want him to have to fight with me ever—or even quarrel. The price is too high after the father disappears.

I glance out the window. We're floating over wheatlands, over farms and small cities—and then the engines change their pitch, and we're making our descent to Kiev as the flight attendant's voice over the loudspeaker begins a long, rambling speech that has something to do with Kiev, its history and its agricultural output.

As we drive in our Intourist Volga toward town we pass through a radiation checkpoint—militiamen with Geiger counters check the car, as they're doing to all vehicles that come into the city, and all produce, or so says the English-speaking airline ground crewman who's hitched a ride with our driver. Nothing more than slightly elevated background radiation here, or so they've been told, he says. And the children are coming back for the opening of school. Josh looks at me and I look at him.

"Am I glowing yet?" he asks.

We check into our hotel, and at the tourist bureau I arrange for a car and guide for tomorrow's trip to Zhitomir, deep into the Pale of Settlement where for centuries impoverished subjects of the Russian kingdoms gathered in small villages, 180 kilometers from here.

We decide to do a little sightseeing on foot up and down the large avenue—the Kreshchatik—that serves as the city's main drag.

It *is* a drag. Thousands upon thousands of people, shoppers, office workers, and students (the kids *are* back and on the street), everyone still dressed in summer clothes since it's a lot milder here than in Moscow where autumn has already set in—but, and it's a big but, there are only the same dull shops with mediocre merchandise in small quantities, and though our hearts light up at the sight of some outdoor cafes, all that you can buy at them are glasses of fruit juice, no coffee, and the ubiquitous ice cream, vanilla, that you find in Leningrad and Moscow, all over. It's good ice cream, but after a while you tire of the same flavor, *and* the fact that just about the only diversion seems to be buying ice cream! I scream, you scream, we all scream *at* ice cream, after a while.

We walk past a large church on the north side of Shevchenko Boulevard on the way back to our hotel and see hundreds of babushkas, the grandmothers of the city, passing in and out of the entrance. Inside hundreds more kneel in prayer, and women so old they seem as dried and blackened as crickets, beg for change in the doorways and nooks inside the building. I hand out a few kopecks, Josh takes some photographs. People seem to ignore us, either so frightened by tourists that they pretend we don't exist, or else so used to them now that it's no big deal to see them. Probably the latter.

Outside we watch an old woman begging. A man comes up to her and takes some tea bags out of his briefcase and drops them in her hand. Another man passes, and drops a coin in her palm. She murmurs a thanks and a blessing, and as the man disappears up the street she glances down at the coin, and mutters what—from the look on her face—must be a little curse.

Dinner at the Homesick Restaurant? *No,* we're forced to eat at the hotel. There is no other place to go for a meal except to the dining rooms of other hotels downtown, and you can't seem to get admitted to those anyway unless you're a guest, or have made reservations through Intourist, or have some other special influence. We figure we'll stay at the hotel and eat.

The menu is varied, all kinds of meat and fish and poultry listed. But there are only three entrées available out of the dozens named—and we order chicken Kiev.

A piano and guitar duo takes the stand. They play a little local folk music, and then some (what they call in the American music business) "identity tunes," that is, music made popular by more famous groups. And what comes first? You got it—"Cheri, Cheri Baby."

"Oh," Josh says. "Modern Talking, very popular in the Soviet Union."

Last night I couldn't sleep very well. Tonight I'm overwhelmed with nostalgia, sadness, and other undefinable emotions. We're going in the morning to the town where my father spent his youth. We're staying tonight in the middle of his home region, and this huge wave of feeling washes over me, and while Josh settles in to sleep I turn my face to my pillow and let the sobs come.

Pa? I call out to him in my head.

No answer.

Pa? Papa?

Then, faintly, far off comes the reply: *It's okay, boy. I'm still here.*

We wake early to meet our driver and our guide, Tanya, a tall blonde schoolteacher who went to work for Intourist when she became bored with the classroom.

It is misty outside, the late summer heat just beginning to seep up through the steamy air. You can't see radiation, but Josh and I know that the city has been affected by Chernobyl. We've walked the streets that street sweepers wash down twice a day to keep the dust from rising, and we've seen the roadways laid bare like a chest in heart surgery as the city switches over to an alternative water system. It's a mental feat to picture the population of Kiev becoming irradiated. They wouldn't have felt a thing, and they won't know for years just how badly they were touched by the accident. Terrible, but it reminds me of the way my father has affected my own life.

There are a few young children on the street, despite the early hour, and these thoughts are also clearly on Josh's mind.

"If my kids are born with two heads, you know, I'm going to have a great time explaining that it was because you took me here to look for traces of my grandfather's life."

So. We roll out of Kiev and head west into the old Pale of Settlement. We pass, in addition to cars and buses bringing people into town, some horse-drawn wagons loaded with vegetables—workers from the state farms on the outskirts who are hauling produce from their own small, private vegetable plots to sell in the city, our guide explains to us.

She's curious about why we're going to Zhitomir and volunteers that she's never been there herself.

I make a vague comment about a grandfather who grew up in the district.

Do you have an address for the family? she asks. She's turned around in the front seat and is looking me in the eye. I glance over at Josh. We've talked about how we don't want to give out this information about our travels, or at least not make any references to Phil's Red Army Air Force days. I did in fact write my last remaining uncle in the Soviet Union a few months before we left on the trip to see if we might visit him, and he responded just before we departed with news that he and his wife were both quite ill and that they were going to be spending the summer in a sanatorium (he didn't say where) and that he wouldn't be able to meet us. Normally he lives in Ovruch, which is in the northwest corner of the Zhitomir district, about another seventy miles away from Kiev than Zhitomir itself. But since he won't be there that town's not on our itinerary.

So: no address, I tell Tanya, and she accepts this. Much of the territory—cities, towns, villages—was razed by the Nazis during the occupation, she explains, and so addresses wouldn't do a great deal of good in a lot of cases, anyway. Although—she reminds us—she hasn't been out this way at all and is only telling me what she has learned from reading histories. She herself comes from one of the old medieval towns outside of Moscow, and only relocated to the Ukraine after she finished school and married and had her child, who, she adds, is the darling of her life.

Her husband?

An engineer who volunteered for work on some construction projects near the Arctic Circle, and has lived there for the past three years.

How does she stand the separation?

She enjoys it. She is a free Soviet woman, she explains, and marriage had been weighing her down for a long while.

Doesn't her daughter miss her father?

Oh, he calls her once a month on the telephone, and he writes to her every week. He does a lot better as a father in letters, as a matter of fact, than he did in person.

We talk about single parenting and divorces and such, and she says that the current statistic on marriages in the Soviet Union is that over fifty percent end in divorce.

A lot in common between our two countries, I say.

The conversation stings me a little, separated as I've been from my two daughters for the past several years. Fathers and sons, fathers and daughters—a great throbbing wound I suffer these days.

Suddenly we pass a sign telling us that we've reached the Zhitomir district and my heart gives a little leap in anticipation of seeing the town where my father spent so much of his youth once he left the little village of Tikhorechka, where he spent the very first years of his life.

Zhitomir. The name apparently means "wheat" and "peace," Tanya explains.

Josh begins snapping photographs through the car windows. The three-hour drive has gone by quickly, and we're soon inside the city limits.

And my leaping heart has fallen back to rest. I'm waiting for some transcendental moment, some emotion to overwhelm me, because here we are approaching old haunts, the childhood places where my father strolled and stared and sniffed the air.

It is odd, or perhaps not odd at all, how the strangeness that Josh and I both felt when we crossed the border seems to have worn off. We can say to ourselves now, Hey, sure, we're in the Ukraine where Phil grew up, and it doesn't seem all that unusual. Perhaps that accounts for the casualness, or sense of familiarity, I feel about entering this particular region?

But since we have no address, and know only that young Fishel walked beneath this particular slab of sky along these pathways, we decide to throw ourselves into a tour of the town. The worst that can happen is to have some knowledge of the profile of a town in the Soviet Ukraine.

We walk its streets, see the food shops—meat and fish, vegetables, dairy products, baked goods—its ice cream parlor, we peek into private houses, walk through the museum, attend the Orthodox church ceremony of Assumption Day—we happen to be passing by and see the thousands of worshippers and go in, and discover that the Metropolitan of the entire Ukraine has come to preside over the event—and end up on the edge of town at the war memorial with a local guide whom we've met along the way giving us the details of the town's battle, and final strategic victory, against the Nazis.

He mentions that Benny Goodman was born nearby, as was Vladimir Horowitz, and, when the territory belonged to Poland, also Joseph Conrad. And I try to imagine young Conrad in these land-locked fields, wondering about the watery places of the world! And I think about my old man as a boy in this region of muddy lanes and wheatfields—could he have figured that he would fly his way out of this world and into another so different?

Then we wander across the ridge behind the war memorial, out of the draft of its oily eternal flame, and find ourselves standing on a precipice looking down at what our new guide calls "our Niagara," a little waterfall that turns the river below into a swirling pool which soon flows gently enough again for several old fishermen to toss in their lines without fear of losing the bait. Boys swim just below the wash of the falls, and with this pastoral scene below, and the warm breeze on our faces, I feel a little tinge of nostalgia—and why not? because who knows but that Fishel once swam there, paddling across the dozen yards or so to reach the near side of the river, as a boy does now, to look up and see visitors standing on the bluff, and raise a hand in a greeting?

FOURTEEN

TIKHORECHKA MEANS "QUIET RIVER," A NAME that came from the broad, placid stream running past the village. Beyond the river to the north were forests of hickory, birch, and pine. Fields of wheat and rye extended to the south, west, and east. Scattered huts were nestled on the outskirts of town amid acres of cabbages, onions and beans, orchards of hops, cherries, peaches and Hungarian plums, and groves of the famous Antonoff apples.

Around the huts with their thatched roofs, whitewashed walls, and tiny windows grew patches of petunias and tall, golden-yellow sunflowers. The silver ribbon of the river snaked among green pastures dotted with flocks of yellow ducklings and white geese and cows in countless herds.

Drought was unknown in these parts. Even during the worst heat of summer the waters of the distant Pripet Marshes flowed into the Tikhorechka and kept it high. The rains always came during summer, late in the afternoons and for prolonged periods after the gathering of the harvest.

Nearly a decade had passed since I had last seen Tikhorechka in 1920. Bathed in the sharp midday sunlight, its rows of wooden, one-story buildings now stood before me again. Despite the brightness of the day and the colors of the countryside beyond, the town looked dismal, wretched, and grey, as only a place of poverty can appear. A dingy bus with cracked windows and wobbly wheels carried me into the town square, the end of a ride that would have been even more uncomfortable than it was had not my wounds healed as much as they had. There, appearing smaller than I had remembered it, was the Greek Orthodox church, tarnished and forlorn, in the center of the dusty expanse. "What an outrage!" I exclaimed to myself when I saw some peasants carrying bags of grain from the church and loading them onto a wagon. "They've turned it into a granary!"

Except for that, the village was as if I had never left. The square, the church, the rows of stores and houses looked as ancient and bleak as ever. As a boy, I had raced barefoot about the crooked streets lined with sagging fences. Now the nameless avenues remained unpaved, there were still no sidewalks, and dust rose in clouds and clung to the high polish on my black boots as I walked. I recalled that during spring and fall these streets were muddy enough to swallow the wheels of a wagon, and in winter the fences were concealed under snow for months.

I remembered, too, the bitter winds that whistled and howled during winter storms. Our house stood on a bluff at the edge of town. When the river froze, wolves, driven by hunger, sometimes came from the woods, crossed the ice and came right up to the barns to try to steal the livestock. Once they ventured close to the ice-encased windows of our house and scratched and howled in the moonlight. The bucket of drinking water in the kitchen was invariably frozen in the morning. Our brick oven and the stove provided scant warmth, but fortunately we all had feather quilts to keep us snug. There seemed no end to my memories, many joyful and pleasant, many horrible. They came back to me in great force, now that my mother was gone.

Here in this village when I was a small boy, the warring armies in the Civil War roared through. Bullets whizzed past our windows and sometimes chipped at the stones before our door. My mother stuffed pillows in the windows at the first sign of fighting, and ordered us under the kitchen table where on some days we remained for hours as the fighting passed through our street.

And here on the outskirts of this same peaceful village a number of people lay buried in mass graves, some victims of the few defenders of the old regime, but most of them shot by the Bolsheviks as obstacles to the Revolution. Some boys had seen some of these executions and had told us younger ones about them, the way the Reds would arrest suspicious looking men and ask them to hold out their hands. If they had no calluses, they were arrested as bourgeois obstructionists, taken to the outskirts of the village, and shot.

A year or so later, after we had moved to Zhitomir, Tikhorechka was overrun by bandits bent on raping, looting, and killing. These marauders were peasants cut loose from their lands, who pillaged settlements some distance from their homes so that they could go about their raiding unrecognized.

Now a provincial serenity prevailed in this, my birthplace. It reflected the townfolk's unconcern with any progress beyond Tikhorechka's borders, their basic indifference to the lushness and beauty that nature had so lavishly bestowed a mile or so in all directions from the godforsaken church in the square.

There was one other change which was painful for me: the few people I saw on the streets were all strangers. At the house of my maternal grandfather, Sholom Cheuse, an old woman sat on the doorstep, minding a small child who was playing in the dirt, digging with his little hands.

"Good day to you," I greeted her, feeling kindly toward the woman though I had never seen her before. I was hoping she would invite me into the house, for I ached to see the place again.

She'd been keeping her eye on me while pretending to watch the child. My uniform, particularly my side arm, may have aroused the suspicion I saw in her colorless eyes and the way she twisted her furrowed peasant face. She said not a word. Perhaps she was deaf. She grabbed the little boy by the arm and dragged him quickly into the house. Though an old house, very likely older than the square, it was still one of the best in Tikhorechka, built of brick and oak and cement many years before by my mother's family, of whom the last was my grandfather Sholom. It hurt me to see it occupied by strangers.

From the top of the elms in the cemetery behind the Tailor's Synagogue across from the square, a flock of ravens rose in flight, their shrill cries drowning out the voices of a group of youngsters who ran across the open space. The high-pitched protest of the flock gradually faded into the distant sky, and the sounds of the children subsided as they walked to their homes. By the time I'd reached the synagogue, silence reigned again. Over the entrance was a sign: "Taras Shevchenko School." As if to ease my nostalgia, the elms in the cemetery whispered to me with their stirring leaves. As long as *we* last, this place will remain a sanctuary, they seemed to say, for some things.

Not far from the Tailor's Synagogue, on a nameless street overlooking the fruit orchards which spilled down to the river, stood the only two-story structure in Tikhorechka—the Volost, or county hall. Its portico was supported by two wooden columns badly in need of paint. An outline of the czar's two-headed eagle had once adorned the portico's topmost point. Bullet holes in the brick testified to the way the insignia had been removed.

"We are open! Come, come inside, if you please, comrade." The invitation came from an open French window on the second floor. There sat an old man with white hair cropped short, whose light and lively eyes were set in a clean-shaven, wrinkled face with pockmarked cheeks. He beckoned me to come up, smiling through a toothless mouth.

"I have no business here, papasha," I said. "I'm just visiting."

"I will be down at once, comrade," he called out in an anxious voice, and vanished from the window. The door at the top of the stairs soon creaked open. With uncommon agility, the old man scampered down to meet me and extended his hand in greeting. Then I saw that he was a hunchback.

"I am Ivan Panteleyevich Karpatin," he introduced himself. Obviously my presence at the Volost worried him. He kept bowing, a little out of breath. At first I felt revulsion at his deformity, then pity which I tried to conceal. I resented his slavishness, his servility and his evident fear of the authority my uniform represented to him. Had I not respected his age, I would have lectured him about how the Bolshevik Revolution had made all men in Russia free and equal, and that no one need fear a man in uniform anymore.

"And who might you be, may I ask, comrade?"

"I am Captain Fishel Isaakovich Kaplan." I shook his hand.

"In the name of the chairman of the Tikhorechka Soviet, I welcome you, tovarich Captain. I regret only that the chairman himself, comrade Dolenko, is not here to greet you in person!" He bowed, looking up at me with his mouth open and his face set in an expression of pleasure at my presence.

"I have no business here at the Volost, papasha," I said again, shrugging, ready to turn away.

"Then, I take it, you are not here in connection with the roundup of the Kulaks? You are not a captain commanding a detachment of the G.P.U.?"

"No, papasha! The G.P.U. lapels are green; mine are sky blue. The wings and crossed daggers on my sleeve mean I am a pilot." He understood my explanation and clearly was relieved.

"Then you operate one of those machines called samolets, one of those things that fly in the air? That must take nerve. I heard tell about flying machines, but never saw one myself. I must see one before I die."

"Good day to you, papasha." I turned to go.

"Please wait, young man, please." He jumped off the step. "Did you say your name is Kaplan?" At my affirmative nod, his face lit up. "Mother of God! I thought there was something familiar about you! You remind me of your father, Isaak Kaplan. I also remember your mother Sonya, and her father, your grandfather Sholom. How is your mother? What? She's passed on? What a terrible thing! How is your father? Run off to America, I think, in the year nineteen-ten, or was it nine or eleven? It was a few years after our war with Japan, I recall. It must have been in the year nineteen hundred and seven, soon after the war, when your father came here to the Volost to register a newborn son. Mother of God! That must have been you, son! Come upstairs and I shall show you the book with the registration. Come!"

My curiosity aroused, I followed him inside. The door led to a bare room with rows of benches in a slight disarray. When my eyes had adapted themselves to the meager light, I saw a portrait of Lenin on one of the walls. On another wall was a portrait of Stalin, staring sternly from the glossy, flyspecked paper. A shaft of sunlight came into the room from a window high on the second-floor balcony. A chandelier of kerosene lamps with smoked-up chimneys hung from a chain, its light forming a square on the unswept floor. The silence in the room was emphasized by the loud buzzing of a horsefly beating against a windowpane.

" 'Isaak,' I recall saying to your father, 'you should Russify your name,' " the old man told me as I followed him up the stairs. " 'You should alter the child's surname a little and make it easier for him to get by,' I said." A door from the balcony led to an office filled with sunlight streaming from the open windows. Rubbing his hands in anticipation, Ivan Panteleyevich unlocked an oak cabinet, opened its doors and, rubbing his palms again, scanned the rows of huge, leather-bound journals numbered in periods of decades. Finding the volume he wanted, the old clerk laid it out on a desk, spat on his index finger and slowly turned the pages. "Here it is! May 20, 1907. A male child born this day to citizen Isaak Fishelevich Kaplan and his wife, Sonya Sholimevna Cheuse. Name of child: Fishel Isaakovich Kaplan. Signed and attested to by Ivan Panteleyevich Karpatin, clerk."

"Ivan Panteleyevich," I said, "can you explain why my father went to the trouble of building a house and then left for America? It must have been sudden."

"Your father was no fool, Fishel Isaakovich! True, he had not intended leaving Tikhorechka for America. He was dealing in animal hides. He bought himself a partnership in a small tannery, and he could afford to use what he earned to put up that house just before he went away. Your father fled to America when I tipped him off through your grandfather Sholom that a police dossier was being gathered because someone had informed on him for calling Czar Nicholas the Second an idiot. I got wind of it because the police and the Volost always washed each other's hands."

I sighed to myself. I'd always felt cheated having had to grow up without a father. I'd even been envious of boys whose fathers beat them without good reason. "I suppose if my father had not taken off for America it would have meant spending many years in jail," I speculated aloud, to justify my youthful misfortune. But Ivan Panteleyevich was preoccupied with the ancient record books, mumbling, reading off the dates, pulling them out of the cabinet and bringing them to the table.

"Is the man named Panas, who bought our house, still living in it?" I asked.

"Yes, Fishel Isaakovich. If you see Panas, don't tell him, but the house and his orchard are soon to be confiscated for a collective farm that will be formed this summer. Your house will be the office."

"I don't relish bringing anyone news like that," I said. "You know, Ivan Panteleyevich, the thousand rubles my mother received from Panas for our house turned out absolutely worthless. By the time we moved to Zhitomir, the czar's money was nothing but colored paper."

The old clerk wasn't paying attention. He had found the records he'd been searching for and proceeded to recount the story of an ancestor of my mother's, a Frenchman wounded and left behind during Napoleon's retreat from Russia.

Only half listening, because I'd heard the story, I thought of the deep love that French soldier must have felt for my great-great-great-grandmother, and the fortitude he'd shown in undergoing circumcision at his age.

"I hope that my ancestor did not regret becoming a Jew later, in 1827, when Czar Alexander the First issued the terrible edicts against the Jews," I remarked, watching Ivan Panteleyevich replace the registers in the cabinet.

"Excuse me for saying so, Fishel Isaakovich. You are the offspring of people whom I knew and respected and you may say even loved, because your grandfather Sholom and I used to play together when we were boys. To you I can talk, yes? To you I can say things I'd say to no other person." Ivan Panteleyevich winked significantly over his spectacles. "If you will hear me out, Fishel Isaakovich, life is like a wheel on a wagon. Yesterday, for instance, the Jews in Russia were at the bottom of the wheel, in the mud, if you know what I mean. Today, though, after the Revolution, they are not at the bottom in the mud and in the dust, but on top of the wheel of life, living in the large cities. Even in Moscow.

No more ghettos. Today the Soviet government is giving the Jews land to settle in Birobidzhan while here it is taking land from the peasants and shipping the poor devils off to labor camps to work them to death somewhere, Siberia perhaps. Do you know what I mean?"

"No, I do not know what you mean! Would you still have Jews in Russia restricted to the Pale?" I inquired sharply. "Would you still deny us land to till the soil? Would you deny *me* a higher education? Your analogy about the wheel is correct, though. The downtrodden who suffered for centuries under the despotic czars are not going to allow that kind of rule to get on their necks again."

"Your speech is high sounding, Fishel Isaakovich. You talk like all the youngsters who've been to the big city and had themselves an education. It could be that you are right about the Revolution, and so forth, and all that. But when it comes to no more czars, that's an open question. No czar? I laugh at that when I feel I should be crying. No, Fishel Isaakovich. No, Russia still has its czars, I am sorry to say. If you know what I mean."

I realized what he meant a minute later when from outside I heard a voice raised in harsh curses. The old clerk dashed to the window, looked out and turned to me, saying he must attend to the transfer of the properties of the arrested peasants who were being brought for this purpose to the Volost.

"Kulaks, they call them these days," the old man remarked, stretching his red, furrowed neck sideways to look beyond the window. "These poor devils were rounded up for refusing to join the collectives. Now their land will be legally taken and they will be sent somewhere, to the devil's mother, Siberia, they say."

We bade each other goodbye as we walked down the stairs where a G.P.U. man was shouting.

FIFTEEN

SOMETIMES, ON THOSE DARK WINTER WEEKENDS, with Til and the boys out of the house, Phil dozed on the sofa and awakened, dozed and awakened, thought back on some of those Russian times, both when he was a boy and when he was a young man, and it seemed like such an incredible tale that if he had not lived it he might not have believed it himself!

This dark morning he had had a little quarrel with Tillie, about what he couldn't even remember—oh, yes, she had wanted him to go north to Rahway tonight to visit friends, her friends, but he didn't really enjoy the company of these people, their little problems, what did they know of serious life and real danger and the kind of worries that wore your life down to the bone? and he wanted to visit his brother in Brooklyn and she said never and started weeping, and he had tried to calm her, and touched her, and she had drawn away, and he had gotten insulted by that, and had slapped her, and then she had said that she was leaving and got the boys dressed and went uptown.

She'd be back, and he would apologize and all would settle back into the usual calm again, the usual calm that he was mostly grateful to live in after the whirlwind of his earlier days—though the funny thing was that from time to time, when he was up to his ears in work at the plant, and Til was asking for money for this or that, and the boys were sick or making noise while he was trying to rest, or he had to sit through some awful, boring evening with people who did not have the imagination to listen to his stories about his adventures or, worse, on a Sunday afternoon when they'd take a drive out to visit friends of Til's who were even more uninteresting (and uninterested) than most, his mind wandered back to those times, to the cold and the hardship and the bullets flying and the lonely expanse of the heaving seas and it seemed to him that for all of the good things in this new life in the United States that something had gone out of it for him—and even as he told those old stories to himself he let his mind wander, so that he could feel again the wind on his face as he took the little ship into a dive or as he heard the after-crack of the guns even as he felt the searing pain in his buttocks, and he was going down, and he was blacking out . . .

And when he awoke to a dark house, without wife or children, he felt such a deep, stretching pang of hunger and misery and even, yes, terror, that he leaped to his feet and put on his shoes and grabbed his windbreaker and rushed out to the car and drove the few blocks along the streets with small wooden and brick houses just like his own to his mother-in-law's place.

"She's not home yet, Philip?" the dark-eyed, buxom woman asked as she opened the door. She always appeared a good ten years younger than her actual age, and she had bequeathed this illusion of perennial youthfulness to her daughter.

"Was she here?" he asked, stepping into the kitchen. If he felt like a stranger in his mother-in-law's house, it wasn't her fault, because he felt like this just about everywhere he went, except at work where on the assembly line he was nothing more than his technical skill and he could dissolve his personality into the particular problems at hand, just the way he could recall taking up one of the samolets and becoming part of the machine as he put it into a dive or roll.

"What's the matter this time, Philip?"

Sarah pursed her red lips and turned back toward the stove where she was preparing something in a steaming pot for the evening meal. If Tillie was not a great cook, she was at least an adequate one and she had learned it from her mother, Sarah, who in addition to running the house was a skilled shopkeeper who managed with Isadore the cigar store on the main street. She had married young and knew from her own life that you grew up along with your husband and that you had to endure a lot in order to make a marriage hold together, and when you changed the marriage changed, too, and sometimes you needed other people in your life so that you could be happy with the one you lived with. That was her philosophy, and when her daughter came over to complain about Phil's moods and Phil's demands and Phil's temper and Phil's this and Phil's that she told Tillie what she thought about such things, except for the part about needing other people, because even though just about everyone in the family knew that she was seeing another man in the candy business now and then when he was in town, they didn't talk about it.

That was certainly one thing that Phil would never need worry about, his wife's loyalty, even through the worst kind of arguments and these occasional disappearances. She was a devoted mother and a sweet and loving person with simple needs. Nothing as complicated as a love affair would ever cross her mind. And as for Phil, he had of course sowed his oats in the old-fashioned way in his younger days, which weren't, he reminded himself, all that long ago. But given the powerful trauma of the discovery of his father's infidelity, not only toward his mother but toward the entire family, there was not much chance that he could ever betray his own wife. He might give her up if he had to, if that meant living in the kind of solitude he sometimes thought that he desired, a solitude that gave him a great amount of quiet in which he could rest and read and listen to the news after a hard day at work. Sometimes in the midst of one of his and Tillie's battles he imagined that he might like to take a little vacation from this household. But that was as far as he got—stopping short of even thinking about such things once the quarrel ended and the house settled down again.

"Oh," he said, finally in response to his mother-in-law's question, "she gets upset sometimes and she doesn't even know why. But where did she go?"

"She wasn't here, I told you," Sarah said. "But she called me. From uptown. She was at the Coney Island with the boys and she wanted to know what to do, could she come over. I told her what I'm telling you now and what I tell her always. Tillie, I said, there's no room for you here, you got to settle these things for yourselves. So, Philip, can't you bend a little when she's getting so upset?"

Phil shook his head and leaned against the table, his hands in his trouser pockets.

"Sarah," he said, "I honestly don't even remember what we were fighting about when she left."

"Philip," Sarah said, "go and get her and take her home. It's cold out, she shouldn't have to walk with the kids."

"I'll go," he said.

"And tell her you love her," Sarah said.

There was a look in her eye, something amused and vital and playful in that look of hers that he could never figure out—he was actually one of the few people who didn't know about her affair—but he noticed sometimes in Tillie's eyes and in her laugh that same lilting kind of affection for others and the world. Sarah was giving him good advice, and he would take it.

"Izzy up at the store?"

"If he's not, I don't know where."

"Maybe she went to the store. The boys love to go over to the store."

"So try it," Sarah said, making a half turn back toward the stove. She had her cooking to do, and she had her house to take care of as well, and it was time to turn her attention back to domestic matters.

Phil zipped up his jacket as he went out the door. There was a little wind off the river and the damp air smelled of salt from the bay. He climbed back into the second-hand Plymouth that he had bought for next to nothing from one of the men on his part of the line and drove a few blocks further north. The houses were a little smaller and more run-down in this section of the small town, just south of the main business district, but he had the eye of an optimist when it came to such things—cars, houses—and he could see a building here, a garage there, that a man could easily fix up and make habitable and attractive for resale.

When it came to energy for work, he could be faulted by no one, and yet . . . and yet he worked at the automobile plant instead of owning his own business of one kind or another. Even some of the most ordinary and (to him) quite uninteresting people he had met through Tillie and her family since he had settled here owned their own businesses and seemed to be making a living at it. When you consider the hours he put in, what with the drive to work and back, he might as well be working at something that he owned. Well, someday he would find what it was that he truly cared about and open his own shop. That was it, wasn't it? to find something that he cared about. Because as much as he enjoyed the work at GM he had to say to himself that it was finally not his business and that he could take it or leave it. Since he had stopped flying, nothing had given him that same kind of feeling.

And since he had left the U.S.S.R.—how long was it now? he was even forgetting the language, that thing, cloud up there, how did you say it—oblako?—nothing had charged him with that same sense of mission as flying had done back then. Life was such a complicated and difficult affair, like nothing he had ever imagined, not even from reading the novels that used to catch his imagination, the Turgeniev, the Tolstoy. He didn't read much of anything these days, he came home so tired and then the boys wanted his time and so did Tillie and there were things to fix around the house, and he did like to listen to the radio, the news and the classical music, except that the Russian composers made him feel so awful and so wonderful at the same time he could hardly listen to *their* music, though he wanted to talk to Alan about Glinka, his favorite composer, maybe the first true Russian composer and the first one he remembered listening to, Glinka, what was that piece? Swift River? Icy River? Stony River? He couldn't find it in the record stores no matter how hard he looked.

But here he was on Smith Street, and now he'd park and go to his father-in-law's store to see if Tillie and the kids were hiding out there.

It was unusual that he was uptown at all, not to mention strange to be walking along the street alone. Except for the drive to and from work he was hardly ever alone. So even with the cold wind on his face he was enjoying this stroll, swinging his arms, craning his neck around at the few people on the street—it was a Sunday, so only a few shops were open—and finding himself in his mind back in another decade, his air force service days, and the way he and a few comrades strolled the streets of Urgench, the desert town north of Khiva, or better yet, the rest and recuperation outings in Tashkent on the other side of the desert, the parks where they met girls, the picnics in the mountains . . .

That seemed like another life. But it was all still fresh right now, fresh on his mind and in his heart, and he wished there were some way he could go back to that feeling, not to that life—that privileged but dangerous life—but at least catch again the feelings of pride and satisfaction, and sometimes after a mission he had to say it, a little glory as well. If he at least could impart to his children something of that life, both its dangers as well as its pleasures, then he could say that he had fulfilled the mission of his middle years.

But right now he felt a little lost and a little confused, what with Tillie taking off like that with the boys. Straightening his shoulders and touching the zipper of the windbreaker he took a few extra-long strides and reached the entrance to his father-in-law's store.

"Phil, what a surprise," said Isadore, a small-boned man who was already going deeply grey on top and at the temples. They spoke in English, but could have used Russian if they had remembered enough of it, since the older man had himself grown up not far from Zhitomir. In certain ways Isadore reminded Phil of his own father, although he was a much thinner man. The sweet look about the eyes Phil remembered from his childhood. But he brushed aside any more thoughts like this, still burning with scorn and disgust for his father as he did. The man was still alive and living in Brooklyn with that woman, as far as he knew. Joe had said something in their last telephone call, that his son Saul had gone to Pessella's house in the Bronx for a visit—and she had introduced a man who was there as his grandfather.

FIFTEEN

Isadore, like his father, was one of those immigrants who had left the homeland because of the terrible times that had come prior to the Bolsheviks, the smoke of pogroms still in the air, and the drastic reality of life-long conscription into the army a constant threat. Phil, in an odd way, had departed both because of accident and design, because of a strange combination of both. And when he had served in the Russian Red Army Air Force he had been one of the proudest men alive.

"Has Tillie been here?" he asked.

"You're looking for her?" his father-in-law inquired. "She didn't tell you what movie she was taking the boys to?"

"No," Phil shook his head, going along with the game. "Which movie house did she say?"

"Let me think," the little, greying man said, "we was talking, and the boys were eating candy, that Alan, *kinnahurra,* he loves that chocolate, and I gave the boys some comics, and so, which? the Crescent, it was, some movie about ships."

"I'm going to pick them up so I better be going," Phil said, turning toward the door.

"Phil, first pick out some tobacco," his father-in-law said, exercising his customary generosity. The boys never left the store without having stuffed their mouths with candy and their pockets with comic books and gum. Isadore knew that Philip smoked a pipe and so he gave him the choice of tobacco and sometimes brought packets home with him so that his son-in-law, who because he worked so hard scarcely ever came to the store, might find a gift when he came by the house.

"I like Prince Albert," Phil said, and thanked Isadore when the father-in-law handed him a tin of the stuff. "I'd better go now because the movie will be letting out."

When he drove the short block to the theater he discovered that it had already ended. And so he drove slowly along Madison Avenue, watching for Til and the kids.

"I don't want to hear it," Sarah had said. "You don't think I got troubles of my own? You take the kids to a movie or something and by that time you'll both be cooled off. So what were you arguing about that was so important enough to make you want to leave him?"

Tillie had been crying a little into the restaurant telephone, trying at the same time to keep the boys, who were sitting in the booth, from seeing that she was weeping. But now when her mother asked about the trouble she honestly couldn't remember. It was just that Phil could turn into such a mean, snarling, *dark* person in a flash, that Russian temper was how he explained it, but that didn't make it any easier to take, because she never knew when it would flare up, and he would seem to settle into it like some beast digging down into a hole beneath a hillside.

This was the underside of the hero, that handsome, dashing young fellow who had rushed up to her at the dance that night in Brooklyn and refused to leave her side until she told him when he could see her again. And if Thelma hadn't invited her to come to Brooklyn for the weekend? And if she hadn't accepted? Where would they all be now? Maybe she would be married now to, *who knows,* a dentist, and living in a house as nice as her cousin Norma, whose new husband was in oil? What a house that was! She had made Phil drive past it just a few Sundays ago so that they could all see what had become of the most successful girl in the family. Of course she hadn't ever been invited anywhere by Norma, but maybe sometime she would get to see the inside of the house. If she went there she would need a new dress. And in her mind she wandered along clothes racks she had recently seen in the Lerner Shop on Smith Street.

"Take the boys to a movie," her mother had said. "I'm cooking, so I got to hang up now."

Tillie glanced over at the booth and saw a head bob up over the back. That Alan was picking on his little brother again! She wanted him to stop that behavior, but he always seemed to find a new reason for punching little Shel or pinching him, for making him cry. There never seemed to be much peace between the brothers just as there seemed to be less and less between her and Phil, though she knew that they all loved each other and never would deliberately try to hurt one another.

It's just that sometimes when she got tired of doing the housework and felt so lonely waiting for Phil to come home from the plant that her mind wandered and she thought of houses like her cousin Norma's and the kind of life she might be leading if she hadn't gone that weekend to Brooklyn. So many turns that might have changed things, so many chances.

"Ma!" Little Shel cried out.

"Tillie, you're still there?" her mother said over the telephone.

"I'm hanging up now, Ma," she said. "I'll take the boys to the movies."

"Good idea," Sarah said.

"Ma!"

She replaced the receiver on the hook and rushed over to the booth. Alan had turned over his brother's milk glass and the stuff was running over Shelly's clean trousers.

"I'll kill you!" she heard herself shout at her older son. "You hear me?" and she raised her hand and slapped his shoulder, and then he was crying and Shel was crying, and she was crying, and Marie, the waitress, a girl she went to high school with, came over to the table to ask if she could do anything and Tillie was so embarrassed, she thanked Marie and cleaned up the boy's trousers and fumbled with the check and her purse and rushed her sons back out into the cold before they could finish the sandwiches she had bought them for lunch.

The picture showing at the Crescent was *Two Years Before the Mast* with Alan Ladd, and as she ushered the boys across the street and toward the movie house her older son boasted about going to a show where the actor and he had the same name—he had such an active mind, that boy, such a vivid imagination, and of course such a mouth, such a big mouth, and when he let his temper get the best of him then you had trouble, when all she wanted was the boys to look nice and do well at school and be successful in the world. That world seemed a long way off, of course. She had her hands full just with the fight with Phil—whatever it had been about—but now and then she wondered what life would be like, years from now, and if she might have some of the things that her cousin Norma seemed to get without even asking for.

But her mind was wandering.

It often did—daydreamer that she was. When Phil told her those stories about his earlier days she could dream on them. It was like watching an adventure movie, and she could picture him in his uniform, as in the photographs, as he flew over the desert, and lay in the hospital with his wounds, his jokes about the nurses made her so jealous, and how he sailed over the Pacific from China to get to San Francisco and the United States . . .

And here she was daydreaming again, recalling how handsome Phil had looked in that new dark suit and with his sweet-smelling pipe stuck between his clenched jaws the night of the dance, and Thelma had looked over and seen him talking to her and she had smiled and Tillie had blushed like a much younger girl, as though no man like him had ever before come over and talked to her. . .

"Ma?"

Alan's voice broke into her revery, and she found herself on the street with the two boys, the wind picking up a little although the sun had come out from behind the greyish clouds passing overhead.

"What is it, darling?"

And she leaned down toward him as she spoke.

"Can we get some candy at Grandpa's store?"

"Sure we can," she said, relieved to know that nothing was wrong, that he was just hungry again as usual, and that her mood, and the fight that had started it, hadn't affected him. As far as Alan and Shelly knew she had just decided on the spur of the moment that she wanted to take them to the movies. Fortunately, they had been playing in the alley behind the house when Phil had slapped her.

(*Now* she remembered!)

She had said that she had wanted to go to the movies.

He had said that he thought that American movies were stupid.

She had said that she heard that one movie called *The Cole Porter Story* was very entertaining.

Who told you that? he had asked.

Somebody, she had said. I just heard it.

You don't just hear these things, Teel, he had said. Somebody must have told you, and I would like to know who.

Why is that so important?

Because then I can decide about the opinion. Stupid person, stupid opinion.

She had all of a sudden begun to cry. And he had come up to her and tried to take her in his arms—but the effect was too rough, and she had cried out even more sharply.

You hurt me!

I did not!

Yes, you did!

Oh, you don't know what you're talking about!

And he stalked into the living room, and then upstairs. And she had gone to the dining room where the large mirror hung behind the serving table and wept even more forcefully at the sight of herself. The next thing she knew she had both children bundled up and was on her way uptown.

"Why are you crying, Ma?" Alan had asked when they first started up the block.

"My eyes hurt in the wind," she said.

"It's not that windy," he said.

"Don't get smart," she said.

"I'm just saying about the wind," he said.

"Don't say it," she said.

"You heard Mama," Shel said.

"Shut up, dummy," Alan said.

"Don't *speak* to your brother that way," she said, giving Alan a little push on the shoulder.

"What did I do?" he said.

"You know," Shel said.

"I don't," Alan said.

"Will you boys be quiet?" Tillie said.

"I will," Alan said. "But dum-dum won't. He doesn't . . ." At her quick jab of a shove he went stumbling along the sidewalk.

"Be quiet," she said, biting through a mouthful of tears.

"Dummy," he said, looking at her and pointing to his brother.

"Do you want to go to the movies?" she asked.

He stared at her a moment and then nodded.

"Then be quiet."

Both boys walked quietly uptown from that point on. At the Coney Island she called her mother, and after that conversation she thought about calling her cousin Mikey, the lawyer, but it was a weekend and he wouldn't be in his office, and she didn't want to call him at home because his wife might answer and she didn't want her butting in on such things as this. Tillie didn't know too much about such things as divorce except that she knew she could get one and end the pain of the marriage, the pain of afternoons such as this, except that then the boys would have no father and she would have to go to work . . . but then something in her mother's voice convinced her not to talk about such things unless she was going to follow all the way through. When she couldn't even convince Sarah that anything besides a little argument was the trouble, how could she convince herself long enough to go through with the whole business, to talk to a lawyer and then go to court, or whatever it was that you did. See, she didn't even know the most minor details about such things! She was feeling a little calmer now, anyway, and they did have a few minutes after the restaurant and she thought that going to the store might keep the boys quiet, so they went to see her father, and he gave the boys candy and comic books, and they got to the movie theater just as the show was beginning. And Tillie immediately fell asleep.

"Mom?" Little Shel was tugging at her coat sleeve.

"What? What is it?"

On the screen seas heaved beneath large ships with sails. A storm, moving them all along toward some inevitable end.

"Alan hit me."

She leaned across her younger boy and slapped into the dark.

"Hey," Alan said with a whimper, "I didn't do anything."

"Who did it?" Tillie asked. "Alan Ladd?"

She stayed awake for the rest of the movie, not thinking much, just watching the screen but not actually seeing it. Images of her own life passed by, the way it was said your life flashed past if you fell into oceans like that up on the screen in front of her: her own childhood in this same town, walking on this same street with her mother, her father's gentle eyes, picnics at the beach, high school days, remembering Norma and how did she get to marry such a rich man as that Hess and live in those houses?, a party where they all drank bathtub gin and got happy and then loud and then sick as dogs the next morning, boys she had dated, tall and short, quiet and snappy, all of them successful in one way or another, opening shops, going to medical or dental school, looking into the mirror and seeing her mother's eyes looking out through her own, a strange feeling, Charleston, Charleston, dancing that dance, watching the door always because he, the one she knew would arrive one day, but whose name she didn't know, would some day enter . . .

She had dinner on her mind as they walked down Madison toward the water, thinking that perhaps she would fix chicken, boil some potatoes, mash them, Phil liked that, the boys liked that.

They were just crossing Gordon Street when a car pulled up alongside them.

"Get in," Phil called from the driver's side through the open passenger window. "I've been worried sick about you," he said when she got into the passenger's seat.

"We went to the movies, Daddy," Alan said. "It was good."

"Was it good?" he asked.

"You should see it," Tillie said.

"But I can't now that you've gone," he said.

"You should have come with me," she said.

"That's crazy, Teel," he said, driving them toward home. "I didn't know you were going."

"What did you do all afternoon?" she asked.

"I told you, I went looking for you. I went to Sarah's, I went to the store."

"You shouldn't fight with me," Tillie said.

"I wasn't fighting. What are you talking about?"

"You know," she said.

"I don't know what you're talking about," he said.

"You know," came Alan's voice from the back seat. He turned around and glanced at the boy with terrible, searing eyes.

"You shut up, or else you'll get the strap."

"Don't be too hard on him," Tillie said. "He didn't mean it."

"Yes, I did," Alan said.

"Alan," Tillie said.

"You're going to get it," Phil said.

"You shut up," Alan said.

"Ow!" Shel let out a squeal.

"Would you leave your brother alone," Tillie said. "We're almost home."

"I want to look at the boats," Alan said. "Let's go look at the boats."

"I have to make supper," Tillie said as the car turned the corner onto their street. "Why don't you drop me off, Phil, and take the boys to look at the boats?"

"After I've been running around all afternoon looking for you? I have to go to work tomorrow, remember?"

"Boats," Alan said.

"Boats," his brother repeated.

"I'll give you boats," their father said, pulling the car up to the curb in front of their house. "If you're not quiet, I'll give you boats."

"Good," Alan said.

"Good," echoed his brother.

"Teel?"

"Boys, you better calm down."

"Or else," Phil said.

Tillie got them to quiet down by sending them up to Alan's room to play while Phil lay on the sofa listening to the radio and she made dinner, chicken, mashed potatoes, boiled carrots with brown sugar the way her mother had showed her, and she worked quickly because every few minutes Phil called to her from the living room to ask her if things were coming along.

"Phil, I can't make things boil faster than they do," she said.

"If you hadn't spent the afternoon . . ."

But she didn't hear the rest of what he said because she banged a large serving spoon against one of the pots on the stove.

"Teel, what was that?"

"Nothing," she called back to him.

"It didn't sound like nothing," he said.

"It was nothing," she said, feeling the tears making her eyes smart and blaming it on the boiling food.

He appeared in the doorway.
"Glinka," he said.
"What?" She dabbed at her eyes with her apron.
"I want to listen to Glinka."

SIXTEEN

ON JUNE FIRST I ARRIVED AT THE VOLSK Military Aviation School for Pilots and Mechanics, and without event was checked in and assigned my barracks. I was not entirely pleased about being here, rather than back with Sasha and my friends at Khiva, but such is the military life. You must go where you are assigned—and I had by now decided to make the best of it.

That first night I wrote to Dunya a long letter in which I confessed that, while I could not be sure of our future together, I nonetheless longed for her and hoped that we would again be together soon, though preferably not as her patient! I wanted to take care of her, rather than the other way around. And that night I dreamed of her, or someone who resembled her, a woman with a shy laugh. We were in a car which I was driving, across some foreign landscape beneath a bright and sunny sky, and from the back seat came the laughter and yammering of young children—two boys it seemed to me as I awakened to bright sunlight breaking through the treetops beyond my barracks window.

Standing and yawning at the window, I saw the courtyard below, and beyond that clumps of foliage of oak and elm and weeping willow around a lake. Nearby was the bathhouse, then the machine shops and a foundry and forging workroom and such. Still further, I could make out firing ranges where cadets would practice marksmanship with rifles and machine guns. On the other side of the fences around the grounds I discerned orchards, and to the east was a hill above which the sun was rising.

I got dressed and made up my bed, and had only a minute to spare before I was scheduled to be picked up for a ride to the school aerodrome. After glancing at my wristwatch, I put on my hat, scooped up my helmet and goggles, picked up my leather coat, and left the room. In a vestibule on the first floor I exchanged salutes with a cadet officer of the day on duty, and hurried outside.

An open Ford sedan driven by a civilian chauffeur slid to a stop on the dew-covered cobblestones before the building. To the right of the chauffeur sat air force Major Kuzmin. In the back of the car sat Captain Gerasimov. After casually saluting them I sat down in the back next to Gerasimov.

"Move over!" the major ordered the civilian chauffeur. "Get out and get in on the other side! I'm going to drive. You sit beside me."

"But I'll lose my job, tovarich Major," the chauffeur pleaded meekly. "I was told not to let anyone else drive this automobile, sir."

"Move over anyway! I've driven a truck a little not so long ago. How am I going to learn to drive an automobile if I'm not allowed to try it? The devil take it—move over!"

Reluctantly the chauffeur complied. His unshaven, bristly face folded into an unhappy frown when the major attempted to find first gear and went into second instead. It took a long minute before the car would move, and then it commenced by bucking and lurching forward past a candy-striped sentry booth at the main gate.

"Do you drive, Captain Kaplan?" Gerasimov asked.

I remembered my dream and almost hesitated before saying, "Never had a chance. But I'll learn."

"Same with me," Captain Gerasimov said. "I'd wager we would have less trouble teaching the youngsters to fly if instead of coming to us on horses they could have first learned to drive an automobile."

I concurred.

"Look," said Gerasimov, "you'll overlook it if I mispronounce your name?" He offered his hand to me. "Mine is Gerasimov Mikhail Petrovich."

"Mine is Fishel Isaakovich Kaplan. My friends call me Fishka."

"And my friends call me Mishka, friend Fishka." He smiled as we shook hands and regarded one another with spontaneous comradely affection.

"The Order of the Red Banner is causing endless speculation among us, ever since you have arrived here in Volsk, Fishka. Obviously you were not old enough to fly combat during the Civil War, when most of them were handed out . . ." The captain paused to hear my explanation, if any, but when he saw me smile and say nothing he continued. "Modesty need not be carried too far, especially among friends, Fishka."

"Sorry, Mishka, but I am under orders not to reveal details of the nature of the operation that earned me the order other than that it was given for rescuing a friend from imminent death in extremely hazardous conditions."

"Well, then, let us turn to other conversation. Ah yes, there is always the topic of women. So let me tell you that my sister-in-law, as it so happens, is due here from Leningrad to spend her vacation with us, and I would therefore like to invite you to have a meal with us next Sunday or sooner."

"I would be happy to dine with you and your family, Mishka."

"But I warn you, Fishka, my sister-in-law is a honey, quite young and as sweet as they come." Gerasimov laughed, and then suddenly became serious. "Say, have you taken up the Grig D-11 before?"

"No, but I studied them back in Orenburg. Speaking of honeys, I understand this airplane is one! It'll be my first time in a monoplane. I can't wait to take her up."

"From this I surmise that you, too, have been trained strictly in pursuit at Orenburg?" And again, without waiting for an answer, he suddenly changed subjects. "You know, Fishka, that last year at this time this school did not yet exist? The first company of cadets was recruited last fall, a company of cadet-pilots from Leningrad. I'm not sure why they chose Volsk. The students and faculty members live on base, but for lectures the cadets have to march to another building, clear across town, and for flight training we have to travel out of town to the school's field!"

"Judging by the strides we're making," I said, getting into the spirit of the quickly shifting conversation, "it won't be too long before we ride in our own Soviet-made cars. And you know, the retractable undercarriage on this Grig D-11 of ours—it's the greatest invention—and the supercharger is sheer genius! Even with the stubby wings, the power we can generate . . ."

"And the speed, Fishka! The extra speed you feel when the landing gear retracts into the fuselage! It's absolutely fantastic!"

"I wonder how this Grig handles with a load of petrol and a maximum load of ammunition."

"Your tongues are wagging, fellows!" The major turned momentarily in the front seat and glared at the both of us. "Do you two not realize that there is a civilian sitting here, taking all you are saying in both his ears!"

"Sorry, Major," Gerasimov said.

The car sped on past some Victorian dwellings which, despite the sunny morning, appeared colorless and drab. A church bell tolled timidly somewhere, as if the bell ringer were afraid to awaken the antireligious out of their Sunday morning sleep. And the church itself came into view when we reached the town square. It was an old and gaudy structure, but beautiful at the same time and stood in the center of a cobblestone expanse within a lush little island of oak and white birch. Formerly white, the once-grand building had turned grey and its paint was peeling. Its stained glass windows were dull and so dark with dirt that they failed to reflect the sunlight. Only the white cross reaching for the heavens contrasted with its otherwise tarnished and worn look.

The houses on the town square were also grand and gaudy imitations of residences I had seen in Leningrad and Moscow. Formerly the homes of the wealthy, these houses stood as mute evidence of the great prosperity of the vanished merchants of the Volga River.

Our car turned south onto a street parallel with the river. We sped past picket fences, past tiny wooden houses adorned with gingerbread designs. After a few minutes we reached a paved macadam road, patched in numerous places, that led us into an evergreen forest thick with lofty fir and pine trees. The bright sunlight, filtered through the thick green trees, was magical–and the sky overhead was a ribbon of blue, like a road itself opening the dense forest to the heavens.

"Begging your pardon, tovarich Major," the chauffeur pleaded, "I beg of you, please slow down. It is easy to break an axle in one of these potholes."

"I am watching out for them, papasha! Don't you see me steering around them? I am watching! I can spot a pothole and steer around it faster than you can blink an eye! I am not a pursuit pilot for nothing." The major drove on even faster to demonstrate his bravado, and then the road began sloping upward, toward a plateau where the aerodrome was built. Soon we came to another candy-striped sentry booth. We braked for an identification check, and the major had trouble getting into the right gear again before we lurched forward toward the flying field itself.

Along a barbed wire fence were lined up rows of Avro training planes with their round, radial engines sheathed in canvas coverlets. Inside the hangars I could see assorted airplanes: De Havillands, Junkers, several German Fokkers, and some American birds. The ground crew was wheeling the Grigorovich D-11 out of its hangar.

The major brought the car to a stop in front of the field offices where a squad of cadets was stationed on rotation duty to guard the field. The newly built offices were panelled with white pine from which sap was still oozing.

"Attention!" a cadet bellowed when we entered the mess hall.

"As you were!" Major Kuzmin waved his hand.

The few tables were set with tin cups and plates and spoons. There was a bowl with sugar lumps and a basket of fresh-baked, sliced black bread. A cadet passed us a kettle and we each poured ourselves tea.

"By the way, Kaplan," the major said to me, "a former classmate of mine wrote me and asked if I would offer you a helping hand should you need one. He is Major Smirnov."

"He was my squadron commander when I was stationed in Khiva. How is he, sir?"

"He is fine, excellent! He wishes me to tell you that the maneuvers your squadron were engaged in have been concluded successfully."

"I'm happy to hear that, sir. Thank you."

"Major Smirnov praised you in his letter and said that he was the one who had recommended you for the Order of the Red Banner. But he neglected to give the circumstances. Would you be so kind as to tell me how you came to earn it?"

"I would be happy to, sir, except that I'm under orders not to talk about it until further notice. I'm sorry, sir." My reply seemed to please Captain Gerasimov and he winked at me as he sipped his tea.

The sudden roar of the Grig D-11 motor interrupted the quiet of the aerodrome. Just as suddenly it settled down to an even, low purring. We finished our breakfast of bread and tea, and after washing up we walked out of the building. The prop of the Grig D-11 was like a giant discus as it revolved in the sun. The low-slung plane had compact aerodynamic lines: its short, stubby wings grew out of a short, fat fuselage, and it literally appeared ready to spring into the air. It only needed a pilot—and as I stood there I felt sure the machine was waiting for me.

An aviation mechanic, Second Lieutenant Komarovsky, climbed out of the Grig's cockpit, and jumped to the ground to greet us.

"The engine is warmed up and the samolet is ready, comrades!" He saluted us and handed the major the plane's log. "If you're taking her up first, sir, will you sign for her please?"

"Very good," the major mumbled as he signed the book. A pair of Red Army men helped the major with his coat, eased the pudgy man into the cockpit, strapped him in, saluted, and stepped back. The major tested the tail rudder by moving it right and left and lifted the wing ailerons up and down. He did the same with the elevator controls, then he revved up the Grig's motor, thus raising a whirlwind of dust. After he eased down on the engine, the major signaled the men to remove the blocks of wood under the plane's wheels, then revved up the engine again until the plane began moving. He taxied out onto the field, glanced at the wind sock on the hangar, and turned the plane into what wind there was that morning. At the instant the ship had sufficient speed, the major lifted it off the ground and was sailing off into the cloudless, cashmere-blue sky.

"Shall we toss a coin to see who will go up next?" Captain Gerasimov asked, producing a twenty-kopeck coin.

"I'll take heads," I said as I watched the Grig disappear into the sunlight.

"Then I've got tails," Captain Gerasimov said, spinning the coin on the top of the fuel drum which was standing next to us.

"Heads! You win," said Captain Gerasimov, not knowing that fate had smiled on him. Or was it that in a long run, it was actually the other way around?

"I will confide in you, Fishka," Gerasimov smiled and slapped me good-naturedly on the shoulder. "When my wife heard you were single she said to me, 'This nice boy is just what Alexandra is looking for.' And frankly, Fishka, my sister-in-law will make your mouth water. When you meet my wife you will know what Alexandra is like because they are identical twins. In fact, I'd be willing to wager that before long you will be my brother-in-law, Fishka. How does that strike you?"

"Ah, but the question is, will Alexandra like me just for myself or because of my career and the Order of the Red Banner?"

"If Vera likes you, then Alexandra will. And Vera will like you because I like you. Wonder no more, Fishka!"

"Did you know that I'm Jewish?"

"Our family is enlightened enough not to be concerned about such things."

"How about Alexandra and her parents?" I asked.

"You'll like having them as family," Gerasimov replied, shrugging the subject off. "Would you care to hear something amusing about my father-in-law? He was walking in Leningrad last month when a couple of longshoremen who appeared drunk approached him and offered to sell him some contraband coffee at five rubles a pound or so. They had stolen it, they said. Well, coffee is a rare item these days, to say the least, so my father-in-law bought twenty rubles worth. Alexandra couldn't wait. The moment her father brought the coffee home she rushed to the post office and mailed us a pound package. But what do you think was in it when we opened the bag? It had printing in Spanish and smelt of vanilla or something, but it turned out to be ground straw, pulverized junk. We received Alexandra's letter of apology yesterday, and was her face red. Hah, hah!"

It was amusing, and I did laugh with Captain Gerasimov–I recall it clearly, for it was the last time I was to laugh for a long, long time.

We were strolling along the hangars, Captain Gerasimov and I, killing time. The second lieutenant, mechanic Komarovsky, got into a truck and drove off toward town. Finally we heard the sound of the returning Grig, then the machine itself came out of a blaze of the sun, swooped around far out and high past the hangars before coming in for a perfect landing.

"Which one of you is taking her up next?" the major asked when we came over and he had climbed out of the cockpit.

"Captain Kaplan," replied Captain Gerasimov. "We flipped a coin, sir."

"Who is in charge of the ship's log?" the major inquired, looking about for Second Lieutenant Komarovsky.

"Temporarily I am, sir," the ground crew's sergeant said.

"Mark me down for forty minutes flying time, Sergeant," the major ordered, removing his coat.

"Care for a game of chess, Major?" Captain Gerasimov suggested.

"Some other time," yawned the major as the ground crew helped me into the cockpit and I began to belt myself in. "I want to go to the reading room and stretch out on the leather divan for a few minutes. My youngest one is teething–kept me up all night."

The Grig D-11 was now at my fingertips. Saluting Major Kuzmin and Captain Gerasimov, I prepared to take off–and a moment later I was urging that marvelous machine to climb. Easily and swiftly the Grig rose and rose until the cold began to creep into the cockpit and numbed my nose and caused me to notice the comfort in the places where I was protected by fleece.

I climbed until the altimeter needle reached the letter *K* crudely scribbled by someone in pencil over the plexiglass. Obviously it meant *kislorod*, oxygen—it was time to turn it on. I had never been so high! But rather than bother with putting on the mask, I flipped the plane over on its belly, checked the climb with a half loop, and eased myself back down. Compared with other planes I had flown, the Grig D-11 was so swift that when I turned back to the aerodrome I was over the narrow part over the Volga and the town of Volsk was far south, barely visible, hidden by the endless forest which carpets the region.

If only I had turned back some seconds sooner! If only I had climbed higher a thousand meters or two! I finished turning and was working my left rudder when I sensed the sluggish reaction of the ship. I glanced at the tachometer, the temperature, oil, and pressure gauges, and saw that my engine was very quickly heating up. Then it stopped!

I wondered if I had enough altitude to glide back to the field, and realized that the squat and heavy construction of the Grig did not lend itself to gliding. I decided immediately that the only thing to do was attempt a dead-stick landing in the river. Even so, if I came down too hard I would knock myself out and drown.

My knees were trembling terribly as I locked the rudder to keep the ship on a level course. I could see the aerodrome on the horizon, but it was the river that I wanted for my landing strip. The river, the river! I held on as tight as I could as the blue Volga rose up to me, reached out for me like my absent mother, and then I was in its embrace and all went black.

SEVENTEEN

ALL ROADS IN RUSSIA LEAD TO MOSCOW, FROM Moscow, back to Moscow—or the air routes do, anyway. We had tried to arrange to fly from the Ukraine to Tashkent in the Soviet Republic of Uzbekistan but could find no direct flight, so we have had to board a plane to Moscow.

In the air I'm again reading *Zhivago,* this beautifully composed and moving and deeply wise book. The passage I encounter now as we sail over the farms and wheat fields that may have been poisoned for years by the atomic accident—the passage speaks loudly to me, the Western artist, on the goal of art, and to me the son in search of the full and final resting place of his father's ghost.

> *Three years of changes, moves, uncertainties, upheavals; the war, the revolution; scenes of destruction, scenes of death, shelling, blown-up bridges, fires, ruins—all this turned suddenly into a huge, empty, meaningless space. The first real event since the long interruption was this trip in the fast-moving train, the fact that he was approaching his home, which was intact, which still existed, and in which every stone was dear to him. This was the real life, meaningful experience, the actual goal of all quests, this was what art aimed at—homecoming, the return to one's family, to oneself, to true existence.*

Isn't that what I've done by setting out on this trip, by travelling these thousands of miles, tens of thousands it will be before we're done, in order to return to my father? to myself? to come home?

And I'm feeling suddenly angry with my father for not having taught me any Russian. I wouldn't feel as though I were travelling in Babel if he had. But then would I be writing the kind of English that I do, which to be sure, is not incredibly stylish, but at least it's my first language. I wrestle with English, but what writer doesn't? Some sound as if they don't. Nabokov, whose work I've never enjoyed, sounds as though English comes easy to him. Wonder what his Russian is like. I'll never know. If I haven't learned Russian in preparation for this trip, I doubt I ever will. Learning English is difficult enough, I think—as I doze off on this flight back to the Russian capital.

Moscow is beginning to weigh on us with its austere breadth and certain boredom. We know that all over the city people are gathering in living rooms or kitchens in friendly talk, listening to bootlegged Western rock-and-roll tapes, discussing the serious matters of art and life, paintings by artists out of favor on their walls, smuggled novels on their bookshelves (*Dr. Zhivago,* for example). But for the tourist seeking diversion there is so little, though we are no longer surprised by this. By now we know that there is no cafe life here, no restaurant-going as we understand it, nothing except movies—and scarcely an English language film to be seen, and so no use to us—and theater for which tickets are extremely scarce, and the traditional ballet and orchestras for tourists. But we haven't done much of that. We're tourists of the heart, on this homecoming journey, taking roundabout as the shortest way back.

Dinner? It is time for dinner, a diversion which is not nearly as relaxing as Josh and I feel it should be. Here it is as much of an effort as just about everything else. We have to go down to the lobby and make our way to the hotel restaurant, and there explain—after the maître d' again tries to turn us away—that we're guests at the hotel. All of this is becoming so boringly familiar. He checks us against his list, and we get a table with other tourists, a toothless Frenchman who proceeds to tell us stories of the Resistance, half in almost incomprehensible English, half in French that we can barely understand. We see a menu that seems identical to the one last night in Kiev, though the baked chicken is off the menu and beef stroganoff is on—still no fish—and Josh orders chicken Kiev again and I the stroganoff and a tomato salad. The Frenchman lurches off, and the maître d' seats a beer-drinking East German tourist next to us, and now we hear stories of a tour on the Dnieper, half in German, half in English. By the time he orders and leaves we've eaten, as well, and Josh wants to go upstairs to sleep. A band is starting up, and on principle I decide to listen to them. It's just too early to go to bed. Josh tells me to have a ball and goes the way of the Frenchman and the East German.

The band opens with some unfamiliar popular tune, and I'm cringing, waiting for yet another rendition of "Cheri, Cheri Baby," but instead the guitar player picks up a violin and begins to play an old Russian melody that I recall my mother humming and singing to me, "Ochi Chernyye," and the piano picks up the tune, and I'm called suddenly back to those days on State Street when my grandfather would play his violin for me and Shel, one eye covered with his patch, the other brimming with tears. My mother was so young, so young (as young as Josh's mother was when we took him to Mexico so long ago), and both of Tillie's parents were still alive, though her father was ill even then, the eye patch the sign of the disease that was already creeping into his liver—but for that time, while the music played we were all there in one place, that small town by the river where it flowed into the bay, and I could love all of it because I had not begun to think, and none of them had begun to die, and my father sat in the small room off the living room on Sundays, at his typewriter, tap-tap-tapping away. . .

All these memories swirling through me, conjured up by this sweet and melodious music, and I'm missing my daughters, watching the fleshy-hipped waitress sidle up to a table, then a swarm of East German teenagers come in for dinner, noisy, bubbling over with their adolescence, and I wish Josh were here to enjoy the spectacle of all these kids trying to dress like him—he could be their leader!

And then the music carries me off again, that gypsylike violin style, Ochi Chernyye, la-dee da-da, and I'm remembering the sounds of the Russian as my mother sang her version of it, and did my father chime in on the chorus? and she's dancing around, and I'm up on my feet, whirling around and about to the beat in my mother's arms, and someone's clapping time, maybe Aunt Bess, and her deep contralto adds to the lustre of the singing, and who knows who else is there? young cousin Marv? certainly Great Gram, and Mama Sarah, all of them singing so deeply and with abandon to the music of the violin . . .

And I'm sitting here stranded, taping my foot to the music, in this Russian restaurant so many years later, like something left wriggling on the beach after an ocean tide of decades has pulled back with the recession of the moon.

And just when I think the music has finished with me the duo begins to play the blues, and I get called home to different old times in the Amboy beach, to my friends who never saw their childhoods, as I did, like a costume to be donned for a play. Where are they now? I never saw much of them again, except for Joe S. who was in the hospital the same time as my father's next-to-last stay, and they took out a brain tumor from Joe and I visited him in his room, his head swelled up under the bandages, his face black and blue, and it wasn't as if he had gotten old but more like someone had pumped out or sucked out or drained out all the youth from him, all the old times in the dirty alleys and the corner lots and the beach and the schoolyards and the basketball courts—God knows you want to live your life, not suffer it as though it's a life sentence! And Ron, an airline pilot now, my father in his old age having had a few good words to say for him about that, and the girls I kissed all gone to fat and married and mothers of children who can make them grandmothers, perhaps some of them divorced, these girls-turned-women, and I hope they look better than Joe did under his helmet of bandages, poor guy.

The years fall away and I'm walking with my mother along Smith Street and we meet one of her friends, a woman like herself with child in tow, perhaps two of them, and she pushes me forward to say hello, and I don't want to be told to say anything to anybody—that's the streak of my father in me, that stubbornness, that damn it all I am here by choice and only the gravest winds of fate and tides of history can move me to do anything I haven't made up my mind to do, either to be polite or mischievous—to turn my back to the crowd or move out from the wall and kiss every cheek and shake every hand in sight. Leaning back in my chair and allowing my spirit to *dig in* to those delicious yet mournful chord changes the guitar player is putting out, I recall getting out of bed in the middle of the night and crossing the cold linoleum on the kitchen floor and feeling my way past my sleeping parents' room and going into the living room and pissing on the wine rug behind the sofa . . .

And the guitar riffs collapse into themselves and the piano player takes over.

These Russian guys have been listening to B. B. King, at least the guitarist has, and the piano player now burrows down deep into the international language of the blues, anguish, the suffering that comes of having discovered that you've been standing on the platform and the train of life has passed this station by, no local stops—and your baby's left you, the best gal you ever had, or she's dead of a sudden illness, or gone off with your friend, and you've seen how much she hates, and made you face up to the end, you've got the blues, the deep down and dirty U.S. Yankee blues, the American national anthem, the we got it all and even that ain't enough I'll always be lonesome capitalist tragic outside looking in, never find my lover, your daddy's left you, give it to another, where's your pretty baby, blooz.

I go up to the guys when they finish and try to talk, but they have as much English as I have Russian—all that they've done has come to me in that old cliched notion of the international language of music, and it suggests that there might be some hope, since it's one of the few art forms that doesn't get lost in the translation, and it makes the Soviets feel what we feel, or at least what most free-to-suffer Americans can feel on occasion, that tragic sense of life that seems summed up in so many Russian novels of the nineteenth century, and in that melody I heard only a few minutes before on the violin.

"B. B. King, *da,*" says the guitarist. "I like B. B. King, *da!*"

And the pianist shakes his head, pointing to the guitarist, "Make jass," he says, "good jass maker," and I put on my best Russian, and shake hands and nod and say,

"Horosho, horosho," good, good, *"pahzhalsta,"* thanks for the music.

And I head back upstairs, my mind full of music and memory, my heart replete with emotions of old times, new places, and I return to the room and undress and fall back onto the bed, listening to Josh's by now familiar, deep adult breathing, and listen to the sounds of the city, and I'm thinking about a number of things, inspired by that music, "Ochi Chernyye," and the blues medley, thinking about old times, Perth Amboy, images of those boys I ran with rising vividly before my eyes, thinking about the way life makes you connect to the chord changes in the blues like no other music, and how the Russian gypsy melodies so different can evoke a similar response, and I'm thinking gypsy, and blues, and Jews, and thinking back on yesterday's travels, on the well-ordered round of Zhitomir, how it was all built up after the Nazis rolled through, a new city arisen out of the rubble of the old, and not after all a place that anywhere near resembled at least in spirit the place where my father roamed about in his youth—unlike, say, Perth Amboy, which every time I visit becomes more and more like the place where I grew up, in fact, year by year becomes more familiar to me than it ever was when I was a child and found the world around me a place as strange as another planet, or a dimension into which my spirit only half belonged. So we grow from the discomforts of first experience into the familiar fit of memory—at this rate nothing will ever seem so real to us as it will at the moment we die!

And I'm thinking blues, Jews, and I'm thinking America, Russia, and I'm thinking America, America, my town, your town, the old life, the New World, the way I felt things then, the way I see things now, how I'll feel things tomorrow, my talented son, my smart, attractive daughters (on their way to school or sitting already at their desks, heads bent to their tasks on paper, pencils in hand, their legs kicking to some internal rhythm beneath the wooden seat as I'm about to tumble over the bluff into that river, the place beneath the falls where boys swim and old men fish), remembering old Jersey, New Jersey, east and west, travels south with my first wife to Texas and Mexico, Josh's first year in the mariachi town of Tlaquepaque, the pungent odor of jacaranda in the dry, hot Jalisco air, then driving west through Wyoming, Utah, Nevada, over the Sierra, to meet the mother of my girls who was then . . .

I'm thinking, and I'm dreaming, and I'm dozing, and I'm supping, supping, now, Hey, Ma, Mama?

I ate at the Homesick Restaurant tonight!

And you thought I wasn't with you in Zhitomir, Oll-an? Where do you think you get all this inspiration from? You think you could just sit down and listen to music and make all these words that give off such feelings? It's in your blood, you've got my blood, that Russian blood!

The blues does it, too.

So you got American blues and Russian blues. That's so amazing?

We never talked about this before. We never talked like this before. We never talked at all.

Because you wouldn't listen. You never wanted to listen.

I couldn't listen. I had a hum in my ears.

The blues?

Not bad, Dad. That's it, that was the sound.

I heard sounds, too. I heard the noise of the wind whipping past my helmet, which is why my ears got bad as I got older. And I had other sounds, the sounds of you and your brother crying out for the first time.

I know that sound.

Yes, you do. And I was hearing the noise of my family, my mother's voice, just the way you hear me now, but you know what?

What, Dad?

I could never hear my father, I tried and tried to remember his voice, I heard when I was tiny, and then I heard it again the one time I spoke to him in New York, when I went to see him, your Uncle Joe had told me, but I wanted to see for myself, I didn't believe Joe. How could it be, our own father doing this to our own mother, abandoning her for another woman, so I went to see, and I saw, and that was the last time I heard his voice.

Sorry.

Don't be sorry. I didn't want to hear him. The bastard.

You must be angry. I never heard you use a foul word the entire time I was growing up.

There's no better word for him. Except maybe . . .

I understand, Dad.

All my life I felt like an orphan because he abandoned us.

I'm sorry.

Sure, thank you, son. You never understood. Because how could you? I worked hard for you and your brother. I wanted you to have everything I never had, I wanted you to have a dutiful father, not a bastard who left you behind, and I wanted you to have a country that you loved, a country you wouldn't abandon.

You didn't abandon Russia, Dad. You didn't have much choice about going back. Did you?

No, I could have gone back. I could have gone from Japan. I could have gone from China. Nobody was stopping me, in fact, they tried to take me back. Did I ever tell you about, well, of course, I did. I told you many times, I wanted you to remember these stories, I wanted you to tell them to your children, I wanted you to make some money telling them, they're good stories. . .

I know, Dad.

And now you think you'll tell them?

That's why I'm here.

Moscow?

Here, in Leningrad, Moscow, Kiev, all over.

Moscow is not such a big deal. My life here was elsewhere. But you're going to Khiva, aren't you?

Don't you know that?

I don't know everything. I'm just following you around, not making your plans.

I know.

But do you plan to go to Khiva?

We're going. Tomorrow. We've been lucky, the timing is right, because it's only been open to Western tourists for a year or so. If we had wanted to make this trip two or three years ago we couldn't have gone there.

It's the right time.

Right.

Everything in its right time.

Yes.

Including your talking to me.

That seems to be true.

I love you, Oll-an. Do you hear me?

Yes, Dad. Papa. Papasha. I do.

And what do you say?

I love you. I loved you in life.

Good. You know how many boys can say this to their fathers?

Some, I guess. But not many. I don't know many.

No, not many. You're a lucky fellow. Luckier in many ways than I was. I mean, I had good luck that saved my life a number of times. When I was hit, when I crashed at Volsk, when I crashed in the Sea of Japan. But you know what? There's one thing I never had, that you almost never had, but now you can say you have.

I think I know what it . . .

Sure you do. I never could talk to my father.

Dad? Papa? Did you even know when he died?

Oh, Oll-an. I never knew. I never knew.

EIGHTEEN

AN INTENSE LIGHT KEPT ANNOYING ME UNITL IT occurred to me that it was sunlight. Out of nothingness, a dark void without pain, I became aware of light and a throbbing in my head. I reached out to explore and learn where I was, and who I was, but awareness came slowly. My fingers found bandages on my head and on the left side of my face. My head was bound all over except for a slit for my mouth and one for my right eye. My left arm was in a cast which terminated with my index finger. There was a mitten of bandage on my right hand, but all my fingers were exposed and when I tried, much to my relief, I was able to move them.

The throbbing in my head was not just physical but musical: there was a humming sound, like telegraph wires singing in the wind. I concentrated and tried to remember where I was, and then it came to me and I could see the river beneath me. But what river? What was its name? And what kind of plane was I in? I knew how I had come to crack up the plane—but what kind of plane was it?—I couldn't remember its designation, except that it was an experimental fighter, a monoplane with a new type of supercharged engine. The name, the name, what was the ship's name? I think I began muttering, wondering why it would not roll off my tongue. The name, the name?

I felt frustrated and helpless and must have passed out again, because when I was next conscious the sun was no longer in my eye but somewhere to the right of me, shining on a water jug on a night table. Somebody had opened a window, and above the buzzing in my head I heard a man's voice and the sounds of a piano playing a pleasant, rhythmic, familiar piece of classical music, as familiar as my own name, which, like the tune, I could hear but not say. I listened to the voice and the piano and was soon able to deduce that the music was accompanying dancers. It sounded like ballet dancers were practicing pirouettes. I was able to visualize boys and girls dancing, making errors now and then, because the man's voice sometimes stopped the music and shouted, "Nyet, nyet, nyet!"

There was something familiar about these shouts. I knew I had heard someone shout exactly that same impatient way, but I couldn't think who or where, although the sound of it led me to a dreamlike vision of a city, half modern, half old, half Russian and half Muslim, a city of minarets and mosques, a city of parks with palms and natives in turbans, skull caps and gilded robes, a countryside with irrigation ditches, donkeys, camels and ancient water wheels, a land of desert and sun. But what was this city, this land? The name, the name?

That dancing, I loved dancing so! My legs, did I still have my legs? I tried to move them. There was a cast on my left leg, but I could wiggle the toes of my right. The rhythmic playing went on and on, coming from a courtyard beyond the window. It was soothing, hypnotic music and it lulled me to sleep.

The third time I discovered myself conscious it was dark. Someone was standing beside my bed and was holding my wrist, counting my pulse. In the twilight of a night-light I could tell that there were two people at my bedside.

"His temperature is way up again." It was a woman's voice, soft-spoken and kind, which reminded me of the voice of my mother. "I don't understand it, Doctor, his fever was over the critical point but now it's on the rise again. Strange."

"Let's try to get through to him, doctor," a man's voice said this time. "Can you tell us where anything is hurting you, Captain Kaplan?" the voice said close to my bandaged ear.

Kaplan? Kaplan! Why, yes! I had somehow mislaid Kaplan in my mind, but there it was! Kaplan, yes, that was me. I felt relieved, elated at hearing my name again.

"Does anything hurt you more than any other? You are hurt pretty badly, of course."

"Yes, it hurts all over," I said through what felt like a mouth full of river gravel. "Mostly my head aches, inside my right ear it hurts more than anywhere." I tried to raise my head, but the pain increased too much. "Where am I?"

"You're in a hospital, Captain Kaplan," the feminine voice said. "You are at the Military Hospital in Saratov. You have been here nearly two weeks." I could barely hear for all the noise in my head.

"Tell me more about the pain in your ear, Kaplan," the man said. "What does it feel like? Tell us if you can."

"It feels tight. It feels like a toothache."

"An abscess?" the woman wondered aloud.

"We will look into it at once," someone said.

Sometime during that night I was wheeled past walls and beneath ceilings, and I writhed under a battery of lights. I was told later that my right eardrum had been badly perforated by a sliver of plywood which was difficult to extract. That day and the day after I spent in continuous pain despite the morphine with which I was injected.

But I was aware of the care I was receiving. There was a young nurse constantly at my bedside, and the woman in white with a voice that reminded me of my mother was Dr. Maria Kapitalinovna Ivanova. The hours and days and nights that followed passed in a haze, a parade of pain and perpetual discomfort. I knew who I was and what had happened to me, but there was almost no detail and I was unable to remember many things. The magnitude of the catastrophe—the crackup—was crushing my spirit just as it had smashed my body. Unable to recall clearly, I began to believe that the crash must have happened because of some error I had made, and therefore my career in the Red Army Air Force was finished.

When sleep could not overcome the pain, I felt myself falling into an abyss. The young nurse kept placing ice bags on my head and giving me sips of water.

"Thank you," I said when she was changing one of my sweat-soaked bandages.

"Are you a Volga German from around here, Captain?" she asked me.

"No. Why do you ask?"

"When you were delirious you said words in German."

"Which words, sister?"

"You did not ask for water when you were burning with fever, you kept asking for 'vasser,' which means water in German."

I wanted to correct the nurse and tell her that it was not German that she heard me speak, but another language, but the word for the language would not come to mind! I tried desperately to remember the name of the polyglot language used by the Jews of Europe, but I could not do it. The name, the name?

Perhaps it was the medicine, I reasoned. But a few days later, when they stopped doping me, I discovered that it was not that simple.

"You say you can remember that you were an instructor at a military aviation school, but you are unable to think of the name of the school. And you are unable to bring forth the name of the town, Captain?" Dr. Ivanova asked me when I confided in her the difficulty I was having recalling names.

"Nor can I recall what has happened, Doctor. That is, all I can remember is that I was going in a glide for a dead-stick landing on the river. The river, what is its name?"

"The Volga, Captain Kaplan! Actually, we find this to be rather common in cases of concussions like yours. The last ten minutes of the experience seem to be totally erased from the brain."

The next time Dr. Ivanova came accompanied by the hospital's chief surgeon, Colonel Bakaleinikov.

"How are we today, tovarich Captain?" he said, obviously without really expecting an answer. "The bridge of your nose is still puffed up a little, but it's mending fine. And I think we can remove the bandage from your left eye now." The colonel nodded to the nurse to do so. "Hmmm, your eye is still puffed and closed, but the scar to the left of it is healing well. We'll leave the bandage off and let the sun at it." By this time on previous visits the doctor would have smiled and walked out of the room. But this time Colonel Bakaleinikov smiled feebly and said, "Do not feel offended, Captain, but I would like to ask you a silly question or two."

"Go right ahead, Doctor," I said.

"Captain, what is the capital of our country?"

I stared into the colonel's face and then looked away. I was able to visualize the Kremlin walls and Red Square, with St. Basil's Cathedral and Lenin's tomb, but I was not able to extract a single name for any of the places I saw in my mind's eye.

"I know, of course, but I just can't say the name," I mumbled, turning crimson with shame.

"Well, then, could you just name a few of our major cities, Captain?"

"I can locate them for you on a map, Colonel. I can even draw you a map of our country. But for some reason I can't say their names."

"Can you tell me what city we are in now?"

"Saratov. We are at the Military Hospital in Saratov, sir."

"Once he is told the name he remembers it again," Dr. Ivanova said quietly to the colonel. "A case of aphasia, don't you think, Dr. Bakaleinikov?"

"Hmmm . . . it appears to be. Partial, at least."

"Can you cure it, Doctor?" I inquired anxiously.

"If nature fails to cure it for you, Captain, then you can cure it yourself by relearning all that you have forgotten." The colonel spoke casually and made it sound that either way I would recover my ability to function normally. The prognosis was promising, but butterflies still swirled in my stomach.

"Will I fly again, Doctor?" I desperately wanted an answer to that question, but I also wanted to change the subject. It was humiliating to have them ask me questions worthy of a schoolchild.

"I do not see why not, comrade," the colonel replied resolutely. "Whether you do or do not fly again is really up to you. Soon we shall allow you out of bed and you can begin to decide what you will do."

"Thank you, Doctor Bakaleinikov, and comrade Doctor Maria Kapitalinovna Ivanova." I was already trying to demonstrate my ability to remember names once I had heard and memorized them.

"Your eye is much better now, Captain Kaplan," Dr. Ivanova said to me the next time she looked in on me. "Do you want me to find you a mirror so you can see what a fine job we did in straightening your broken nose?"

Dr. Ivanova was sympathetic to me and tried her best to help cure me of my various afflictions. She was a rosy-cheeked, cheerful, and friendly woman in her forties in whom I must have awakened certain motherly instincts.

"I am still more concerned with the damage inside my head," I said.

"Oh well, then, let's practice, Captain Kaplan. The Bolshevik Revolution has emancipated Russian women. Had not the revolution taken place under the Czar, I might still be only a Sister of Mercy. Can you tell me what the revolution has done for you?"

"Before the Revolution my people were a minority in . . . in this great land of ours . . . in . . . Russia. Before the czar was overthrown my people were not allowed to till the soil or live in large cities like . . . Moscow."

"Can't you tell me the minority population to which you belong?"

"I know, Doctor. The name is on the tip of my tongue, but my tongue is useless . . . I do not know! The word that is, Doctor. I am of a people who some twenty centuries ago were vanquished by the Romans who exiled them from their homeland. Of ten tribes there are only two now who are identified as . . ."

"You are Jewish, Captain Kaplan," Dr. Ivanova supplied with emotion. "The Jews of Russia were contained mainly in ghettos of the Ukraine, save for the privileged merchants and artisans who lived under special permits in the major cities, such as Moscow, Petrograd, Kiev, Kharkov, and so forth."

"I am Jewish, of course, Doctor. How awful of me to forget!"

"You must rest now, Captain."

The humming in my head accompanied by a windlike rushing in my right ear had gradually ceased. The cuts and bruises on my body had shrunk, become encrusted, and were visibly healing. The casts on my leg and arm were weighty and they itched terribly, especially in those places I could not scratch. I began easing out of bed by sitting on the edge of it, and then, with crutches, began hobbling about my room—and later I ventured to a vestibule down the hallway.

There were the usual portraits on the visiting room walls, but I tried and tried to think of the surname that went with the familiar face of "Vladimir Illich." After an hour I gave up. "Face it, fellow," I told myself, "if you cannot remember Vladimir Illich's surname, you're in trouble." It was the same with the other portraits.

In the visiting room sat a six-year-old youngster reading a magazine. "Name me the leaders on those portraits, little fellow," I asked.

"Oh, he knows them, comrade," the boy's mother said. "He's smart."

"Name them all for me, then, will you?"

"Oh, very well." The boy looked up at me and smiled. And then he named them all. "That one with the smile is Vladimir Illich Lenin. The ones with the hats are Comrade Stalin and Comrade Voroshilov," the boy went on. "That one is Kamenev, that one Zinoviev."

I felt as if I were the owner of a vast warehouse which had been burglarized and from which countless items had been stolen. Day and night, every minute awake, I was busy adding up my losses, trying to take inventory of the knowledge I might have once acquired but was now missing. The clean-shaven and ever-cheerful Colonel Bakaleinikov, with his short-cropped greying hair and compassionate eyes, came to see me during his weekly rounds and helped me with my mental inventory.

"You did fine when we had our talk last week, Captain," the colonel would say. "Now . . . I've been told that you're a qualified aeronautical engineer. I will not ask you any formulas, or calculus, since I do not know that myself, but let's try to establish the degree of aphasia you have suffered. How much is nine times nine?"

Aware at once that the multiplication table, as I had memorized it, was beyond recall, I began adding nines instead of multiplying them. "Nine and nine is eighteen, eighteen and eighteen is thirty-six, thirty-six and thirty-six is seventy-two, and add nine is eighty-one. Nine times nine is eighty-one, sir."

"How much is three times nine?"

"Nine and nine is eighteen and nine is twenty-seven, sir."

"I will see that you are given a book with the multiplication tables, Captain Kaplan. Do you think you can memorize it for me by next week?"

Before he returned I received a visit by Air Force Captain Phoma Iosifovich Feldman. I felt less sorry for myself when I saw this young man with his sunny disposition despite the fact that his pilot's wings were sewn on a folded-over sleeve which was pinned close to his elbow. Under his half arm the captain carried a light briefcase. In his good right hand he held a book and some recent magazines.

"Captain Kaplan?" Feldman smiled.

"So I am told, sir."

He handed me his bundle and removed his cap. "Something for you to read, Captain."

I thanked him and we shook hands.

"I took the overnight boat here from Volsk," he said, pulling up a chair. "I'm on my way back to Moscow, to the office of the Air Force Advocate General. I've just defended Second Lieutenant Komarovsky, the engineer mechanic who was in charge of the Grig D-11 you piled up."

"Grig D-11—that's it," I mumbled to myself. "So, there was an investigation. And there were charges?"

"Yes. Komarovsky was court-martialed. It came out during the trial that your attempted emergency landing was most skillful. There were three flight instructors on their way to the aerodrome who heard the Grig coming in on a glide path in an attempt to reach the field. They stopped their car, and when they saw that you realized you could not reach the aerodrome you dovetailed the ship toward the river. You went right over their heads as they sat in the car and you did succeed in making a perfect three-point landing on the water—but that ship's no boat, as you know, and it cracked up like wet cardboard near the shore. You're lucky those boys were there to pull you out of the drink."

"I'll thank them," I said. "But what happened to the oil in my machine? My engine ceased, you know!"

"We know. The court decided that it was Komarovsky's fault. The men of his ground crew testified that there was an oil leak in one of the gaskets of the Grig's engine, but that Komarovsky refrained from fixing it until it had been in use a certain number of hours. Komarovsky's contention was that he had a standing order for the men to watch the oil level and keep adding oil as needed. The oil level of the Grig D-11 was not checked when Major Kuzmin returned from his flight. Gerasimov testified that Komarovsky had left his crew and had driven off in a truck into town. Did you see that also, Captain Kaplan?"

"I did."

"Komarovsky was sentenced to ten years at hard labor. I had hoped that you might know something upon which I could base an appeal for at least a review of his sentence." He looked at me to see if I approved of his sympathy for his client.

"I wish I could get hold of some ordinary school boy's geography maps!" I said, browsing through the reading matter Feldman had deposited on my bed. "I've forgotten the names of everything, little brother!"

"Yes, I know," Feldman said in a low voice. "That's why the court-martial went forward without your testimony. You should not have let it become known, Kaplan, if you could help it. It will not help you when you are finally released from here."

"It's too late now, Captain. I wish you'd been here to advise me the day I woke up here. So, they know about my mental lapses at Volsk!"

"Yes. It was stated during the trial that Lieutenant Komarovsky's negligence had cost us the loss of a million-ruble samolet and a first-class fighter pilot. When they said that in the indictment I thought you had been killed."

"I wish I had been! I'm alive, but I'm an idiot."

"Don't be so hard on yourself, Captain. Remember that your record is a brilliant one, and it will be taken into consideration. They let me examine your file before I left Moscow for

Volsk. I thought I might find something to use in behalf of my client. I noticed that you served in Khiva, Kaplan. That is where I left my arm, you know. I was under the impression that the counterrevolutionary resistance by the Basmachi in Turkestan had ended at least five years ago."

"Basmachi . . . Turkestan . . . Khiva." I repeated to myself, relieved at remembering these names again." So you were there, too."

"Yes, but some time ago."

"The embers of the fire you helped put out flared up again, Feldman." I managed a feeble smile. "I was just doing my bit."

"I understand. I'm not forgetting that, and neither are you!" Captain Feldman cheerfully rose to end his visit.

"Do you think they'll give me another chance?" I said.

"It's hard to tell, Kaplan. In my case I was assigned to study the rudiments of Soviet law." The captain shrugged, reaching to shake my hand. "You must attempt to convince the doctors that the lapses of memory are of a temporary nature."

Captain Feldman pumped my hand warmly and wished me well—and later that day a bookstore messenger delivered to me a gift from the captain, an atlas which must have been expensive and must have taken some time to find.

In the following days I became totally preoccupied with learning and relearning, filling in gaps in all subjects, from arithmetic and astronomy, to memorizing dates of the succession of Roman emperors, and the names of the Roman and Greek gods. And when I read about the Trojan War, I allowed myself to become sidetracked and figured out how many board feet it would take to have built that wooden horse.

Thus I kept busy through the rest of summer of 1929 and hardly noticed when autumn came. The nearly naked sycamores and stately oaks beyond the windows were shedding their last leaves into a rain-washed courtyard and a deserted street. Through the crevices in the window frames the wind was whistling with the ominous sound of the coming Russian winter.

It was then that a brain specialist, Dr. Bereznekhov, came all the way from Stalingrad to examine me. The doctor questioned me endlessly and looked everywhere, into my ears and eyes, inside my mouth and up my nose, and then the learned little man questioned me some more and scribbled down everything I uttered.

"It is nothing for you to worry about, young man," he said soothingly. "What is your rank?"

"I am a captain."

"But you're so young! How old are you, Captain?"

"It should be on my medical record, Doctor. You have it. I saw it."

"But I want you to tell me, Captain."

"I was born in . . . the year nineteen hundred and . . . I am about twenty-two years old, Doctor," I stammered, not remembering exactly.

"Tell me the date of your birth, please, comrade Captain!" My plight did not seem to move him. He seemed callous, perhaps made immune by all the years he had been practicing his profession. Pencil between bony fingers, he adjusted his pince-nez, and his cold, insensitive stare penetrated me. I stared back at him as calmly as I could, knowing that this old man was about to decide my fate—even if the decision was already known elsewhere by the same judge who had already decided the doctor's fate.

In fact, at that moment, perhaps due to the injury or concussion my head had suffered, I seemed to know that the doctor was ill and that death was on his heels, ready to take him any day. And I sensed that the old man envied my youth and the lifetime of years I had yet ahead of me. And I in turn envied the knowledge the man had accumulated in a lifetime, learning which would soon turn to waste. A shiver passed through me when I imagined the fertile brain in the little old man's head being devoured by worms.

"Dear God . . . how awful!" I said aloud.

"Oh, do you believe in God?"

"I will confide in you on that subject providing you do not put the information on my record, Doctor," I said in a low voice.

"I won't, Captain, I am merely curious. Also I wish to know what is so awful, young man."

"Yes, Doctor, I believe in God, but I can no more visualize Him and propose to understand Him, any more than most people can understand the laws of aerodynamics, or the circuitry of a radio which enables us to talk to one another. Yes, I believe in God, Doctor!"

"How refreshing it is to hear you say that. You have just given me hope that your generation is not unlike mine was, Captain Kaplan. And as for your affliction, that is, your difficulty in recalling names, it is most assuredly a temporary block, a blood clot perhaps. Keep relearning what you can so that when and if your injury no longer handicaps you, you will only be reinforced in your ability to recall names. Your memory will be twice as good!" Now the doctor was friendly for the rest of his visit, talking about his life and dreams, and, despite my previous reservations about him, I was sad to see him go.

The morning of the day before I was to be discharged from the hospital I awakened and found that the world had turned white overnight.

That same morning the doctors gave me the customary periodic medical examination given to air force personnel. Besides twirling round and round in a rotating chair, which was routine, I was made to operate switches, to turn them on and off to achieve certain results–the ringing of a bell or turning on of a light. Failure to carry out the instructions correctly, they told me, was tantamount to creating a pilot error equivalent to an aerial disaster.

But I did everything calmly and accurately. The lamps lit, the bells rang, and the technician clicked his pencil and smiled. When they made me stand up on the whirling chair, I managed to remain upright. And when I was given something to write, and a pistol was fired behind me, still my handwriting remained even.

When the exam was over I was told that I had passed with flying colors and they all congratulated me heartily. But how cruel fate can be! The next morning I received an honorable discharge from the armed services of the U.S.S.R.

The discharge was based on the fact that I had not passed the mental exam performed by Dr. Bereznekhov. So I had been right about him all along, and correct in assuming that he had been sent to pass a final judgement on me.

My discharge had various footnotes which informed me that I was now free to pursue any career as a civilian, and that I could apply for another mental examination for the purpose of reapplying to the armed services, but not before six months from the date of my discharge.

Colonel Bakaleinikov came to my room with an orderly who had my belongings. It all seemed like a bad dream. I was studying my discharge, reading and rereading the letter and hoping that I would awaken. Colonel Bakaleinikov had picked up the voucher which had fallen out of the envelope and whistled. It was for more money than I had ever before seen at once. There was also a voucher in the envelope which was to be exchanged by me for a railway ticket to any destination of my choice in the U.S.S.R., providing it was not closer to a border than three hundred versts.

"If you wish we can have your pay voucher cashed for you, comrade Kaplan," Colonel Bakaleinikov offered. "Also let me suggest that as soon as you arrive home, or wherever your destination is to be, you must not venture too much outside. Don't forget that you've had pneumonia."

And Dr. Ivanova came in. She was glad, she said, that the people at Volsk had had the foresight to send me items of warm winter issue, including my flying helmet and my leather coat. "I want you to wear your leather helmet instead of the regulation hat," she said. "And how does your foot feel, Captain, now that you are wearing boots?"

I felt fine physically, I told the doctors, though my spirit was weak. I had never been a civilian, I explained. I had been a young boy once, but never a civilian.

The doctors made me show them that I could lift my duffel bag, but they would not allow me to carry it downstairs to the panel truck which was to take me to the railway depot.

The world outside the hospital felt different and unfamiliar, if only because I did not know what it held for me. Even as we drove to the train station, I had no idea where I would go.

I was not accustomed to making such decisions—for several years now they had always been made for me.

This new world was white and crisp and cold, with snow that creaked underfoot. But there was no wind as the door of the panel truck opened and I was let out at the train station. For the first time in my life I found myself truly on my own.

N I N E T E E N

HE LEFT HOME WHEN HE WAS FOURTEEN AND he never came back."

That's how Tillie explains her son Alan's various wanderings, outings, adventures, misadventures, matings and mis-matches. But leaving home became for him a process that was much more complicated than, as she saw it, merely running away. Running was only the physical part. Every boy carries his father's house with him on his back like a snail's shell and moves slowly away from the man who mated with his mother. Alan wasn't any different. He ran, but he ran toward home without knowing it.

The first time he made an attempt to break from the oppressive daily round of school and home he knew very little about his motive. Driven by youthful desire, he wandered to the water's edge, to the Jersey shore where young girls and boys gathered in order to take each other's innocence in rituals worth the study of serious anthropologists.

Alan had first discovered Bradley Beach around the age of ten or eleven when Tillie convinced her husband that he must take her on a weekend vacation to the shore. Phil at this time in his life didn't think much of vacations. He worked hard all week and didn't believe that packing the car and driving to the shore and staying the weekend in a rented room was the most restful way to recover from the workplace.

"Perth Amboy and my house are good enough for me," he would say from his vantage point, lying prone on the living room couch. "It's a nice place and I can stay right here and rest. If I want a vacation I can go to Joe and Sadie's at Greenwood Lake. The boys like it there."

"And what about me?"

"Oh, Teel!"

But Tillie wanted to go somewhere away from Perth Amboy even if only for the weekend, and there was no way that Phil would convince her ever again that going to the lake was fun. She dug her heels in and wouldn't budge.

"If you want to go there you can take the kids and go by yourself. I'll stay here."

"Oh, Teelie!"

"Don't Oh Tillie me! You heard what I said. That Sadie is a . . . a . . . peasant, and I won't spend time with her!"

"How can you say that about my brother's wife? How can you cut me off from the only relatives I have here? Don't you ever wonder what it would be like if you had to leave Perth Amboy and New Jersey and the United States and live forever in a strange country? Wouldn't you like to now and then see someone from your old family, from your old way of life?"

"It's not strange here," Tillie said. "And that woman insults me."

"How does she insult you?" Phil asked, grudgingly raising himself up off the couch on one elbow and showing some interest now in her remarks.

"None of your business," Tillie said.

And she said then and there that she was going to have a weekend in Bradley Beach if it killed her. With the boys. And with Phil. If it killed him.

"I just think it's terrible the way he treats you," Aunt Bess told her when she described Phil's reaction to her suggestion. "You can't always do what he wants to do. You've got your rights, too, Tillie."

"I do, don't I?" Tillie said, and began thinking of the plan that within a few weeks would have them driving down toward Bradley on a Friday after work.

A strip of sand along the coast south of Red Bank, Bradley had been staked out by the North Jersey Jews (just as the fundamentalist Christians had long before settled into Ocean Grove further up the beach). They streamed down this way all summer, some for weekends only, some for weeks at a time, some for the entire season. The houses that in winter held only aging landlords were opened in the hot part of the year to transient tenants such as Phil's family.

"We're paying for this?" Phil said in a lamenting voice as soon as he saw the room where the four of them would spend the weekend.

"We're going to be out at the beach," Tillie argued. "The room is not so important."

The room wasn't entirely unpleasant, with two large double beds and wide windows overlooking the street, windows whose white gauzy curtains shielded the room from the hot July sun and at night blew inward on the wings of the offshore breeze. It made Alan think of curtains on a stage set. In fact, he saw all of outdoors Bradley as a stage set, and he was an audience of one, watching from the window as crowds of teenagers strolled back and forth from the boardwalk, studying the boys for habits of style that he might imitate, and scrutinizing the girls as though they were visitors from another planet.

That night he crawled into bed alongside his brother and slept a strange sleep, dreaming of his mother who lay with Phil in the other bed, dreaming that he was back in Perth Amboy and was suddenly awakened by her narrow, dark face looming over him in the shadowy upstairs room of the Lewis Street house, just back after their abortive move for a few years to Rahway, fifteen miles to the north. (They had moved there so that Phil could be closer to his job at the auto plant in Linden, but where Tillie had grown homesick for her mother and Aunt Bess, and so from which Phil, trying to please her, had grudgingly moved back to Amboy.) And then Alan awoke and listened to the steamroller bass of his father snoring, and watched the curtains streaming in as if on the power of the rays of the streetlamp rather than the wind from the sea.

The next morning they went to the beach, where hundreds of bathers had much earlier established their claims and where thousands more would crowd them as the hours went by. Pale as a slug, Alan wandered aimlessly through the breaking surf, digging in the sand and watching the holes fill up with salty spume, kicking water at his little brother, soaking up the sun. By afternoon he was nearly baked—or fried. Phil suffered only on his arms since he had covered up after an hour or so, and besides his hirsute nature seemed to protect him from the rays of that searing August ocean light.

"You stupid," he did say when he noticed as evening settled upon them that his older boy was in pain.

Tillie covered Alan with salve and sent him out on the street where all the teenagers were stalking. With his red face and white shirt and trousers he appeared something like a signal flare in the Bradley dusk.

"Oohh," came a rousing cry from one of the porches. "He glows in the dark!"

Alan rushed on embarrassed, and found himself staggering stiffly along—the very touch of the cloth of his trousers on his nearly crisped legs was agony—on the street that paralleled the boardwalk and the ocean beyond, drawn as if by magnetism toward Mike and Lou's, the hot dog and hamburger joint that was the landmark hangout for all the high school and college students for miles around.

Mike and Lou's! The name itself took on mythical proportions in the mouths and minds of teenagers from all over Jersey—for it had become known as the place where you might meet someone who would love you as much as you had come to love yourself. And all these kids with their braces and complexions heated as much by hormones from within as tanned by sun from without, with their horrid nasal voices and their rolling, lifeless eyes—eyes like that of calves about to be slain by sledge hammers and turned into veal—these kids in their summer whites and striped T-shirts and deck shoes and snappy fingers and rings and earrings and highly waxed, souped-up Chevys and ducktails and crew cuts and—the girls—breasts breasts breasts and lips that only years later he would kiss and cheeks he would touch and hands he would clasp and dreams he would have in the comfort of his own affections, how they became to him, still a child, like gods and goddesses—that summer when he glowed in the dark like a lamp and returned lonely to the rooming house bed and listened through the night while he burned to his parents' snoring.

Yes, so if recognizing and giving in to sexual desire is something like leaving home, then Alan had left even before he was fourteen.

TWENTY

THAT DAY IN SARATOV, AS I WALKED INTO THE railway station waiting room, it occurred to me that for the first time since I was a teenager I was free from all military regulations. I was a free agent, free to go and do whatever I chose to do, yet I was lost, dismayed that my military career had come to an end, and worse because I had no home to which I might return.

I caught a glimpse of myself in a mirror in the back of a buffet and saw that I looked pale and haggard, with hollow cheeks, and without the satisfied smile I used to have. It was especially difficult seeing myself in my flying helmet in a place so far removed from an aerodrome, in a place associated with trains instead of planes. It was hot inside the waiting room. I unbuttoned my coat. My tunic and the trousers felt loose. I had lost weight.

At the buffet the girl served me the only hot food she had on the day's menu, fireman's cutlets. The meat tasted old, tough and greasy. At the next table I overheard a conversation going on between two women, one of whom was a Volga German.

"My son, he is an engineer," she said. "He graduated from the Leningrad Politechnic Institute, my son did! In Zlatoust though, in the Ural Mountains he wrote me, they are working him as a draftsman. That is why my son will not be back there after his vacation is over. He refuses to do a mere draftsman's job even for an engineer's salary, that's what my son wrote to me."

At the air force academy I had excelled in drafting. I could draw the finest letterheads in freehand, and my mechanical drawings and topographical tracings were always neat and I finished them accurately and fast. Drafting, engineering draftsman's work, that would be something I could do well.

I rose and wanted to salute the woman, but instead crossed the room to consult the railway map on one of the walls, to see where exactly Zlatoust was located. The name itself was enticing and totally unfamiliar to me. Zlatoust, or Eastern Gold, or the Golden East, whichever in ancient Russian. There it was, right on the Trans-Siberian Railway! From the map I went to the ticket agent's window.

"Put down the name Zlatoust on that free ticket voucher of mine, please!" I said to the man on the other side of the window.

"Change trains at Samara, comrade," the cashier said as he handed me the validated voucher.

So here was another little factor in my unfolding fate, a conversation overheard in a train station waiting room!

Now either the ordeal of travelling so soon out of the hospital had proven too much for me, or perhaps it was the greasy cutlets I had just eaten, but as the train reached Samara, suddenly I began to feel ill. A weakness overcame me, a turbulence within my stomach, and I made it to the washroom just in time to vomit. And immediately after that I passed out.

When I awakened I felt wet and cold and dizzy, and suddenly cold water cascaded over my head and chest, falling onto me from the palm of a bearded patriarch who towered over me. Above the mane of grey hair was a murky bulb burning on the ceiling. The meager light of the bulb mingled with the light of day and the cold air streamed in through a broken window.

"Dead, is he?" I heard someone ask.

"Dead drunk, more likely!" a voice replied.

"And he's . . . naked!" someone snickered.

"Can you get up, or did you lap up too much?" the man above me asked. Behind him other men were pushing forward. Some were laughing, and others were simply curious—only a few had compassionate eyes.

A police whistle shrilled a short blast. A member of the G.P.U. militia was making his way through the crowd outside the partially opened door.

"Out of the way! Out the way," he said. "Where is the body?" The bystanders in a chorus informed the militiaman that I had been resurrected, though a man with a flare of frivolity informed the policeman that it wouldn't be long before I froze back to death.

"It's God's truth!" a peasant woman swore, "he's kneeling there stark naked."

"When I wish information from you I'll ask for it," the militiaman said, brandishing his revolver in one hand and his whistle in the other and wading forward through the crowd.

"We found him lying there, sleeping it off," somebody volunteered.

The militiaman's eyes twinkled with amusement when he saw me, arms huddled in and dancing a jig. "It's against regulations to parade around naked in public except in the bathhouse!" he said.

"I w-w-was robbed, c-c-comrade," I said with a stammer.

"Stop bleating! Speak up!"

"I am c-c-cold, c-c-comrade!"

"Now then, tell it to me again! What's your name?" said the G.P.U. sergeant at the G.P.U. station several hours later.

"I told you, my name is Fishel Isaakovich Kaplan! Why are you so reluctant to believe me? My head aches! I told you who I was! And I told you that I'm a veteran, a captain by rank, honorably discharged from the Red Army Air Force! This bump on my head I suffered in your station washroom has not helped injuries I sustained during an aircraft crackup I had this summer. I was discharged from the Saratov Military Hospital only yesterday. I am suffering from memory loss, and this may be why I may not be answering all your questions to your satisfaction."

Never had I been treated so shabbily before, and I tried desperately to control my temper during that interrogation.

"Personally I am inclined to believe him, Sorokin," said a G.P.U. lieutenant who sat by, sipping tea. "If he were not telling us the truth, why then would he dream up a non-Russian name like Fishel Isaakovich?"

"We'll send off a query," said the lieutenant to the sergeant, "so you can stop questioning him for the time being. Let the man be for a while, until we hear from Saratov."

"Just so!"

With the crook of his forefinger Sergeant Sorokin summoned me. I followed him to a door he had opened for me and behind which he shut me as soon as I entered. I found myself standing in darkness, and when a light went on after a while I found that I was in an improvised prison cell. In a corner was a pile of straw which had been slept on and which was mostly shredded into a millet mixed with dust. The wooden door that had been locked on me had an inside door consisting of iron bars which had been left ajar. There was a barred window, boarded over from the outside—otherwise the room was bare.

"I don't deserve this," I protested and banged on the door. "I am not a prisoner here! You have no right to treat me this way!"

I pounded on the door with my fists until the light in my cell went off!

"You lousy, no good bastards," I raged at the top of my lungs, "The Air Force High Commander will hear of this! I will write to General Budenny about this! It wouldn't surprise me if Comrade Stalin himself hears of this outrage!"

A clerk they called Petrushka and who was slightly dim-witted came to me during the night to give me tea and some bread, and as he stood at my door he said that he was glad for me that things were working out, that is for the wire that had come from Saratov.

"Say, this is wonderful! At last! What did the wire say, Petrushka? Did it just now arrive?" I came awake and felt alive again for a moment. "Does it say what I am to do? Did they send any instructions?"

"Did not the lieutenant tell you all about it? Oh I see, he's not here now. So. And well. The telegram which is on his desk is addressed to his superior, the company commander. But if the lieutenant did not tell you about it, comrade Kaplan, then I'd better not tell you lest I find myself in hot water."

"Read it to me, Petrushka, please! I give you my word of honor that I won't tell anyone what you did! Read it to me, Petrushka, please."

"If you promise, sir. If you give me your word of honor, sir, then I will tell you what's in this wire, but there isn't much."

Petrushka was a boy not long from his village, a boy not yet contaminated by callousness. When he returned from the lieutenant's desk with two pieces of paper I could hardly contain myself through his hesitant reading.

"It says here, it says, that you are now a civilian and are therefore no longer subject to military jurisdiction. It says here, it says, that any infractions of the law you may have committed may be due to a mental affliction you have suffered as a result of a crackup of a military aircraft, and allowance should be made for any and all manifestations of this mental illness."

"What else, Petrushka? Does it not state whether I was to be given an issue of clothes and money to get me home?"

"No. It merely confirms that by rank you were a captain and a holder of the Order of the Red Banner—Holy Christ! Imagine that, sir."

"Nothing about giving me winter issue and a few rubles?"

"Nothing, sir. This is what Lieutenant Konotopsky is asking in this other telegram, sir. He is asking for a clearer disposition."

How long does it take to get an answer to a telegram?" I asked Lieutenant Konotopsky when he came into the office the next morning. "But you have no right to keep me locked behind bars!" I shouted, unable to contain my indignation. "You have no charges against me."

"You're right, absolutely right, Captain Kaplan!" he agreed. "You see, we have received word that you are who you say you are, and officially we are no longer detaining you. But tell me, where are you going to obtain clothes to continue your journey to Zlatoust? As a matter of fact, I went late yesterday to my superior, Captain Golovolissy, to discuss your case. While I was there, he called the local military commissary and asked them to issue you clothing. You know what? They told us that they cannot issue winter or summer wear to anyone without a voucher. Otherwise, they said, everybody would line up for a handout of military issue. My superior says that you should remain in our custody until we receive a voucher for an issue of winter clothing."

"At this rate I'll be here all winter!"

"Listen, Captain, by now the railway detachments of G.P.U. all over the Soviet Union have been alerted to be on the lookout for some joker wearing a full-length black leather coat, an aviator's helmet perhaps, an air force officer's tunic, and custom-made boots," the lieutenant recited calmly and in a monotone. "The G.P.U. are on the lookout for anyone masquerading in such attire or using your identity papers or showing off the Order of the Red Banner. I doubt if we can recover the money for you, but there's the chance that the perpetrator will be caught and summarily shot."

"Well if the G.P.U. is *that* efficient, can you not obtain a voucher from Air Force Headquarters through Red Army communication channels?"

"We are trying and I'm sure we'll succeed, Captain. We need time though. Given the circumstances, please try to exercise a little more patience."

"Could I secure a loan from some organization?" I wondered.

"If you belonged to some labor union, and if you had a membership card to prove it, the local union might give five or ten rubles to keep you in borscht and bread." Konotopsky said. "As I told you, Captain, we are no longer officially detaining you. You are technically free to go. But even if you had all the money that was taken from you, you couldn't purchase a military winter issue of clothes since they're not for sale, and I doubt you could find a store in Samara that could sell you an overcoat ready-made, if you know what I mean."

"I know one thing . . ."

"What's that, Captain."

"I'm stuck here, naked, in this G.P.U. hotel of yours!"

Later that day, a day that was becoming dark and ugly outside, Captain Golovolissy stormed into the office followed by Lieutenant Konotopsky. "Who is the typist here? Sit down and take this down: 'To whom it may concern. Spravka.' You have that? Take down the rest! 'The bearer of this spravka, former Red Army Air Force Captain Fishel Isaakovich Kaplan, and holder of the Order of the Red Banner, was recently discharged from the Saratov Military Hospital for medical reasons resulting from a plane crash . . .'"

"Tovarich Golovolissy, excuse me," Konotopsky said when the captain hesitated in his dictating of the temporary identification document.

"What is it? What?"

"Shouldn't we do something about a clothing voucher first?" Konotopsky suggested. "The captain is practically naked, you know."

"Ah, yes! It slipped my mind. As if there isn't enough paper work to sign, he has to come along! Let's do this, let's make out a voucher for an issue of *used* winter clothing, Konotopsky," he said. "That's more quickly acquired. Just make sure there is no insignia on the lapels! Understood?"

"Yes, sir!"

"The spravka will get you a ride on a train to Zlatoust, Captain Kaplan. It's only a stone's throw from here. Speak to one of the ticket agents at the station, Konotopsky. Come on, let's finish, so you can put him on the next train!"

"Yes, sir!"

"Now . . . where were we? Oh, yes! Take this down on the next paragraph! 'The bearer of this spravka is therefore to be given all possible consideration, and keeping in mind that he has suffered some apparent brain damage, and, after his release from the hospital, had his condition further aggravated when at Samara, this former fighter pilot and veteran was apparently beaten and robbed of his uniform, his money, and all his other possessions.' Put my title to it and I'll sign it and place the seal to it."

"Yes, sir!"

Although I didn't really care for the tone of the spravka which made me sound more dangerous than decorated, I couldn't have been happier than if I had been awarded a second Order of the Red Banner.

TWENTY-ONE

I'VE HEARD THESE NAMES SO MANY TIMES before, Tashkent, Urgench, Khiva. *Khiva!* And read about them now so that they're engraved on my living mind as well as in my family memory. But when I see them typed on our airplane ticket, and see our bags packed and ready at the door, and know we're leaving Moscow, heading for the airport, and that we'll be spending the night in a city three or four thousand miles away in a part of the world that I've heard about only before in a history that is fused with myth, stories from the mouths of dervishes—images out of Hollywood films in which slant-eyed warriors in leather helmets ride across the dusty steppe—then I have to marvel at the way in which past and present, illusion and reality, hope and dream and actual possibility, come together in our lives now and then, which is not often.

We check out of the hotel and are soon heading southeast out of the city, toward Domodedovo Airport, the largest in the Soviet Union and one of the world's largest. We drive and drive just to reach the outskirts of Moscow, past endless high-rise apartment buildings under construction and entire blocks of recently completed apartments, until finally after half an hour we leave the city behind and travel past woods and well-farmed clearings where many makeshift wooden houses stand alongside garden plots. Here we could be in the middle of rural Michigan, except that the road is broad and new and signs every few miles point us toward the jetport.

We can see large airplanes drifting lazily in descent toward the horizon before we come upon this huge aerodrome in the country, like Dulles in Virginia, and our driver swings to the left, passes through a security gate, and drives us out onto the tarmac and across the field to the Intourist door off the runway. There we go through the usual processing, ticketing, x-raying of our few pieces of luggage, and then we repair to a waiting room where some disconsolate dark-browed, curly-haired, and mustached students remind us that our destination lies quite near the Afghanistan border.

American voices resound through the hall. I look up to see a face strangely familiar—of all people, a student from my old days of teaching at Bennington College—leading a small group of Americans on a tour of Siberia and Mongolia. We exchange hurried greetings, but then she has to head out for their flight. Small world? No, still quite large, but shrinking.

This is also the gateway to Siberia, but it is the south we are interested in. The departure signs tell us that we can catch flights here for Novosibirsk or Irkutsk or Tashkent, among other places. Even Ulan Bator. If seeing these names on a map seems exotic, or seeing them on the pink itinerary sheet of an American travel agency is odd, try sitting in the waiting room and looking up to see them spelled out on the departure board! It couldn't be more weird to me than sitting in a room looking up at a board that says, "Mars flight, 2100 hours," or, "Next Venus Trip, 0730."

An Aeroflot attendant leads me and Josh downstairs and out onto the tarmac where we walk with an Intourist guide a few hundred yards to where the airplane is waiting. As usual we've been told to board ahead of all the Soviet passengers. We're the only Westerners on the plane—and two Ethiopian students, man and wife, appear to be the only other foreigners. We find our seats, settle in, and notice that some of the flight attendants have Asian features, and the pilot who boards just after us appears almost Chinese. This is a part of the Soviet world we rarely hear or see much about, the Central Asian Soviet Republics. In a few minutes we're in the air, rising through clouds that quickly hide Moscow from sight.

We had wanted to go to Orenburg first, where Phil did his flight training, but we couldn't get a visa. Orenburg, gateway to Soviet Asia! We should be flying just above it now, or to the south of it. The voice of a flight attendant bursts through on the static-filled loudspeaker in our cabin, and I make out the name Volgograd, and I realize that we're flying southeast along the Volga, the river that for a time cost my father his memory.

Beneath the clouds now, according to my map, should lie the northern coast of the Caspian Sea, and ahead of us the beginning of the Asian steppes, and the borders of the Aral Sea.

I read a little, then must let my mind drift, remembering my father's account of his journey east, the call to report to Tashkent because of the three other officers who were lost in the supposed crash in the Urals, the flight across the mountains and the desert in formation with his comrades from Orenburg. And now here we are flying this same route, though tens of thousands of feet higher above the steppe, and hundreds of miles faster. Who knows but that one day Josh will take this route again, perhaps even with a child of his? And that that child will bear children, for after all he might be a she, and those children will in turn take this journey, to see where we had been, where Phil had been, to know where they are going!

Time out of mind? Time in the air. A time to think, a time to dream.

Good, Oll-an, my father's voice speaks gently in my ear. *You've come far, you've come this far, so far so good.* A feeling of great warmth washes over my head, down over my shoulders, over the rest of my body—I feel his love pouring over me, the way you hear Born Agains talk about how God's love comes over them.

Do I actually hear this voice? Or am I making it up in my head? I don't know. Do the Born Agains hear anything real?

Did Joan of Arc? Do schizophrenics on the street hear actual words coming from mail boxes and street lamps? Writers certainly hear voices in their heads all the time, and dialogue becomes an act like taking dictation. But there is hearing and there is *hearing*.

My father's voice doesn't come to me like the voice of the flight attendant over the loudspeaker telling us—I can make it out—to look to the right of the aircraft for a glimpse of the Aral Sea. But it comes to me. It comes.

Down off to our right, to the south, the upper shoreline of the Aral Sea comes into view through the haze, a high-white shade on its surface in the brilliant afternoon sun, this large inland body of water in the shape of a fat outstretched hand in the middle of the brown steppe. I'm reminded of the Salton Sea in the southern California desert, and of the Great Salt Lake.

The other passengers appear to be dozing or reading. Josh is asleep, his Walkman earphones perched on his head. I check the map, compare the tiny spot of blue on the page with the lazy hand filled with water below, half-fused now with the hazy air all around it.

Soon our engines change pitch, and we begin to descend, in the early stages of our approach to Tashkent. We are low enough now that we can see the first signs of the Kyzyl Kum Desert below.

And the sun has fled far behind us even as we have raced eastward,

And the lights begin to flicker in the darkening sands below, where we see the shadowy outline on the far horizon to the southeast, of farmlands,

And we sink further into the dark,

Into a sea of deepening desert,

Homing in on lights ahead, the desert sinking back and below,

And if I had been born the son of an Uzbek khan, or the son of a water carrier on the mountain road between Tashkent and Alma-Ata, or the offspring of a cart driver at one of the oases on the way to the Hunger Steppe to the south, a country boy, child of the desert, to whom the city meant nothing but loud noise and trouble,

Then my heart could not have leaped less high than it does when our aircraft goes into an easy left turn, then straightens out and rides smoothly for a few miles more before touching down on the tarmac at Tashkent.

Tashkent!

Though it is not the Tashkent that my father knew, this is a city with the same basic layout and the same name, rebuilt almost entirely after it was razed by a major earthquake in the early 1960s. Supposedly only half a dozen of the pre-earthquake structures still stand. If true, this may be one of the most remarkable reconstruction efforts in modern times, because this is a *large,* sprawling, semitropical capital. From the car on the way to the hotel we see parks and the ubiquitous apartment structures, women of a dark, quasi-oriental cast holding children on street corners, men in shirtsleeves, wearing their shirts untucked like Caribbean guayaberas. The air is warm here, after Moscow veritably springlike. People push baby carriages along the pavement, despite the hour, and children stroll along by the entrance to a park. Ethnic Russians walk the streets in light clothing, looking like Midwestern Americans who live in Puerto Rico or Mexico, Guam or the Philippines.

My father fought for this, nearly lost his life for this. The old men you see on Soviet streets walking with their chests weighed down with war medals—my father might now be one of them, strolling with a cane to help keep himself steady, a grandchild perhaps at his side, in the warm night air of Tashkent's mild autumn. Like the old fellow passing by the hotel just as we arrive and our bags are unloaded from the car, an old man whose eyes meet mine because I allow mine to linger, my father might have lived his life out as a hero of the Soviet Union, and somehow been happy.

And suddenly I wish he could have achieved that, stayed within the borders of his country, worked in the war effort against the Nazis, distinguishing himself for his untiring labor, the hours he put in, worrying about his family—stayed with a lovely Russian woman from Siberia, or met someone from Irkutsk on the train back to Moscow, and disembarked at her stop and followed her home and married her, raised children with her, and with great and trying sadness left her to fight in the Great Patriotic War—and say that he survived, survived the bombings and the shellings and even the dangerous missions that he would have flown against the German Aircorps, and then was awarded medals, and promoted, and somehow survived through the Stalin years, keeping his mouth shut and his eyes straight ahead—say that Stalin figured that he needed a *few* well-trained officer-pilots left alive—and come into retirement during the Khrushchev "thaw," and watched his children enter the professions and make him proud, and worried about Soviet-U.S. relations since his brother and his sister still lived in the United States (amazing, how he lasted under Stalin with relatives in that country, but last he did), and wrote letters to the air force newspaper about international politics, saying that it was important to support the left-wing parties in Israel because of the base for an eventual socialist government for all peoples in the Middle East, and that we ought to have patience with the seemingly intransigent American government in order to ultimately achieve world peace through their cooperation—and say that he decided that he would like to move to Tashkent for his retirement, the place where he spent some of the best years of his youth, and since Moscow meant little to him because he had no real place there—as an officer of Jewish ethnic affiliation he had never been promoted very high or engaged in the innermost discussions of military strategy—and so say that he moved here with his wife because as it turned out one of their children had decided to emigrate to Uzbekistan, having listened all her life to the stories about his old days there, to take up, say, a post in the health ministry, and here it came to pass that on a warm night in September he went out for a stroll, thinking about the old days when he had raced through the air against such oncoming darkness as he had seen overtake the desert just this twilight time of night, and he was walking on Karl Marx Street just before the entrance to the new Hotel Uzbekistan when a black Volga pulled up and two men, a father and a son, tourists, climbed out of the car, and he thought to himself, these could have been my boys if I had had another life, they look so familiar, and his eyes and those of the older tourist met—but only for an instant or two before life called out to each of them and they had to look to other business.

This night in Tashkent is one of sleepless anticipation. I am worried that nothing real can match this feeling of what I hope to find out there in the desert, *back* there in the desert, actually, since we have to fly about six hundred miles back in the other direction, *west,* across the Kyzyl Kum to Urgench, the main town of the fertile valley that hugs both shores of the Amu-Darya River, where we will stay overnight and then take a car and a guide the thirty kilometers south to Khiva.

I listen to the sounds of the Tashkent night, a few cars rolling by, a little night bird song—here in the North Asian dark it seems that some birds persist into the deep evening.

"Are you nervous?" I ask Josh, so that I can ask the question of myself.

"Not really," he says. "I want to try and get some good pictures, though."

"There should be a lot to shoot."

"Probably."

"The desert, the town, supposedly it's some huge oasis between the two deserts, the Kyzyl Kum and Kara Kum. Tamburlaine once ruled here."

"Tamburlaine," Josh says.

"The big khan out of Samarkand."

"I remember something about that. And Genghis Khan and his horse soldiers, who ruled most of the civilized world. They came through here too, yes?"

"And then came Phil, your grandfather."

"A little bit later."

"But still part of that story. Strange. . ."

"Weird," Josh says, and pulls the covers over his head. He dissolves quickly into sleep and his breathing sounds more hoarse than usual, a stomach bug that's affected him is working his system overtime, I guess. Sorry, sorry. He'll take the pills we brought along and feel better soon.

We're some fifteen floors up in this supposedly "quake-proof" building, but I lie in the dark and worry a while about the entire place coming down around our ears. That's one part of me I don't like, the part bequeathed to me by my father in his middle to late life, the behavior we used to call—before feminism—"old womanish." What should I call it? Can't say cowardly. Think of all the heroics he performed in his youth. Wish I had a name. Old mannish? But then he has been with me on all the airplane flights so far, assuring me that he was holding up the wings.

Still, I can't quite ditch this stupid and no doubt unwarranted sense of trouble. There'll be no quake, at least not tonight. It's twenty-five years too soon for another major upheaval. Twenty-five? My father came here some fifty-six, fifty-seven years ago. Flying low over the desert, east of Aral, north of the Afghanistan border, coming in over the dunes and seeing the green sward of the farmlands around Tashkent and the rising peaks of the mountains behind it, and what did he know that he was flying toward?

He had his orders, he had a pretty good sense of pleasure and adventure, and that would have been enough—and yet look what else the future delivered to him, the future he flew toward in full control of his faculties and his airship but without any awareness of what the years ahead might bring except more of the same that he was enjoying at the moment. Siberia. The Orient. America. The rest of his life, my mother, my brother, his two granddaughters, me, and this sleeping presence alongside me on the other bed, my own son.

My father's future, now my past: I feel that time itself, like some great winged oriental bird, has wheeled around in air for us to meet it. The night bird sings me to sleep.

TWENTY-TWO

THE MONOTONOUS CLICKING OF THE RAILS, THE muffled rumbling of the train hurtling on and on obliterated all measure of time. How long had I been travelling? In the dark, warm niche of the upper berth I could not tell if it was light outside or if it was night. Had it been an hour or a day since I had left Samara? I kept slipping in and out of a sweating sleep, and when I awoke I felt hungry and nibbled at the crust of bread and sipped at the bottle of water one of the two G.P.U. militiamen had given me as I boarded the train. When after one of these sessions of dozing and waking and eating I felt the train slow down, I gathered my strength and launched myself from the berth only to feel underfoot the soft limb of the person sleeping in the berth below me.

"Assassin!" a woman cried out in a sleep-choked voice, and thwacked my foot with a fist.

I leaped past her, sniffing the sour odor of her night breath, and rushed from the compartment toward the door at the end of the corridor, desperate for a taste of fresh air. No one else stirred as I worked open the outside door, which took some pulling. This made me dizzy again, and as I stepped down into a curtain of driving snow my legs went out from under me and I found myself sitting on the icy ground. It took all my strength to get up again, with the wind trying to hold me down like a hand of ice.

The train had stopped, and a few cars ahead a lantern bobbed through the rifts of snow. Then suddenly the train gave a metallic screech and started to jolt its way forward.

It was all like a dream, what happened next. My head was spinning, the wind was blowing against me, and my knees gave out again.

I sat down once more in a bed of snow as I heard the conductor's shouts sound through the icy air, and the shrill answer of the locomotive's whistle, and I could hear the train cars bang one another and their wheels begin rolling over the rails. I tried to call out over and over but gradually my voice faded with the sounds of the train as it vanished into the dark woods to the east.

I was stunned, sitting there alone in the cold quiet of a white night in the wilderness. My ears were the first part of me to feel the stinging frost, next was my nose. The snow on my face and hands and inside my neck bit into me, stinging as if it were powdered glass.

I saw my hat. Somehow I managed to pick it up and pull it over my ears. Where was the station? It would not take long to freeze to death out here. Then I saw it, a forlorn looking shack just ahead. I found my feet and began walking, then running toward the building. It was an oblong building with windows, the panes of which reflected the light of the waning moon. In the whiteness beyond the station shack I could see huts, but all of them were dark.

The snow creaked under my feet as I hurried on, racing to reach the shack. Then I suddenly heard another sound, one that sent new shivers down my spine. Wolves. Then I saw a whole pack of them, crouched among a stand of white birch. There was another howl, and then the leader came lurching toward me, bouncing up and down through the snow field, as the rest of the pack got off their haunches to follow. Fortunately I was on a trampled path which ran along the rails, so that by running full tilt I was able to reach the shack quickly despite the numbing cold.

I wasn't prepared for my next shock. I grabbed the door handle, pulled, turned, twisted and pulled. It was locked. My fingers stuck to the metallic knob, and to pry my hand loose I had to tear at it. I stepped back and jabbed my foot through one of the panes. Feverishly I reached inside and turned the door lock open.

When I had smashed the window, the falling glass made a sudden tinkling sound which apparently frightened the animals and caused them to stop for a second or two, even made them draw back a bit before they resumed their race to reach me. These were the seconds that saved my life. My palm again froze to the doorknob, and I had to breathe on it to pry it loose. I freed myself and stepped fuller inside just as the leader of the pack reached the building.

Inside I at once felt relieved, safe despite the fact that it was a dark and dismal place that smelled of dust, tobacco, smoke, and mice. I tripped over a scale. I upset a sled standing against a wall. Once I became accustomed to the darkness I went into the waiting room. Between two smooth benches was a cast-iron potbellied stove. It was still warm, but inside I found only embers.

I grabbed the sled, smashed it with a crowbar, and used it as kindling. Behind the stove I found a bucket of coal. I kept shoving the kindling and pieces of coal into the smoking stove and blew and blew at the smoke until I became utterly exhausted. Still no fire!

I searched for matches all over the station but could find none. Again and again I tried to make a spark in that stove, and although some smoke curled toward the flue, I could not raise any flames.

I felt sleepy. It made sense to find something to cover the window frame with the broken pane of glass, to keep out the cold, although I knew that without the stove going it would make little difference by morning. The flimsy building constructed of clapboard was cooling rapidly. I stumbled over a bundle of newspapers and used some of them to plug the window frame. The wolves had been waiting all this while. One of them jumped up and sunk his fangs into the roll of paper as I pushed it through, and I watched as he also caught his mouth on the broken glass. The entire pack was well aware of my presence in the building, and soon they were flinging themselves against the door. I had seen the hunger in their eyes, and now I could hear their snapping fangs and the scraping of their paws against the panels.

The cold was beginning to weigh me down, but with the last of my strength I tore more newspaper and stuffed the shredded pieces into the stove. Then I sat down to rest on the smooth bench. It felt so good to stretch out there in that room full of shadows and moonlight. Through my drowsiness I could hear what sounded like the wolves devouring one of their own, perhaps the one who had slashed himself. But I hardly cared about what was happening outside the door—all I wanted was to sleep.

Then I dreamed that I was in my Uncle Yankel's house in Zhitomir, in the ramshackle house near the bluff where I swam as a boy while Uncle Yankel fished the river. My mother was there and my aunt Rachel, and my grandfather Fishel was there. My mother was smiling and stroking my hair just as she always did when I was a little boy.

"Fishel," my mother said to me. "Go to America to your father, your brother Josiah, and your sister Pessella. Go there, angel! It's not for nothing that God gave you wings to fly, even as birds do."

"Do that, Fishka," said my uncle Yankel. "But you are going east instead of west, son!"

And my grandfather Fishel, who had a white beard and wore a prayer shawl over a white gown, as when the Jews bury their dead, spoke to me soothingly and said, "The world is round and is forever moving swiftly through endless voids and is thus suspended in the firmaments. It matters not which way you travel. East or west, eventually you will arrive in America if it is so predestined."

Then I felt a stabbing pain in the fingers of my right hand and the dream vanished. The pain persisted and continued until I fully awoke. There was light coming from the potbellied stove! The side of the stove was crimson and the heat it gave off was bringing me back from a sleep that could have become eternal.

"My brother's name is Josiah and my sister's is Pessella!" I rejoiced in remembering. "Oh, Mama, mamochka mine, how alive you are in my heart and mind!" I sighed as I thought about the meaning of the dream. Go to America . . . just like that! Easier said than done. The idea was crazy, I told myself and got up to feed coal into the stove. It was almost morning, light enough to see the destruction I had wrought in my feverish haste to build a fire. The bundle of newspapers which had been neatly tied was busted open, a roll of papers was stuck through the door in place of the missing pane of glass, and there was the smashed sled, most of which I had used up as kindling. There was also the broken glass of the lamp, and lumps of coal strewn around the station. From the window I could see the village, not far away. My stomach began churning at the sight.

Before opening the door I listened a little to the arctic silence of a winter day just being born in a world where everything was tempered by an icy cold. Draped in white, the firs still glistened—but in a yellow light dispersing bluish shadows, rather than in the silver shimmer of moonlight.

Outside I saw no traces of the wolves and wondered if I had dreamed it all, their attack and the fear they had inspired in me. But the snow that had fallen through the night, and the wind which made it fly sideways, could have easily erased their tracks.

The sun still lay hidden behind white mountains to the east, but I could feel its presence as the light grew and warmed this frozen world ever so slightly. I made my way along fresh sled tracks toward the village. The snow creaked underfoot as I alternately walked and ran, waving my arms in an effort to generate some extra warmth.

Beyond a rise I found the main street. Rows of huts ornamented with gaudy rafters and doors and windows overdone with wooden filigree, stood behind fences. Further up the street I turned and found myself in a sort of town square. There was an onion-topped church without a cross and a brand new building constructed of new logs which was unmistakably a store. The store stood half on a hill and half on stilts with a stairway leading down to a small wooden bridge over a frozen stream. Nothing stirred on the street or in the square, until from the side door of the store I saw a woman emerge holding a broom and a pail. The charwoman descended the stairway and walked through the snow to the stream where she dipped a bucket into the water through broken ice. However, before turning to return to the building, I saw her look furtively about, reach into the folds of her coat, and then hide something in the snow which she smoothed over with her broom.

"Ahah!" I said to myself. "The old one has helped herself to some goods and I hope it is something edible!"

I waited until she climbed back to the store and then I slid down the slope until I reached the spot beneath the bridge. Wrapped in a woman's kerchief I found two paper packages. One contained a paper box of safety pins, a paring knife, two fishing hooks, and a can of Scandinavian sardines. The other package held about a kilo of assorted paper-wrapped candies. I despised myself for taking what was not mine, and I hated myself for toying with the idea of confronting the cleaning woman and trying to blackmail her into stealing some new clothes for me in that store, and perhaps taking me to her home and giving me a hot meal.

Halfway up those steps I learned that I did not possess the makeup of a blackmailer. I could not find it in me to threaten to expose the poor charwoman as a thief. But I kept the items I had found and left the kerchief on the steps to let the charwoman know that someone had seen her steal from the store. This might at least induce her to stop helping herself to the merchandise. I smiled to myself, leaving behind a trail of candy wrappings as I went. I was so hungry that I considered trying to bite through the sardine can. But the candies were filled with jelly and, though they were brittle and cold, they were loaded with the energy I needed to keep going–wherever that might be.

Back at the village square, I saw another peasant woman pulling a sled loaded with a makeshift charcoal stove, a cauldron with a cast-iron cover, and a number of bulging burlap bags, all tied securely with a hemp rope.

"Matushka," I called out to the woman. "This sled of yours, it's loaded with enough for a horse to pull. May I lend you a hand?"

The woman shied away from me at first, but with a second look she saw that I was young enough to be her son and that I was smiling and that it was correct of me, according to custom, to address her as "little mother."

"You just passing through?" she asked of me, looking straight ahead.

"Was on my way to Zlatoust. I got off the train and it left without me. I am cold and hungry, Matushka. I am perishing." I was not exaggerating. "If I don't perish from hunger, it will surely be from this cold. Because even if I were of sturdy Siberian stock, like yourself, I could not last much longer dressed as I am in these rags."

The second-hand uniform and coat the G.P.U. had acquired for me in Samara were not only disgraceful in their disheveled appearance, they were worn so thin that there were holes at my elbows.

"No money for a train ticket this close to Zlatoust?" the woman asked.

"I have but one ruble, Matushka, and I am looking to buy something hot to eat with it. Is there anywhere I could find warmth and food around here?" Meanwhile I took hold of the rope and helped the woman pull her sled.

"You have not any mittens, boy! Put your hands back into the pockets of your coat before you freeze your fingers!" She talked to me as she might a child. "I'm going to the railway station myself, as I do every morning to sell food to passengers. The train for Zlatoust is due in an hour. In two hours there is one going the other way, for Ufa. You can take your pick and go either way."

"I'm going to Zlatoust, Matushka. I may look like a tramp, but I'm not."

"I believe you, boy! You're not a swindler or a highwayman, I know them when I see them, and I shall do what Christ wants me to do for you, inside here." She pointed to her bosom. "Christ tells me to feed you, boy. Those are potatoes in that bag and you'll have as many as you want without charge."

"Do not give them for nothing, little mother. I'll pay."

"You will need the money for a train ticket! It's exactly one ruble to Zlatoust from here."

"Will you then take these?" I said, offering her the things I had found, save the package with candy and the sardines. I wound the rope with which she was pulling the sled around the crook of an arm and helped her tug.

When we reached the railroad station, I helped her trample a spot in the snow where we could set up her vendor's stand. She lit the charcoal stove, placed some snow into the cauldron, and before long I was feasting not only on hot potatoes but a chunk of reheated meat. By then there were other women vendors setting up their stands with the food items they had to offer. Now that the sun had risen it was a brilliant winter morning. But still the air felt almost too cold to inhale, as if the oxygen had frozen and turned into needles of gold.

The stationmaster, an ex-serviceman in a Red Army greatcoat, arrived on foot and surveyed the domain with satisfaction until he noticed the broken windowpane on the station door. He rushed inside, then right back out, looking perplexed and obviously searching for the culprit. Intuitively, or perhaps I was the only strange face he could see, he rushed over to me and yelled, "You're under arrest!"

"Why?" I inquired, continuing to eat my meat and potatoes as I stomped in the snow to keep warm.

"For damaging certain government-owned items of property. You broke into the station and you spent the night there!" He accused me as though he had actually witnessed me doing it with his own eyes.

"You leave him be, Matwevich! You hear?" my woman benefactor demanded. "Stranger that this lad is, he is not the only one passing to and from on trains past here!"

"Who are you?" the station attendant demanded. "Where is your passport? I have the right to see the passports of passengers."

I produced my spravka and handed it for him to read. The attendant read it slowly and kept scratching the back of his fur cap. Finally he made an effort, smiled, and handed the letter back to me.

"The train for Zlatoust will be here in twenty minutes, tovarich Captain," he said and saluted courteously in a soldierly manner.

I returned his salute. "Will you sell me a ticket?"

"There is no need for that, Captain. Seeing that you have been robbed, I will ask the train conductor to oblige you and allow you to ride free of charge, at government expense, sir."

The woman kept staring and nodding her head at Matwevich, unable to get over his courteousness. There was an unmistakable smile under the stubble on the stationmaster's face now. A moment before he was ready to arrest me, to rage about the damage I had inflicted, and now all was forgiven and forgotten. The woman crossed herself, probably to ward off the magic spell which came over Matwevich, no matter what might have occasioned it.

When the train arrived the stationmaster spoke with the conductor, who waved me aboard. I sat down in one of the compartments where there was a seat available among passengers of both sexes. A petite young woman looked at me, turned up her little nose, and did not once look me in the eye again. When the conductor happened by, she called him over and complained loudly that I had stared at her and made her feel nervous, and on top of that, she said that I smelled. Would not the conductor be so kind as to move me somewhere else, she said, to the baggage car perhaps where derelicts and tramps such as I would not offend people such as herself. The conductor bowed to the young lady and said, "Yes, your highness, yes! I shall ask the young man to remove himself. But only if he wishes to do so on his own free will."

"By all means," I said and got up.

"And if you'd care to know who that young man was," I heard the conductor say as I left, "then I will tell you that he is a national hero who . . ."

The passengers in the next car scarcely noticed me. They were peasants going to sell their produce on the free market at Cheliabinsk, and I sat happily among them with their bags of cabbage heads, strings of mushrooms, onions and garlic, and pleasant chatter. I might have once been a hero of sorts but, if nothing else, the last few days had made me comfortable with the most common people of this earth.

TWENTY-THREE

BOYS AND GIRLS, I HAVE AN IMPORTANT announcement to make."

The teacher in a brown dress from which dangled many darker brown bows and twists of cloth drew herself up to her full height before the blackboard of Alan's eighth grade homeroom in the old grammar school on Barracks Street. The site was named for the British military bivouac that stood on this little rise above the center of town during pre-Revolutionary War days. But nothing that happened in this school had much to do with grammar or revolution. It was a miserably dull, lackluster institution that did more to hold back from the work force for a few years the proletarian kids from the ethnic neighborhoods around the town than prepare anyone for further study. Its greatest attractions were all extracurricular: the after-school duels with fists and rocks by some of the best street fighters in town, or generally goofing around with friends. The upper reaches of the school where most of the auditoriums and classrooms lay held little for the students that was compelling—Christmas programs when the boys rolled ball bearings down the slightly tilted aisles, poetry classes during which time ecstatic middle-aged women read James Russell Lowell aloud with the passion of lay ministers, and by their actions rolled boulders between most of the students and art. (In the sub-subbasement of the school were the fabled "salt mines," the detention halls for the unregenerate. Given the level of instruction in the upper levels it wasn't unusual for boys such as Alan to sometimes find themselves threatened by teachers with deportation to the nether regions if they didn't improve their behavior in class.)

There was something about the way most teachers carried themselves before these groups of adolescents that gave away their deepest views of education: stiff, unyielding, undialectic, undemocratic, the facts facts facts school of learning, which meant to boys such as Alan and his crowd—Joe, Ron, a few others—that things went, in Tillie's often-used phrase, "in one ear and out the other." Just about anything that any of the boys said to one another about the most trivial subjects seemed more important at the time of its saying than even the most obviously important statements—dates of examinations, the nature of written assignments—made by the teacher in the front of the room.

The boys sometimes quietly played the "mother" game: "Your mother and my father had a party under the boardwalk and nine months later out came you." "Yeah, well *your* mother and *my* father . . ." It went on and on, until one of the boys broke into laughter too obvious and loud and everything came down on their heads. Or they passed notes: "What's black and blue and red all over?" "I don't know." Answer: "Your mother." "Chuck you, Farley and your whole fam damily." "Eat shit, white boy." "Fuck you, Charley." "White you, Jew boy." On and on and on and on. Or they would find certain of their female counterparts at work on such matters as filing their nails surreptitiously beneath their desk tops, or delicately poking at the pinching material of their (for most of the girls) newly acquired foundation garments: at the lower rims of cups that cramped their burgeoning new breasts, at waistlines where panty girdles dug into deepening folds of their flesh.

"Boys and girls! May I have your attention please!" And this witch in brown rapped on her desk top with a ruler.

"Boys and girls!"

Joe reached over and tugged at Alan's shirtsleeve.

"Which are you, jerk-off?"

"Shut up, already," Alan whispered, wondering about the teacher's apparent urgency. Maybe a boiler had blown in the basement—or the fuses for the other half of the school burst into flames. Both things had happened before, and either meant that they would be sent home early, the greatest and most sought-after event of all.

"Hey, stupid," said Mark Kaplowitz from his other side. "You want to hear what she says?" He was calling this to Joe across Alan's shoulders, a daring act since the teacher could see him clearly from where she stood.

"You're the one that's stupid, birdbrain," Joe called back to him.

"Oh, yeah?" said Mark.

"Yeah," said Joe.

"Children!" the teacher said again with a punctuating rap of her ruler.

"We ain't children," Joe said in a whisper. "We're . . ."

"Joseph, what did you say?" Finally she could not ignore his flagrant disobedience.

"I said we ain't . . ."

"Aren't."

"Aren't children. That's all I said, Mrs. . ."

"Very well." Now that she had everyone's attention she plunged on with her announcement. "We have just been notified of some important world news. Premier Joseph Stalin, the Russian dictator, has died." She cleared her throat, and before she could say anything further, a great cheer went up from the classroom.

At supper that night his father talked about the news.

"This will be a very good turn of events for the Russian people," he said, in an unusual burst of speech while the news still played on the radio.

"Shush, Phil," said Tillie, "don't you want to hear the rest?"

"No," he said, "I'm talking, Teel. Turn it down, won't you?"

"I'll do it," Alan said, leaping from his chair. "What, Dad?"

"It will be a very good thing. Stalin was a terrible man, for the Jews, for all Russians. There'll be rejoicing now that he's gone."

"Rejoicing?" Alan said.

"What's that?" asked his brother.

"Shut up," Alan said to his brother.

"Don't speak that way to him," Tillie said.

"Tillie, I'm talking," Phil said.

"What is it, Dad?" Alan asked, noticing a very strange look in his father's eye.

"Stalin's dead," he repeated. "I could . . ."

"What?"

"I could almost go back."

"Don't be ridiculous, Phil," Tillie said.

"Ridiculous? It wouldn't be ridiculous. I had to leave because of Stalin."

"Why, Dad?" Alan asked.

He looked at his older boy and something seemed to pass between them that Alan could hardly detect and certainly not explain.

"After supper I'll show you something," said Phil.

"Can I serve the rest of the meal now?" Tillie asked, poised at the side of the table, watching this odd and uncharacteristic exchange between father and son.

"If the Communists ever take over here, I'll be the first one they shoot," Phil said later in the living room.

Alan shrugged, not understanding much of anything of what his father was saying.

"Look at your hands, Oll-an."

The boy looked at his hands.

"No, no," said his father. "Turn them palms up. Do you have smooth palms?"

Alan nodded.

"Then, God forbid, they would shoot you for being bourgeois."

The boy was growing uncomfortable with this talk and looked around the room, wondering about what was going on at the "Y" that evening, wondering about which of his friends he should call first to make plans.

"What's that?" he said.

"Bourgeois? For not being a vorker. If you are a vorker, then you have callused hands. During the Russian Revolution, only those who had callused hands would live. I remember hiding in our house and listening to the bullets flying back and forth. Stut! Stut!"

Alan shifted from one foot to the other, embarrassed now at the enthusiasm with which his father was telling this anecdote, something he recalled hearing a number of times before when company came to the house.

"Stut! Stut! Stut! There was shooting in the street and my mother put up pillows in the windows to stop the bullets and she made us lie on the floor under the table to keep from getting hit. We lay there for days."

"What's that got to do with your hands?" Alan asked in a slightly hostile voice.

"Hands? Oh, because the people they were shooting, the bourgeois from the town, they showed their hands and when the Bolsheviks saw that their palms were smooth they took them out to the edge of town and shot them."

"That sounds pretty stupid," Alan said.

"It was more than stupid," Phil said. "It was awful."

Alan shrugged, tapping his fingers against his palms, noticing his palms' smoothness.

"Is that why you're always writing about it?" he asked.

Phil shook his head.

"I'm writing stories in the style of Ilf and Petrof, two Russian writers whose work I always loved. You should read them. But first . . ." and here he reached up onto a shelf and pulled down a book that his son had never seen before, the title of which was *Ten Days That Shook the World.* "First I want you to read this sometime. It will tell you a lot about where I came from."

But Alan put the book aside. He didn't want to know where his father had come from. He had enough trouble figuring out what he himself was doing here, in Perth Amboy, in New Jersey, on this continent, on the planet, in the solar system. Despite all the affection his mother gave him he still felt lonely a lot of the time, and there were long hours when it seemed his heart would swell up like a sack of ice and freeze him from knees to throat, particularly when he listened to certain kinds of popular music.

He often fled the house when he felt a spell of that odd, cold pain of loneliness coming on, and by his sophomore year in high school he fled most often to the house of Lynn and Lloyd Winick. Lynn was a former professional actress who, with her husband, a local businessman, had founded an amateur theater company that the boy was welcome to join. In fact, because of all those afternoons and evenings he had spent at the Winicks' house and at the theater, Tillie had made her famous comment that he had left home at the age of fourteen and never came back. But why should he have stayed at home when all he could do there was hole up in his room and read science fiction magazines and novels and listen to music—or quarrel with his father?

"Come down and listen to music," Phil said to him one Sunday afternoon from the doorway of the upstairs room.

Alan looked up from his book with a certain amount of scorn.

"I'm reading, Dad."

"No, come down. I want you to listen. It's Rimsky-Korsakov. You have to listen to the native melodies in his music, because they come from Russian Asia where I once lived."

"You and your Glinka," Alan said. "That's all you talk about. Him and Rimsky Whore-sakov. I like Eddie Fisher and Dave Brubeck, Dad. Why don't you listen to some American music?"

"Because it stinks, that's why. Your music stinks. Now do you want to come down and listen?"

Alan shook his head. "Do you want to go to the next Yankee game with me?"

"You know I hate baseball, son. It's . . ."

". . . not as exciting as Russian soccer, I know. Well, fuck you."

"What did you say?"

"You heard me."

"You said such a thing to your own father? How dare you speak to me like that?"

The angry Phil charged up to his son, his eyes flaring with rage, and with a wild rearing back of his hand, hit the boy on the side of the head. Alan spun around, stung with pain, and rocked back and forth in convulsive sobs.

"I'm s-sorry," Phil said to his son's trembling back.

"Get out!" Alan screamed, flinging his book across the room with such force that when it hit the far wall it broke open at the spine, showering the floor with its pages.

"You shouldn't curse at your own father," Phil said.

"Fuck you," Alan said under his breath, and shut his eyes against the light. He reached up blindly toward the bookcase alongside the bed and found the dials of his radio and turned it on and allowed the voice of Eddie Fisher to drown out his father's apologies.

With these hands
I will cling to you . . .

"Ahhhh, damn it!" he heard his father's voice over the noise of the singing. Alan lay there a while, and when he sneaked a look his father had gone.

"Alan?"

He turned again at the sound of his mother's voice.

"What, Ma?"

"Alan, you shouldn't fight with your father. You've made him very upset."

"He shouldn't have hit me, Ma."

"He didn't hit you. He never hit you."

Alan's head still ached a little from the blow, so he knew differently.

"He lied to you, Ma."

"He doesn't lie to me, either, and I think that you owe him an apology. He loves you very much and he only wanted you to come downstairs to listen . . ."

"To Rimsky-Whoresakov, I know."

"Please," his mother said.

"Please what?"

"Please go easy on him. He's had a hard life."

"Well, he's a liar. A liar flier. Maybe he lies about all of it. Maybe he's . . ."

"You stop this," Tillie said. "It's not right. So you just stop."

"I'll stop," Alan said, and turned up the music.

"Please," she said.

He turned it down a notch, and he turned to her again, and he could not help but smile a little, and that made him nearly sick.

> *First the tide*
> *Rushes in . . .*

The music went on through the afternoon and evening and night.

On the eve of his fourteenth birthday Alan joined the youth group at the temple and was immediately conscripted, voice unheard, to sing in the Friday evening musicale. Its director was Cantor Gershon Ephros, a sour-faced, hunch-shouldered man in a dark suit who always wore a slight stubble of greying beard on his narrow cheeks. Ephros, or so he himself informed the group, was known in modern music circles as a composer of Sabbath music that had won secular acclaim.

His songs made Alan's skin crawl. He was an admirer of Eddie Fisher and daring smut like "Roll Me Over in the Clover" (which a few of the boys had picked up from a selective reading of *The Naked and the Dead* that Joe kept hidden behind his comic book collection in his room). The dissident hymns that the cantor wrote for them chilled Alan's chest and made his teeth chatter.

It was love that kept Alan in the choir, but not love of music. He wanted to stand in the immediate presence on Friday nights and the minimum of one rehearsal a week of Ruthie Eisemann, red-cheeked, long-limbed Ruthie, who wore plaid jumpers over plain white blouses and a single, dark blonde braid that burst from the back of her head like a unicorn's antler in reverse. Ruthie and Alan had played together as children, scrambling around with a bunch of other kids in the loft of her family's garage at birthday parties. They had attended the same schools until sixth grade, when her parents put her into a preparatory school in New Brunswick; until Alan joined the temple youth group he hadn't seen her for several years, and now he couldn't see enough of her.

It was for her that he mooned hours away listening to "With These Hands." It was for her that he suffered the teeth-gnashing hymns of Cantor Ephros. It was for her that he endured blurred hours of school and unbearable nights at home. He lived for choir practice and for the Friday evening service when they performed.

The Sabbath Bride
Beckons
Our hearts take on life

They were singing Ephros's newest composition, a simple poem that he had turned into a living outrage of sounds the likes of which Alan had heard before only when alley cats humped outside his bedroom window.

At sundown
The World
Glows with
A joy

The boy couldn't imagine how the congregation of shop-keepers and professional people was going to sit through this one, but he bore down and sang out each note as though he were spitting up during a visit to the dentist.

Bride of
Sabbath
Lovely bride
Bride glowing
With
Beckoning Joy

Out of the corner of his eye he watched the sopranos open wide their mouths like hungry baby birds. When skinny Donna moved between him and Ruthie, he edged out of his seat, pretending to glance down at the dark open space of the auditorium below their perch in the choir loft, and then up and over at Ruthie.

"Con-cen-trate!" shouted Cantor Ephros over the roar of the organ and the shrill cascade of their voices.

Bride lovely
Bride peaceful
Peace peace
Peace peace
Peace

"Piece? Piece?" Alan knew exactly what Joe was chirping about, at least he knew what he wanted to be saying. A well-scrubbed boy whose mother always dressed him in new bow ties and clean white shirts, he was the first in their gang to say words like *quif* and *quim* and *balls* and *boobs.* And the enlisted men's chorus from the Mailer novel he had secreted from his parents' room became the boys' national anthem.

Half past one
The fun had just begun

Even as they lifted their chins toward the ceiling in anticipation of the conclusion of the cantor's new tune, which if done properly might not have reached heaven but surely would have shattered glass, Joe leaned toward Alan and sang the vulgar soldiers' prayer in his ear.

"Joseph!"

How Ephros heard or saw Joe when his back was turned and their voices were screaming music he didn't know.

"Not me!" Joe yelled.

The cantor waggled a finger at him and then attacked the organ for the conclusion of the piece.

Lay me down
Roll me over

Joe spurted out another bit of song in Alan's ear, and they giggled along with Berenice one row over. But Ruthie, lovely Ruthie appeared to be carved from marble—not a quiver crossed her face or mouth, half open as she sang so that Alan could see the slick wetness of the netherside of her underlip, and the furtive, fleet action of the tongue.

Peace
Peace
Peace

Alan snorted like a horse. The cantor led them through the last few bars of the song, then stood at the organ, turned to point a finger, and silently ordered the boy from the loft.

"Me?" Alan whined. "I didn't do anything."

But Ephros kept his finger in the air until the boy slid out of the row and sauntered from the choir loft. He glanced back at Ruthie before he shut the door, but she appeared not to notice.

It was winter outside; he was dressed in trousers that rasped like steel wool across his thighs. His eyes stung. He felt humiliated, but also singled out for his love. He could think of nothing but wandering the two blocks southward toward her house, where he meandered in the dark up her driveway and, like a sleepwalker in comic strips he read each Sunday, entered the garage and climbed the stairs to the loft.

A single lamp had been glowing downstairs in the Eisemann house as he passed it. Through the small, triangular window at the head of the loft, he could see the driveway and a corner of the house. When a new light flicked on—in the upper room on the driveway side—he knew that Ruthie had returned home.

By kneeling and cramming his face into the left-hand corner of the window he could catch a glimpse now and then of her pale figure—the white of her blouse, the gold of her hair passing back and forth before her mirror. His posture required of him more concentration, mental and physical, than life had ever called on him to produce. His knees ached, his eyes twitched. Something scraped across the attic floor and he started, bumping his head against the window frame. A small black cat sidled up to him and meowed. He grabbed it by the neck and hurled the howling thing sideways into the dark.

Ruthie's light winked out. He descended the stairs to the garage floor, head aching, knees weak. His skull pressed against the hard, wood frame, his nose stuffed with odors of damp, cold wood and the ancient fumes of automobile oil and old rubber tires, he had squinted in the dark lost as though dreaming. He didn't remember the long way home.

"Look at you!" Tillie started out of sleep from her berth on the living room couch.

In the light of the living room Alan noticed that sawdust and glistening strips of deep, dark grease had accreted to his knees and cuffs.

"I fell."

Her expression changed as quickly as a river churned by a fierce, sudden wind.

"You hurt yourself?"

And then her face softened into a yawn.

"Who was with you?"

"Joe."

"So we'll get your pants cleaned. No more trouble. Go to bed."

He didn't sleep for what seemed a long while, falling rather into a restless reverie in which he stood his watch again at Ruthie's bedroom window and undressed her over and over again. He remembered hearing his father's bedside alarm ring loud and clear, and the next thing he recalled he was being awakened by the ringing of the telephone.

"Feel all right? You felt like you were on fire. I let you sleep." His mother sounded further away than the office downtown.

"Yes, Ma," he replied. And then he raced to the bathroom to throw up.

A week passed before he returned either to school or choir practice. When he came back there was something new in the air. The first thing that happened was that Ruthie slid down a row in the middle of a rehearsal, leaned forward, and whispered, "Which do you want to see?"

He looked around for Berenice, or one of the other girls. He couldn't imagine that Ruthie was talking to him.

"Which?" she said, showing some annoyance.

"Which what?" he said finally. By that time the cantor had turned from the keyboard, daring him to say another word.

"The show, silly," she said. "We're going to vote pretty soon."

"What show?" he asked, staring at the flat of her braid, which lay like a golden rope across her left shoulder.

"Walk me home and I'll tell you."

The season must have changed—or his fever returned—he felt so warm as they left the building. She asked him how he was feeling and he thought for a moment that she had read his mind (and he was still sure that she had somehow seen him up behind the window in the garage). Finally he decided that she had registered his absence the week before and was merely being polite.

"Fine," he lied. His head stung from the burning within, and his chest shivered against his breastbone as though he were facing a cold arctic wind. Perhaps this was the way the cantor's music was supposed to make a person feel—cold and lonely and confused, the modern secular way, so that you'd run home to Temple or to Mama and ask to be taken in. He felt frightened without really knowing why, as though he were treading the familiar path toward Ruthie's house while blindfolded, afraid that he would trip at each step.

"We get to see a show every spring," she was saying. "Didn't you know that? We get to vote and the Temple buys us the tickets. The one I want to see is *Kismet*. It's from music by the Russian composer Borodin."

"I've never been to a show," Alan said, "Except for Radio City with my parents." He didn't know why he kept on talking—he never liked to talk with his friends; joke, sing, shout, maybe, yes, but not talk. But in the short time that it took to walk the distance from the temple to her block, he had told her about a number of things he never could have imagined saying to anyone. The only thing he didn't mention was the night spent in her garage. She must have known something about how he felt since they hadn't gotten more than a few steps beyond the curb of her corner when she stopped, turned to him, and right there in the frosty air under the street lamp asked him if he wanted to kiss her.

Alan stepped back and looked around. The only presence besides themselves was a low, black Chevy parked with the motor running just beyond the driveway near the front of her house. The same way he learned the past summer to step into a ball and hit a single, he stepped up to her and swung his lips to her mouth.

A week went by in which he felt as dizzy and otherworldly as he had during his feverish illness. The streets echoed with his off-key renditions of popular love songs.

With these hands
I will cling to you
Forever and a day . . .

And like a gooney bird just before flight he raced along the beach that bordered their town on the south where the river entered the bay.

First the tide
Rushes in . . .

He sang into the wind. The memory of her tongue lingered in his mouth like words he sometimes thought but never said. He lived for Fridays, but when Ruthie missed a practice he worried about her absence through the weekend. By the next practice, he could scarcely see straight. In school he spent most of his time imagining her padding down the halls in all her antelope grace, or flitting back and forth before her bedroom mirror, shedding clothes the way a butterfly sheds its winter wrapping. He arrived early in the loft the next Wednesday, having brought with him as an excuse Joe's copy of the Mailer which Joe made him swear on pain of eternal humiliation that he would return within a week. The loft was brightly lighted, but the auditorium below lay deep in shadow. He thought that he heard voices down there in the pool of dark but then decided that he was mistaken. He opened the book and attempted to read something other than the pages the boys had already aged with their probing fingers.

The door to the loft opened, and Alan jumped in his seat. Donna Cohen smiled in the darkened doorway.

"Oh, you're early, too!" Her squeaky voice and forced smile made him uncomfortable.

"I'm reading," he said, his own voice sounding to him unnatural and strained.

"What are you reading?" she asked as she settled onto a bench.

"Nothing you'd like." He held up the cover.

"Oh, *Naked!*" Her squeal turned his stomach.

"No, *dead!*" he said, fiercely cruel with this girl whose chest was as flat as his own.

She fluttered her eyelashes, and he didn't know whether she was going to laugh or scowl or cry, but then the door opened again, a few more kids entered the loft, distracting both of them from their little encounter. He looked for Joe, but he wasn't there. Neither was Ruthie. Stepping past the new arrivals he went to the door and looked down the winding staircase to the auditorium. Behind him the other kids chattered about the annual trip. Several of the girls were talking about a show.

"Danny's seen it and he thinks it's wonderful," he heard Ruthie's voice drift up the spiral stairwell.

A deep male voice grunted assent. A few girls giggled loud enough to make heads turn in the loft. Ruthie appeared in the doorway, towing by the hand a tall, dark, curly-haired boy about twice Alan's height.

"Hi, everybody," she said, her eyes skipping past Alan like a swift stone across the surface of a pond.

"What's going *on* here?"

Cantor Ephros was trying to step past them through the door.

"Cantor, this is my friend Danny, he's studying history at Rutgers. Do you mind if he visits tonight?"

The cantor for the first time in a long winter smiled as he came into the loft.

"He's got a voice?"

Alan heard Donna whisper to someone behind him. "He's got a Chevy."

TWENTY-FOUR

THE TROUBLE WHICH HAD FOUND ME IN Saratov followed me to Zlatoust. Without identification papers and a passport I was forced to show people the spravka, and it was the content of the spravka that caused problems. As if my appearance were not enough to repel people, those who read the spravka thought there was something wrong with my head. As I looked for jobs that first day, people no sooner read it than they began to politely but firmly ease me out of the office without so much as an interview.

After spending a day of futilely seeking employment and encountering the same treatment in the personnel offices of all the plants I had called on tirelessly, I finally gave up. I was again tired, weak from hunger, disgusted at the callousness of the people I had seen that day, and I had no money left at all.

I decided to return to the Zlatoust railway station, if only because I knew that the waiting room would be warm. The hike from Zlatoust proper to the railway station was about three kilometers, and uphill all the way. It had been a relatively warm and sunny day but now it was cold again, and as I walked I couldn't help but wonder what would become of me. Then, in the twilight of evening, I saw a building—not the train station, but a taller building—which with its several twinkling lights seemed for some reason to smile upon me. I stopped to look at it, and then I saw—from the sign over its door—that it was a public clubhouse. And if it was public, could I not at least rest myself there?

The front hall of the clubhouse was lined with benches and smelled of new white pine, stale tobacco, and the tantalizing aroma of pork simmering in sour cabbage. The smell of the food drove me half out of my mind, and I held onto the benches as I made my way toward the source of the smell. I found a door which was ajar that led into an apartment with a spacious kitchen. There were two beds beyond a partially opened curtain, a commode and a potted palm, while the rest of the room contained a heating stove and a cooking stove, a pantry, and a large dining table with two benches.

A handsome woman in her early thirties was tending one of the stoves. A child of three and another boy about four played on the floor. When the children and their mother looked in my direction it was without surprise—apparently they were used to people popping in unannounced.

"Aren't you a little early?" the woman said. "The club is closed until seven-thirty, comrade!"

"Please forgive me," I pleaded. "I've just come in from the cold. That is, I was attracted by your warmth here. I am homeless, you see."

"Are you ill?" She sounded genuinely concerned.

"I don't know. I am too hungry to tell."

"Let me fetch you a glass of milk." The woman went to the pantry for a jug of milk, some of which she poured into a pan and placed on the stove.

"I have some candy for your children," I said meekly.

"No candy just yet for them, thank you. Not before they have their supper."

"Mama, Mama, is he our uncle Miron?" the elder child asked. "Uncle Miron always brought us candy."

"Miron is my brother. He lives in Simbirsk," the woman explained. She poured the hot milk into a glass and brought it over to me.

"Drink it slowly. Sip it," she said and went off to bring me a chair. "Sit here and rest a while and tell me how a young man of quality and good looks has allowed himself to sink into your sorry condition. You speak well; you must be well-educated."

For a moment I could not speak. The woman could not have been older than me by more than ten years, yet for the first time since I had discovered manhood I found myself attracted to an older woman.

"My name is Maria Ivanovna Kusatina," she said, making me feel at ease. "What's yours?"

"Fishel Isaakovich Kaplan," I told her, seating myself.

Her voice sounded musical to me. And as I watched her moving at the stove, preparing supper, I realized that I had fallen instantly in love with her.

"Are you harboring some kind of a secret, Fishel Isaakovich?" Maria Ivanovna smiled when she came over to take the empty glass. Unhesitantly I took out my spravka and handed it to her.

"So, you're a hero, Captain," she said. "You should have no trouble establishing yourself."

"You're the first person to comment so kindly," I said. "This is the only document I have, and without other documents it seems I cannot get a job."

"Well, at the very least, Captain Kaplan, I would think that with your education you should have little trouble obtaining a position on the railroad. I should know this. Before I was married I was a secretary to the depot manager. What sort of a job on the railway do you think you could do?"

"Engineering draftsman," I said.

"My husband was an engineer," Maria Ivanovna said, her voice becoming low, changing to almost a whisper.

"Is he away?" I inquired.

"My Shura is no longer among the living. He was an engineer on a locomotive. A pipe on an incoming freight was sticking out and struck and killed him instantly. I took this job as janitress and cook here at the club to keep my family going. It pays well. My Shura was about your height and size, Captain Kaplan. I still have his things. I could sell the clothing I saved to you."

"I have no money to pay you, Maria Ivanovna."

"I will trust you to pay me when you begin collecting your pay."

"I don't have a job, Maria Ivanovna."

"Nor will you get work dressed the way you are! In the trunk under the far bed there is a lambskin jacket, boots, a Sunday suit Shura wore only once, and shirts and underwear and things. Go right now, Captain, draw the curtain and change. Put the things you have on outside the curtain and I will take the bundle and put it in the trash. After supper I'll write a note to old Prokopich, the attendant at the bathhouse. He will put you up for the night. He will let you stay at the bathhouse until you find work and a family with whom you can board."

Everything, even the boots, fit me perfectly.

Old Prokopich, the bathhouse attendant, received me graciously and set me up with a cot in his room next to his own bed. And in the morning I bathed for the first time in what seemed like a year, and even shaved with Prokopich's razor, and then the two of us shared a breakfast of tea and bread.

"If it's a job you're seeking, son," the old man said to me, "go directly to Leonid Mikhaylovich. Be it technical or clerical or who knows what, see Leonid Mikhaylovich! He'll hire you on the spot."

It wasn't long before I was being interviewed by this Mikhaylovich in his office. He was a man in his late fifties, clean shaven, with greying temples and meager hair on a shining bald head. He had blue eyes, a severe mouth, and tight, thin lips. As I watched Leonid Mikhaylovich relax in his swivel chair I sensed that at another time, during the days of the Czar, before the Revolution, he had held a position of power far greater than that of a manager of railroad employment. "Yes, we can use you as a draftsman," Leonid Mikhaylovich said curtly to me after glancing at my application. "When can you start working if I hire you? And where is your passport young man?"

Before handing Leonid Mikhaylovich my spravka I thought it best to explain how I came to possess it in the first place. "This is the only official document I can give you for the time being. Copies of my credentials should arrive here as soon as I forward my address here to the headquarters of the Red Army Air Force in Moscow."

Leonid Mikhaylovich pursed his thin lips, leaned back in his chair, and screwed up his face into a grimace as he read.

"It says in this spravka that Zlatoust is your home, whereas a while ago you said you came here because you heard that there are jobs available. If such is the case, young man, let me advise you that there are far better jobs to be had at our depots further east. We could put you on the Moscow-Vladivostok express, to ride free, of course."

"No thank you, sir." I said. "I cannot go, if only because I must pay for these clothes I have on."

"You do not sound as if you have a brain injury to me. I'm just a little bit surprised you're willing to work on the railroad."

"But I am. I'm quite willing."

"Well then, we should get on with it."

I was put to work making tracings of pattern details for machinists and carpenters who were making railway freight cars, but it did not last long. To my dismay I discovered that my left hand failed to fully coordinate with minute movements of my right. In fact, it was worse than that, one hand seemed to interfere with the other now and then, and sometime it seemed as if one hand did not know what the other was doing, or was going to do.

So all too soon, after serving less than a week as a draftsman, I was back before Leonid Mikhaylovich asking for another job. Mikhaylovich did not seem surprised that things had not worked out for me. Worse, there were no other jobs that I was suited for, he told me, except as an ash cleaner. Frankly, it was work no one wanted, he said.

"It's a dirty and dangerous job, and it's the lowest on the pay scale of the railroad. One has to slide into the ash pit under the wheels of a locomotive and scoop hot ashes and pieces of burning coal out of the grating under the locomotives with a scooper. And you'll have to work nights, straight through, year round—and wear a mask to protect your lungs from the ash dust."

"Could I obtain a free railroad ticket after I work for you three months?" I asked. "I might at that time like to go to Vladivostok."

Leonid Mikhaylovich's face lit up. "Of course, young man! You will be entitled to a free pass to anywhere you like, even if you quit. Ah, yes! Vladivostok! Our back door into the world. If I were only young again, that is where I would go! Vladivostok! Good idea. Just think of it!"

Along with my badge number I was issued special work clothes, mask, and boots that I was to use on the job. With this bundle under an arm I watched a woman ash cleaner working under a locomotive. It was not the kind of a job one had to learn.

My shift was hours away. In the meantime I wanted to find a new place to stay before I reported to work. I did not relish the idea of continuing to live in the bathhouse. Old man Prokopich was kind but he did nothing but talk, talk, talk, endlessly telling and retelling the story of his life. If I were working nights it would be even worse. So I went to the clubhouse to ask for the advice of Maria Ivanovna.

"But a bathhouse is just the place for one working with ashes," she said as she served me lunch. "It will take plenty of hot water and soap to clean your neck and ears."

"Yes, I suppose so," I said, somehow disappointed. "I will report back to Prokopich after work, at two in the morning."

"Then again," said Maria Ivanovna, almost in a whisper and without looking up, "why not stay here with us? At two in the morning you can wash up in the pantry. I'll have hot water ready for you on the stove."

"Hot water? That would be nice, but . . ." I became flustered.

"Hot water and a towel–it will be ready and waiting."

"But where would I sleep?" Now I felt guilty for having hoped of something like this.

"She looked up and smiled at me. "I will unfold a cot for you to sleep on–in the library. If you are neat about it."

"Neatness is one of the habits inculcated into every soldier. A cot in the library . . . would be wonderful," I mumbled, suddenly full of longing for this warm and beautiful person, and my mind racing with expectation of what she might have in her mind.

She could apparently see what I was thinking.

"You are a good and decent man, Fishel Isaakovich, and I know you will not take improper advantage of such an arrangement. So, it is settled."

She got up from the chair and sprinted across the kitchen, lithe and lively like an adolescent, to one of the beds in her apartment.

"Listen," she said, summoning me with a smile, "you can lie down on my bed here and rest until it's time for you to go to work."

"What about the children?" I wondered. "Won't they disturb my sleep?"

"Unless it is snowing the children always play outside until sundown," Maria Ivanovna assured me. "However," she stretched and added with a yawn and a smile, "to play it safe, you had better draw the curtain."

Next to the ash pit was a hut with a potbellied stove where the ash cleaner spent his or her time while waiting for the locomotives. Some nights there were as few as two or three locomotives that came to have their gratings cleaned, and sometime there were as many as ten. The men on the crews were kind to me, the lowly ash cleaner. It must have been the dirtiest and most undesirable job on the Trans-Siberian line, at least I saw none worse, and the men on the crews of the locomotives took care that I should not be hurt. They would not allow me to slide under the tender until the engineer had secured the brakes, and whenever a locomotive converged on me while I was still in the pit they made certain there was no steam being discharged where I lay.

I liked the solitude around the ash pit during the nights when the locomotives did not choose to come. They would maneuver in the yards, they would come in for repairs or to be turned around in the roundhouse, but for some reason there were some nights when not a single locomotive rolled to the ash pit. It was quiet then, though one could hear the clank and hissing of steam in the distance.

The sky over the ash pit was not limited by the tall firs of the taiga which began just beyond the embankment of the railroad. Most nights the constellations stood out in brilliant clarity, and with the aid of a borrowed astronomical map I rememorized most of the stars. And on other nights when there was little work for me to do, I read books borrowed from the library by lantern light in my hut.

Out here alone on these winter evenings under the brilliant sky, I recovered some of the inner calmness I had known prior to the plane crash, and gradually I felt that more and more of my old self was being reborn. But with my mother dead, my father long gone to America, and separated from my brothers and sisters, I decided that I had to push myself forward to the borders in the east instead of going back to Moscow and the old ways. My life as a flier had taught me that—to surge ahead, to push on. But to where? I had only the faintest idea.

In December I had written the Red Army Air Force about my disposition and when I might again take examinations, both physical and mental, for my reinstatement to active service. In February of the new year, 1930, I received the following disheartening reply, along with a package.

"Comrade Reserve Captain Kaplan: Pursuant to the present policy of the Politbureau of the U.S.S.R., the Red Army Air Force is in the process of demobilizing into inactive reserve a maximum number of its officers in order that their services may be utilized by our expanding industrial effort which presently lacks the required numbers of engineers and technicians. In view of this policy, you are ineligible to return to active service unless a recall is initiated by an office of the Red Army Air Force Command.

"However, we are taking this opportunity to inform you that the documents pertaining to your honorable discharge from the Red Army Air Force, as well as the Order of the Red Banner, along with items of uniform including a flight coat, tunic, and so forth, which had been taken from your person in Samara, were recovered by the G.P.U. in Poltava and forwarded to this office. The items recovered did not include any money. The documents and items listed are being forwarded along with this missive.

"We are glad that you have at last communicated with this office. We trust that you will distinguish yourself in civilian life as you have in service.

(Signed) Adjutant General Red Army, Department of the Air Force, D. S. Gavrilenko."

The items in the weighty package could not balance out the heaviness in my heart.

In March the Siberian snow still creaked underfoot at night, and if one inhaled the bitter, icy air too quickly it stabbed one's lungs like a spear. But in the morning the sun would rise over the mountains and the snow would shine and glisten and the air would fill with warmth. The days were still short because the sun also set early over other peaks to the west, again plunging us into a valley of ice and dark shadows.

In the evening of just such a day, when I was not working, Maria Ivanovna came home and told me in confidence that she had seen a decree from Moscow and that soon it would be announced that all jobs in the Soviet Union would be frozen.

"Do you mean I won't be allowed to quit my job here and go to Vladivostok to find myself a better job?" I asked her.

"Not to Vladivostok or any other city. You may be stuck here for the rest of your days, for all I know. In important matters such as this the local Communist party secretary is tipped off in advance so he will not be caught with his pants down, and that's who told me. He was a close friend of my husband's, and now he pursues me by keeping me in his confidence. Of course he said I should not tell you. So we must be careful. But if you're going to go, you'd best go now."

I thanked Maria for the information and felt still more weight on my heart. I felt sorrow for her, that I had to leave. And for myself, I was sad, too, that I had to move on yet again. But move I had to. Zlatoust was no place to spend the rest of my days. I remembered that odd dream, too. And I thought, fleetingly, of my father, and my brother, Josiah. Would I ever see them again?

A week later, as long as I dared wait, I gave Leonid Mikhaylovich notice that I was quitting my job. In turn he told me that government regulations had recently changed and he would not be able to give me the free railroad pass that he had promised me when I started. Somehow I was not surprised, and to the man's credit he seemed sincerely sorry that he could not do this one small thing for me.

"You've been a good worker after all, Fishka. I wish you luck. Will it still be Vladivostok?"

"Yes," I said, "if I can make it that far on the few kopeks I've saved."

Picture the scene at the station on the day of my departure: tears glistened in Maria Ivanovna's eyes as she held the hands of her children. I would miss them almost as much as I would her. But since we had never allowed our affair to be in any way public we did not even kiss, though I waved and waved and waved, like a schoolboy, as the train pulled out of the station. At that moment I was certain that I wanted a family of my own, but I feared that I could never settle down to make one.

Of my long ride east on the Trans-Siberian there was nothing but boredom and snow, white, always white, as I looked out the window at the endless landscape, mountains and forests, covered with snow, but even after nearly a week I did not make it all the way to Vladivostok. After days and days of that blurring whiteness, against which I played out my regrets about leaving, and after nights of yearning desperately after Maria Ivanovna—and after countless stops at meaningless stations where babushkas sold the same hot potatoes and meatless soup—we finally put the taiga behind us and reached the far eastern capital of Khabarovsk where, purely for the exercise, I got off the train and paced the platform in the warm sun. It was there I heard someone call out my nickname.

"Hey, Fishka!" Out of the corner of my eye I saw someone rushing after me. "Over here, Fishka!" I turned and saw an air force officer waving his hand at me. His face was familiar, but it took me a moment to remember him as a former classmate way back at the Leningrad Military Academy.

"Hey, Kaplanchik," he yelled as he lunged at me and gave me an affectionate bear hug.

"Seriozha Pivovarov," I was finally able to say after catching my breath.

"One and the same, Fishka! I'm stationed here at the Khabarovsk Air Base. But let me look at you, droog! You do seem a little older, . . . and why in the world did you remove the insignia from your uniform?"

"I see you are a captain?" I mumbled. "So am I. Only I piled up a plane and they put me into the reserves."

"Well I'm glad to run into you, Fishka! Are you on the Moscow-Vladivostok express? I just put my wife and two little girls on it."

I nodded.

"Well, you're going to have to get off and finish the journey tomorrow, Fishka, because you're going to stay with me for a visit tonight. Just get your things. I won't take no for an answer."

I was so happy seeing my old friend I didn't care if I had to purchase another train ticket to complete my journey, even if it took every last kopek I had. I stepped back up on the train just long enough to gather my duffel bag.

"At your service, Captain Pivovarov," I said back on the platform, effecting a salute.

We walked through a cobblestone square beyond the station where Sergei pointed to a Fiat convertible. "I borrowed this from the motor pool. Unlike our runway, the road to the field is not paved. I drive with my old goggles so as to avoid getting dirt in the eyes. The plane I fly is an Illyushin bomber, no need for my goggles there." He threw an arm around me and looked me deeply in the eyes. "You graduated first on the list and they sent you to Orenburg for further training as a fighter pilot. So what happened?"

"A lot, droog. I graduated and Sasha Kadikoff and I were sent to Tashkent, and from there to Khiva, . . ." I hesitated for a moment before going on, aware that I was about to risk my tongue but—now that I was hopelessly out of the service—also savoring the very danger of it, "where the Turkomen tribesmen were in rebellion. They shot down Sasha Kadikoff and I landed and picked him up on my wing and flew him out before the Basmachi arrived to cut both our heads off." I didn't mention the Order of the Red Banner.

Pivovarov whistled low. "So where is Sasha now?"

"The last time I heard he was still stationed in Khiva. I hope they're finished up with the Turkomen by now."

Pivovarov was quiet for a long moment, then pointed out in the direction of the embankment along which we were driving. "That's the Amur," he said. "Great salmon, delicious caviar. Good sailing, too."

I stared out at the broad, shimmering river, remembering other waters, other days. "There was a river in Uzbekistan," I said, "over which we flew from Chardzhou to Khiva. It was called the Amu-Darya. Funny, you could take a glass of water from that stream and there was murky, desert dust of some kind suspended in it. No matter how long the water stood it never cleared. But we drank it. We were thirsty. We had to drink."

"So how did it happen that you piled up the plane, Fishka?" my old comrade asked, breaking into my sudden reflective mood.

"Some son of a whore neglected to add oil to the engine of a Grig D-11 when he damned well knew it was leaking oil and due for an overhaul!"

"Why were you put in the reserves?"

"Because the medics thought I needed more mending even after I spent an entire summer in a Saratov hospital."

"Isn't the Grig D-11 one of those pudgy Tupolev types?"

"Pudgy, yes, but pudgy like a mean bulldog."

"We have one of those on the base," Pivovarov said. "It's an experimental job flown only by our test pilot. In fact, our General Delenko was making inquiries for a qualified unmarried fighter pilot to fly this bird. Apparently the first test pilot just got married."

Oh, I thought, feeling a great surge in my heart, how willing I would be to take his place! "So, you've seen action here on the Manchurian border?"

"Very little. Except for the occasional incursion over the line, things are pretty quiet out here. But say, Fishka, I thought we cleaned out the Basmachi down in the resort in 1923 or '24?"

"They flared up again in 1927. It's a state secret—you're the only one I've told. There was one Djunaid Khan who led the uprising. Sasha and I were actually quartered in one of his captured palaces in Khiva. You should have seen the Persian rugs we had in our room!"

Pivovarov's apartment was in one of the officer's barracks in the civilian quarters of the base. It was past noon when we arrived there and Sergei left me to go to the mess hall to see if there might be some lunch left. When he returned, successful in his quest, we settled in and ate like men returning from a long flight. I felt quite at home with Pivovarov, comfortable in the way that only old comrades can be. After lunch Sergei said he had some things to attend to and invited me to have a nap while he was gone. But it was not long before I was awakened by a knock at the door.

It was a young soldier with a message. "Captain Pivovarov asked me to tell you that he is registering your presence on the base and intends to see General Dolenko to find out if it would be possible for you to return to active duty, tovarich Captain."

I smiled to myself, and fell back into dreamy sleep. Pivovarov himself came back I know not when. I found him standing over me and grinning when I opened my eyes. I could hear the familiar music of propellers in the distance. Formations of multi-motored planes were returning from their day's missions, coming in overhead for their touchdown on the field. I thought I could make out and segregate the sound of the Grig D-11's engine being revved.

"Well," Sergei Pivovarov said, "I just saw our General Dolenko, and tomorrow at six sharp he will meet you at hangar number seven. I have an idea what he has in mind. We have a little monoplane made in Italy with a very powerful motor—a Hispano Suiza, I believe. It's a sleek, fast little ship he uses to test pilots. Usually he takes you up and tells you to take over the controls. He allows you to do what you like and lets you land the ship wherever you like, within a reasonable time, of course."

Was I dreaming? It seemed quite impossible to me that anyone could be saying what I thought I was hearing. Nonetheless, I treated it like reality. "Sergei," I said, "I have not been up since my accident."

"To me, Fishka, you appear no different than when we were learning to fly at the academy that first year in Leningrad. The instructor kept telling us that you and Kadikoff were naturals and that both of you were born to fly. Remember what the major said about you two? Give Kadikoff and Kaplan a good strong wind and they could fly a wooden gate."

"I would not let you down, Sergei."

"The general said that you can undergo a medical right here on the base. But should he request your recommission it will have to go through the Air Force Command in Moscow, and that could take weeks if not months, so meanwhile you should continue your journey to Vladivostok, Fishka. After tomorrow, that is."

"Civilian life stinks, Sergei. I know I won't be happy again until I get back into the service."

"Well, Fishka, the way you give an account of yourself tomorrow may bring you back."

General Dolenko was a short man in his fifties. On his left sleeve he wore the crossed daggers of a fighter pilot, and on his tunic two Orders of the Red Banner! I saluted the general. He did not bother to return my salute, as he was busy pulling on his helmet and goggles.

A soldier handed me my own helmet and goggles and before I buttoned my leather coat I made sure the general noticed my decoration. Out of the hangar men rolled out a slick monoplane, a dual control job. The general squeezed himself into the forward cockpit, then motioned me to climb into the rear. While the engine was being warmed up I watched the gauges and imagined how the control stick of this plane would respond to the touch of my gloved fingers.

"Here we go, Captain." The engine awakened into a powerful roar as the general throttled us forward. We lifted into the air after a short run.

The altimeter soon registered one thousand meters and the order rung clear into my ears: "Take over, Captain!"

"Taking over, tovarich General!" With this I pushed the throttle of the engine forward on my own and pulled the nose up, putting the plane upside down in a half loop. Then I did a half wing-over and banked the plane into the opposite direction. When we were behind and above our take-off point I repeated the same maneuver and then dovetailed the plane into a slow and smooth approach to the air field.

"Sorry, General," I said into my microphone when I heard the man gasping for air.

"I must be getting old," he mumbled. "Head her back to the hangar, Captain!"

I took the machine in slowly and carefully, afraid that I had somehow lost the general's favor with my acrobatics.

"Did Captain Pivovarov tell you that we are working on improvements of the Grigorovich D-11 here at Khabarovsk?" the general said as we climbed out and turned the ship over to the ground crew.

"No, sir," I lied.

"I understand you have had at least some experience with that aircraft, Captain, and if all goes well with a medical, and providing Moscow can approve your recall to active duty, I think I could use you to fly ours."

"I would be delighted, tovarich General," I said. "I'm anxious to resume duty in the service of my country."

"And to Comrade Stalin?"

"And to Comrade Stalin, sir."

Pivovarov was taking me back to the Khabarovsk railroad station, driving with a devil-may-care bravado that sent the last remnants of melting snow flying against the fenders of the car. I had passed my physical with flying colors and it had been a wonderful three days on the base with Sergei.

"Remember how we used to march on the Nevsky Prospect in Leningrad during military parades, Fishka? Rifles on our shoulders, we performed as one in perfect formation? Can you remember the cadet song we sung in those days, Fishka? How did it go?"

At the top of our lungs Sergei and I sung:

Higher, and higher, and higher,
We skillfully fly our birds,
And in every propeller breathes
The peacefulness of our borders.
Our nerves are made of steel,
Our eyes pierce every atom,
And you can be sure that to every ultimatum
The Soviet Air Force will give its right reply!
Oh higher, and higher, and higher,
We skillfully fly our birds,
And in every propeller breathes,
The peacefulness of our borders . . .

TWENTY-FIVE

IT'S EARLY MORNING, AND WE HAVE TO CATCH our plane to Urgench. We ride back out to the airport through a light haze, though the desert heat hasn't yet risen. The streets are relatively empty, but clean, and there's not much traffic, no bustling, hustling streets. There is clearly a trade-off here, with health care and schools and crime-free living and no enormous extremes of poverty and wealth in exchange for the excitement that a city such as this, with its semitropical atmosphere could generate were it composed of very rich and very poor and a lot of entrepreneurs between. There is clearly a living Uzbeki culture lurking beneath the Russian here. In the lobby we saw women from desert towns in their flowery long skirts and turbans, and the driver has tuned in the radio to a whiney, sinuous eastern melodic sing-song of what must be the local music. This must be something like a Soviet Puerto Rico, with two cultures melding in odd ways, clashing in others. If there don't appear to be the visible problems our Puerto Rico has, there is a certain quietude, even dullness that seems to have come with the triumph of the Soviets over unruly local customs and chaotic social practices.

My father helped shoot Russia's way into this place, though his last fifteen years or so—his benign decades—he wouldn't have thwacked more than a mosquito or a fly. Think of the last years of some old Roman soldier who in his twenties had marched for the empire in Spain and North Africa. Or an officer for the King of Spain on expedition to the Netherlands. A British sergeant in the American colonies, at Saratoga, say, with the shot whizzing about his ears and marking the trees like the beaks of a thousand native woodpeckers? Or that same sergeant, my father's mother's father's father's father, who took the wound in his leg and dropped out of the line of march on the retreat from Moscow?

This airport seems old enough so that it might be the same aerodrome that Phil flew into when he arrived in Tashkent, and I look at this sky of his as we take off, then down at the desert, the rising waves of heat now appearing like kite streamers emerging from the ground up.

Our forty-two seater, a two-engine Russian jet, goes into a turn and heads west. Most of the other passengers are Uzbeki women, in their flowered robes and turbans, most of them leaning forward, arms on the seat back ahead of them, their heads pressed against their arms.

It was easier for this plane to lift off the ground than for me to burst through this weight of heavy anticipation in my chest. I take deep breath after deep breath and glance over at Josh. He's got his Walkman on, I hear the faint chush, chush of drums from his headphones, and he's got his eyes closed.

What's he seeing behind his closed eyelids? He lives by an admirable rhythm, listening to his music, then opening his eyes on the world and taking his fine photographs. But what's he seeing now? Anything resembling my vision? As we fly across the desert, approaching the old battlegrounds where my father made his small war against the rebellious Uzbeks and Turkomen, I realize that this trip is both like coming to meet him again *and* coming to meet myself, the self I could not have admitted to before.

I look out the window and see high misty peaks rising out of the clouds to the south and southeast, the Afghanistan border, the mountains of the Hindu Kush!

"Josh?"

"What?" It's been a long trip. He's sick, tired, grouchy, but willing to listen, if only for a moment. With a quick movement he slips off his headphones and cocks an ear.

"The Hindu Kush!" I point out the window to his left. "Josh, do you realize we're flying just north of the Hindu Kush?"

And below us are the dunes of the Kyzyl Kum, stretching all the way to the low mountains on the nearer horizon—and at the height Phil must have had to fly over the sand, just imagine how the low peaks and the immense rising stature of the Hindu Kush must have appeared. With the hot desert wind in his face, and the roaring of the engine, flying those small biplanes must have been something like riding a large motorcycle with wings, racing through the constantly rushing waves of wind!

The oasis town of Tamdybulak appears below us, which puts us, according to the map, about half way to Urgench. A few roads spoke out from the green patch in the middle of the sand but are soon lost to sight among the dunes. Those mountains that stretch from the Afghan border west to Kashmir and east to China's westernmost province fade now into the mist behind us to the south. I focus my attention on what lies ahead. My heart is beating like the drums on Josh's Walkman. To come here, so far, all these years.

Thank you, Phil, I say to him in my mind.

It was nothing, he says.

How can you joke with me at a time like this?

Why not? You always complained that I never had much of a sense of humor. But let me tell you, son, if we didn't have a sense of humor it wouldn't have been so easy to get through some of the rough times. Ah, look, there's the river, the Amu-Darya!

I peer past Josh's shoulder out the window, and motion for him to look, too.

"The Amu-Darya River," I say. "In ancient times it was called the Oxus. When the khans ruled here, after Tamburlaine the Great, who came after Genghis Kahn . . ."

"Cut the history, it's too early in the morning."

"You ought to know these things so you can place what you're seeing in context."

"I'm placing, I'm placing, give me the book," and he snatches the guide book away from me and presses his face down against its pages.

Just like you.

Is that so?

You should have seen yourself sometimes, so quick to anger, you couldn't take any information from me about life, let alone advice. But you were a good boy, and never deliberately mean.

But sometimes I was mean in effect?

You hurt my feelings. But what did you know? I understand that I failed you sometimes, too. I didn't understand enough about how you needed an American life. I didn't encourage that, and you needed me to. I wish you and I had gone to some ball games together.

Oh, it's okay.

No, no, you're just saying that, Oll-an. I wish I had done more. But I was lost in my funk about leaving my country, and lost in my self-misery.

Self-pity?

Sure, call it that. I was an orphan of sorts, you know. And on top of everything else I wanted to be able to tell my story. After all I had lived and all I had read, I wanted to do that, too. But after all, you can't do everything, and how many lifetimes is a man supposed to live? I made up my life out of the things I did, I was like a hero in one of those old-fashioned color adventure movies, don't you think?

You were, sort of.

When you were little I wanted you to read T. E. Lawrence. Did you ever read him?

Now that you mention it, I think I remember the book lying around the house. A thick volume? a lot of pages that I think I once ruffled through. *The Seven Pillars of Wisdom?*

Dots the one. I wanted you to read it.

I never did until I was grown, and then I thought it was sort of crazy.

I'm not thinking about the philosophy, Oll-an, I'm thinking about the adventures. What did you think about his adventures?

Fascinating, that part.

And mine?

Fascinating, too. You're like him in certain ways, a kind of Jewish Lawrence of Arabia.

You're making a joke. But I accept it as a compliment, Oll-an.

I meant it as a compliment, as much as a joke.

Thank you very much.

Have I hurt your feelings?

You've tickled my funny bone.

Father, Father . . .

"Hey," Josh breaks into this dialogue, "doesn't this desert ever end?"

Below us it seems to go on forever, a desert into which you could fit Nevada and Utah and Arizona and still find room for part of the Midwest.

I'm listening closely to my heart, I'm hugging my ear to the wind within the aircraft and the wind without, I think I can hear the sound of another older engine, of more than one engine, of gunshots, shouts of men on horseback, the steady patter of the guns for the airships, the spat-spat of the old machine guns fired by the veiled men in their filthy, flowing robes as they see the ships on the horizon.

Do I see a walled city below? Some oasis? A swatch of dark green against the brown desert, seen through a scrim. Is it really there? Or does it appear with the sounds of the old, straining engines and the spat of the rifles and the shouts of the Uzbek horsemen?

And it's gone, faded into the brown haze rising from the brown sands. And we're descending now, into the heat of the desert morning, into the heart of the matter.

I've never been further from home—and never closer to completing this spiralling circle in time—from my father's memory (lost and regained) to my own life to Josh's.

Urgench.

We step down out of the aircraft into a hot soup of light and dust, the entire horizon giving off a glow that seems brighter than sepia but slightly duller than the brilliant views you find on seacoasts and atop high mountain ranges. This is a town between two deserts, the Kyzyl Kum and Kara Kum (Red Desert and Black Desert, respectively). The armies of Alexander the Great marched through here, after the Persians had been thrown back behind their own boundaries by the earlier Greeks, and later came the horse soldiers of Genghis Khan who rode out of the steppes of greater Mongolia (now Siberia) and conquered much of what was then the entire world.

Cities such as Urgench melted easily under the heat of that army and became part of an empire that extended nearly into the heart of Europe. Here in this place of about a hundred thousand people you can see clearly the effects of that ancient conquest, with the cast of the inhabitants looking unlike most people that I've ever seen before, a fusion of Arab and Oriental features, appropriate since we're walking here along the tarmac midway between the Arabian Desert and China proper—no, well, I'm mistaken, since we are much closer to China than Saudi, that's certain, but the facial features of the people on the walkways now, the men in shirtsleeves and cheap synthetic trousers, the women in that cotton blend of many colors in large floral design, appear to have blended perfectly the major characteristics of both adjacent cultures.

Urgench has far fewer Russians on the street than Tashkent. The Intourist guide walking with us across the tarmac to our car is an Uzbek. So is the driver. All around us we see women in native dress, their skins as dark as East Indians, their features delicately Oriental.

Our drive through dusty, paved streets to the Hotel Khorezm is short. I'm so excited I'm finding it hard to breathe. But I don't want to lose my control, and I don't want Josh to see me this way. Why? Why? In Kiev as we were going to sleep I hid my tears from him. And now again? Why? I think back far and long to times when I saw my father lose his control—and I allow myself to remember those angry fits, a snarling, bearish ranging about the house, his voice a nasty, almost brutish kind of roar.

I hated him when he lost his temper, but it must have been more of a case whereby when he lost his temper I grew frightened not merely at the possibility of immediate physical harm, the harm that would come to me, the pain I would feel if he caught me with the buckle of the strap from his trousers which he waved wildly over his head, but I was also suffering from primal sexual fright and jealousy and my own rage and terror at the image of what he must be like when he and my mother made love, that is, out of control and rampaging, if not raging, like a bull, a bear, a wolf, a jungle beast—and feeling the loneliness of the bird thrust from the nest, the fear before the prospect of flight, fear of sex and death, the two great unknowns that lie before us, just as the third, awareness before birth, lies behind.

I can understand a little now about why I don't want to lose control in front of Josh, but I resolve that next time when I feel like it I will just give it over.

We check in and go up to our second-floor room. The hotel has an air about it of recent construction, though everywhere you look it seems about to have begun to decay. The new tile is slightly soiled with fungus. A lizard slithers away over the edge of the railing on our balcony. The room is large, musty, the bathroom dank. The bottom of the tub appears darkened with some nasty stain. In Moscow we risked sitting in these tubs. We don't do it here.

We lie down on our beds for a little nap and awaken in time for lunch of rich and spicy soup with meat, and then a meat dish with rice tasting of the same spices. The local bread is moist and tasty. We drink of course only mineral water, as does everyone in the room round us—all men, mostly Uzbek. The manager is a woman, as are all the waiting staff.

Some sixty years ago all the women here would have been veiled, if they ever appeared on the street at all. I'm not sure about the intricacies of Islam on the subject of women, but it's clear that the Soviet influence has stripped away a number of the veils in domestic arrangements here. I'm not sure that this is all bad, since one of the few things I've learned in my own life, about women, about family arrangements, and perhaps about the world and nature, too, is that the more veils that you strip away, the more you discover—the more you learn, the more you deepen and make more complex the mystery of all things.

What will I learn about my father when we get to Khiva? What will I learn about myself? About me and him? About me and Josh? About the three of us, strung along time like wash on a line, arms stretched toward the heavens, feet dangling inches above the earth?

In the heat of the afternoon we head out to the bazaar, where we discover beautifully arranged mounds of apricots, oranges, grapes, all varieties of peppers, and dozens of other spices. Nowhere else in the Soviet Union have we seen such a fine array of fresh fruit–and bountiful vegetables, too, in another section of the market.

Uzbeki women swathed in their colorful robes jerk their heads toward us as we pass. Come over, try *our* grapes, we'll give you a good price. Old women, young women, in their reds and yellows and greens and blues, the beautiful cotton cloth that the region produces as a by-product of growing cotton for all of the rest of the Soviet Union. Men in short-sleeved shirts and gabardine trousers wander through the market, dark hair close cropped, their naturally tanned faces creased from life in the sun.

We wander over to the clothing section, booths that vend bolts of cloth, plain winter coats, caps, combs, shoes, the quality of the merchandise lower than anything you find in the U.S., stuff that would make K-Mart goods look like items from Rodeo Drive boutiques. No folk craft at all available here either, only the drab outerwear, and the colorful cloth for the women's saronglike dresses and turbans.

We linger before the caps, and the vendor asks us if we're Yugoslavs. We tell him where we're from, but he doesn't believe us. Does he expect capitalist devils to spout fire from their nostrils? No other Westerners here, and only a few ethnic Russians.

Josh buys a blue cap for the equivalent of four U.S. dollars–expensive by Soviet standards. With his new purchase on his head he could pass for a Yugoslav. Or a western Russian. Strolling through this marketplace he makes the picture of the young Captain Kaplan. I thought that on this trip I would somehow possibly find myself as my father. How often I've felt in certain situations that Phil was superimposed on my own personality or I on him. But here is Josh looking like his grandfather when the old man was the same youthful sport Josh is now.

It occurs to me that everything could turn out to be anticlimactic now, after seeing Josh in this light. Is this what I've been so anxious about? We walk slowly back to the hotel,

Josh taking shots of passersby, of the posters on the walls, of statues. And I'm breathing deeply of the hot, particle-misted air. Sweaty and tired, we've been away from home a few weeks now, under the stress of the present, carrying the past around with us. My eyes water—tears from the irritation of epiphanic images, my son and my father as one.

TWENTY-SIX

THE TRANS-SIBERIAN RAILROAD DELIVERED ME into Vladivostok late in the afternoon, and with duffel bag over my shoulder I emerged into the street and followed Sergei Pivovarov's directions. I turned left to the trolley line that would take me up to the old Nobel Barracks where I found a room for the night.

The following day at the shipyards I got myself a job overhauling carburetors for internal combustion engines. I located a drawing board barely large enough to suit my needs and began producing the drawings and blueprints for forging and machining parts. And—after a week—just as I was becoming really involved with the project of duplicating the work, I received the news for which I had been hoping, a telegram from the Air Force High Command in Moscow telling me to report to the Vladivostok military commissariat in order to be recommissioned into the armed forces of the U.S.S.R.

Ah, my second mother, the Red Army Air Force! I was issued a splendid new uniform of fine English wool, and on my left sleeve I placed my wings and two crossed daggers.

After returning to the Khabarovsk Air Base, I learned that the machine shops had facilities for modifying aircraft. In charge of the current experimental plane, the Grigorovich

D-11, two mechanics and Major Yakov Evgenevich Yakovlev, an aeronautical engineer, and General Dolenko, the commander of the base. I was the pilot elected to fly the not-yet-operational fighter.

When I was first allowed to enter the hangar I noticed that the ship, unlike the same model I had flown and wrecked at Volsk, had panels merging with the trailing edge on the wings. I could also see that both wings were attached to the fuselage with hinges and could be swivelled and then folded.

"Those are hydraulically operated flaps, Captain Kaplan," Major Yakovlev explained to me. "When changed to the right angle, they can aid the pilot in slowing the landing speed, as well as give added lift on take-off. You'll get to try the new system yourself tomorrow. The flaps have been tested first in wind tunnels at Tula, and they've been flown by test pilots on air bases in eastern Russia. Tomorrow, after I show you how they operate, you'll fly over a designated part of the field where we can observe with binoculars if the carriage retracts correctly and the wheels fold as they are supposed to into the wells in the wings. We did quite an extensive job on that."

"With the wings folded, Major, we can ship entire squadrons of these samolets on the platform of a single train," I observed.

"Right you are, Captain. And they can also land much easier on the deck of a carrier."

"Do you think we need carriers to defend the Soviet Union?"

"That is a political question, Captain Kaplan. Now then, you will notice that the feathering on the wings is still plywood. That's because we might have to change the accesses to the guns and to the ammunition. Our next assignment is to make improvements on that, and also find room for an auxiliary fuel tank. Oh, yes . . . they also want us to trim the weight of the machine guns. So train your mind on how we might anchor the guns differently."

"Just so."

"About the engine—this model's engine is different from the one you flew at Volsk. It's been replaced with one that operates with a supercharger that enables the plane to fly higher."

I began flying the next day, and within a week I had engineering ideas for the machine gun placement and auxiliary fuel tanks. How fantastic it was to be in the air again, soaring higher than any bird and looking down at the earth as it tipped left, tipped right. It was during those days that I became convinced I had been born to fly, so clearly so that even the worst vicissitudes of life could not keep me down.

After six weeks we had the new auxiliary fuel tank installed and General Dolenko ordered a long distance test to determine fuel consumption.

I rose with the sun that fateful day. I ran ten kilometers, did calisthenics with the officers, and ran back for a shower before breakfast. Major Yakovlev met me in the mess. "Well, Captain, all is ready! Your only stop is to take on fuel at the Ussuri landing strip near the Manchurian border. They will find you and escort you to that landing. As you know, the supercharger will enable you to rise higher than anyone has before over the Sikhote Alin Mountains. If you should for some reason find yourself over Manchuria or Korea, and you're challenged to land, your orders are to shoot down the enemy and return to our territory. And, of course, under no conditions are you to let our ship pass into enemy hands."

"Just so, Major! Orders understood. May I ask about the weather conditions?"

"The meteorologists say you have the sun with you both ways. However, they do qualify that they have no information about the weather over Manchuria or Korea."

Soon after I climbed into the morning haze I started searching over the green carpet of the taiga for the tracks of the Trans-Siberian railway, and when I found them I set my compass for south. There was so much for me to do I hardly had time to think or revel in the realization that I was at the controls of my country's most advanced fighter plane! Where I had formerly despaired of ever flying again, here I was in complete control of my destiny—or so I rather foolishly thought.

I flew on for hours until ahead of me I saw the silvery ribbon of the Ussuri River. Lake Khanka, like a sea, also lay ahead of me and to the right. Forbidden Manchuria glowed in a haze under my starboard wing.

"Identify yourself!" a voice rasped in my ear. I glanced to my right and left and I saw two Tupolev fighter planes with crimson stars on their stubby fuselages.

"Good morning, comrades!"

"Say corn in Russian, comrade!"

"Kookooruza, comrades," I said. This was unexpected on my part since it was not part of the password.

"His accent is okay." I heard another voice say. "It's fine, follow us and land."

"Understood," I said.

"Hey," cried out the other, "you have no wheels!"

"I have wheels," I said, letting my landing gear down.

We landed in tandem, but as the two stubby little planes rolled on and on, I, thanks to my brakes, had practically come to a stop."

"Hey! Very fine," I heard one of the pilots say in my earphone.

"Never saw a landing so slow and so short, Captain," the lieutenant in charge of the ground crew muttered as I climbed down to the apron.

"So far it's a secret," I said. "Let's keep it that way."

"I'm the officer of the day," another young lieutenant said on the run. "We knew you were coming, so I ordered the cook to save you some borscht and kasha."

"Thank you for that," I said.

It was a wonderful lunch, though a quick one. I only had the time it took to refuel the Grig. Then it was back into the blue sky, the ground receding quickly from my sight. The town of Spassk passed beneath me. The Trans-Siberian rails led me to the Sikhote Alin Mountains, and I rose and set my compass for the return to Khabarovsk.

But then over the Sea of Japan I saw rushing in my direction a dark and billowing mass that was swallowing both sea and sky. The oncoming storm moved in my direction like a cannonball, and I was crazily racing toward it at the same speed. When we met I was tossed in the other direction like a ping-pong ball, and my compass whirled. I shoved my throttle all the way forward in an effort to maintain any forward momentum at all . . . and stalled.

In order to stay aloft I let the tail wind take me where it would. It rushed me along with the force of a thousand locomotives. There was a hole in the clouds and I could see by the horizon that I was flying sideways and turning upside down. Somehow I started my engine again and righted the ship, but then I felt my port wing creaking and cracking at the hinge.

Rain was pelting the cockpit and I could barely see the wing—though what I could see was terrifying enough. A piece of the plywood was being ripped away, rivets and all. The forward hinge holding the port wing at the fuselage was cracked, and the one-inch aluminum bolt locking the rear hinge had a sheared cotter pin. Any more stress and I'd lose the port wing!

Then, as suddenly as the wind had come on, it passed. Beneath me I could now see water, a sunny but turbulent sea. I looked for land and saw none, and my four main tanks were almost empty.

Fear iced up my bowels. I turned east and kept looking for a ship, a fishing boat, a dinghy, anything afloat. Beneath me, horizon to horizon, was a watery desert rippling with tiny waves and an occasional whitecap.

"Dear God," I prayed, and suddenly I remembered when I was six and we still lived in Tikhorechka where I attended a religious school taught by an old rabbi in the old Tailor's Synagogue. A great sadness came over me.

It was time to switch on the auxiliary fuel tank, and I could not find the valve because tears were welling up in my eyes. Tears blinded me. It was clear in my mind that I was about to die. Suddenly I began to recite the words of the Twenty-third Psalm, words that I had been made to memorize when I attended Hebrew school. The auxiliary tank, once switched on, had only enough fuel for a few minutes of flying. I decided that when the engine died I would go into a dive and finish myself off quickly. In the meantime I kept on searching the horizon, hoping against hope to spot a ship in time for me to reach it while there was fuel left in the tank.

I struggled to remove my boots and threw them from the cockpit. Next I shed my coat and draped it on the dashboard lest I smash my face, but then shouted with desperate anger and flung it into the void outside.

The engine sputtered and died.

I dove toward the sea, but at the last moment, just before I reached the surface of the water, I pulled up on my stick with all my might—and as the nose of the Grig rose to the horizon, my port wing folded over. The plane lurched to one side and went knifing through the waves. I was catapulted from the cockpit like a clown from a circus cannon. I saw the starboard wing racing after me as if it were the fin of a giant shark before I plunged, head first, into an oncoming wave.

I tried to swim upward toward the murky light. To my surprise, I surfaced and I gasped with relief. It took me a moment to realize that I was under the port wing, which had sheared off from the fuselage, and was rising and falling with the waves. Thank God, I cried to myself, that it was made of wood. I grabbed the protruding pipes and a wire-harness dangling from inside the wing, and when I had regained my breath I climbed on top. I stood up, spitting and coughing, to let the warm breeze dry me.

Now and then the chilly water rolled over and lapped at my feet. The underside of the sun was touching the crimson waters in the west, heralding the coming of night. It could take days before I would reach land or meet up with a ship. Saved from drowning, I might die of thirst or hunger or exposure to the elements.

Then, in the twilight, I saw on the horizon what looked like the smokestack of a ship moving north. If it were true, then I was in a very heavy sea lane—and if I did not drift away in the other direction I would probably encounter more ships. But then darkness came. The sky was overcast and I could not see the stars. It was cold, cold, cold, but I curled up in the center of the wing where there was a dry place and somehow managed to sleep.

Just before dawn it became even colder. My teeth began to chatter, and the icy waves lapped at my limbs. My left eye had swollen shut and my right one twitched. But, as the sky began to glow in the east, I could see well enough to recognize the outline of a freighter.

The silhouette of the ship grew as it moved alongside me about a kilometer away. As the sky grew lighter and lighter I took off my shirt and waved it until my arms ached. And then I saw the bow of the freighter beginning to point in my direction!

But what of the khaki shirt with my insignia on it? What of the red star on the wing? Without thinking any more of it I stripped off my shirt and spread it over the star and secured it with my belt. My revolver and holster I threw into the water long before the ship, the S.S. *Zuisa Maru,* arrived at my side.

TWENTY-SEVEN

HOW FAR FROM HOME DO YOU HAVE TO RUN IN one direction before you understand that you've circled more than half the globe and are now racing *toward* it?

Alan certainly didn't know of such distances, nor anything at all about the physics of nostalgia, when he left for college. But a few months at a small liberal arts school in Pennsylvania had him gasping for breath. Aside from a brief sojourn in Boy Scout camp when he was about twelve—which should have warned him since he nearly wept through the entire weekend, so homesick did he become in the northwest Jersey woods—he had never spent more than a day or two away from home, and those days, overnights to be specific, had been in the rooms of Mama Sarah above the various candy stores that she and Ed had purchased.

"So you want to leave Lafayette and transfer to Rutgers?" Phil's voice sounded weak somehow over the telephone, as from a great distance. "That's okay with me." He cleared his throat and Alan, on the other end of the line, breathed easier.

Before the call his chest and throat had tightened up on him in anticipation of what he feared might be a difficult conversation. What did he know about how his father would react? Coming home might appear like failure to a man who had travelled so far to find his place in life. Coming home might seem like caving in, and no matter what happened, for a boy born and raised in the industrial wilds of northern Jersey the need to keep up the outer show of confidence—even swagger and spunk and bravery beyond foolishness—never left his mind.

"Yeah, Dad," Alan heard himself saying, "I just don't like it here out in the sticks." The young man could feel the sweat running down his sides despite the coolness of the dormitory hall where he stood hunched over the telephone. "I think it would be better for me in a bigger place, one closer to the city."

"So come home," Phil said without hesitation.

Alan pressed up against the wall and began to weep.

But when he returned home at the end of the school year, the acceptance to nearby Rutgers in hand, he found himself once again spending so little time in the household that he had to question his desire to live nearby—so far, that is, as he was capable of questioning anything about his life at the age of eighteen. Perhaps there were boys his age who could look at themselves with some sense of consciousness, but not this boy, the flier's son; he skidded along the pathways of life like a kid pushed ahead of a massive roll of California surf.

In philosophy class he read that "the unexamined life is not worth living." But what did he know about examining?

He did not know.

"You know a lot," Tillie said to him one night after he had had a violent argument with his father, and what were they arguing about in those days? about civil rights? Phil didn't want his son involved in demonstrations that might turn violent themselves. Or was it about Zionism? That argument began in his college years and went on for decades, "but how much you really know we'll find out!"

Fortunately he seemed to know enough so that after his arrival back in Perth Amboy, when his father suggested that he live at home and commute to Rutgers, he declined.

"I better live out there, Dad," he said.

"Are you sure, Oll-an?"

They were sitting together on folding chairs on the front porch of the Lewis Street house, where they had moved after their return from Rahway. It was a summer weekday afternoon, but Phil was home. After years of working at General

Motors as an engineer he had opened his own television repair business at home. He enjoyed the independence of working for himself, even though it meant that as many as three nights a week he went out to make house calls like a country doctor, and he also enjoyed the liberty of some long hours at home without anything to do: if he finished what repairs he had sitting on the bench downstairs, he could try once again to make some stories at the typewriter—tap-tap-tap-tap . . .

"I'm sure, Dad," Alan said.

"You could live here, your mother could cook for you and take care of your laundry."

"You wouldn't have to worry about a thing," Tillie added from her vantage point at the front door.

Phil turned at her voice, annoyed somewhat that she had been listening without making her presence known, but pleased that she was agreeing with his suggestion.

Something in the offer put Alan off, he couldn't say exactly what—well, he could if he put his mind to it, it would have meant real difficulties if he wanted to see some girls, and he did want to see some girls. So, new desire helped him to snap this old cord. Ah, desire, desire, desire!

"I'm going to take a room in the dormitory and then see what else is around," he explained.

"If you have to," his father said, some of his pain showing in his voice. This love of his for Alan! It was almost . . . carnivorous! and the boy didn't understand it much at all, in fact he felt nearly always repelled by it! Suffocated by it! It was as if his father, having put behind him all of that former adventurous life, now lived only to crush any possibility of such action out of his son's days to come.

"Here," said his mother, handing over a large sack of groceries for his new room at Rutgers.

"You take this, too," his father said. It was a manuscript. *Of Fate and Flight* was printed on the title page, in ink, with the careful lettering of a trained draftsman.

"What do I want this for?" Alan said. "I'm going to have plenty of work to do at school."

Phil cocked his head to one side, and said, "I thought that if you had a little time you could read it, and rewrite it, and we'll make a best-seller together."

"Dad . . . ," Alan protested.

"Take it," Tillie said.

"Do you want me to do my courses or to read this sh–?"

"Dot's all right, Teel," his father said, withdrawing the manuscript from his son's reach. "I'll keep it here until he's ready."

"Ready?" Alan said.

"Do you have enough socks?" his mother asked. "Do you have enough underwear?"

The boy nodded, and carried his belongings to his car, the second-hand, plum-colored Henry J–its fins and dachshund-like shape making it one of the oddest vehicles on the road–that Phil had bought for him for a few hundred dollars from a local barber.

"You ought to read it sometime," Phil said as he accompanied him for one last trip to the car. "It's got all sorts of good stories in it, my training in the air force, the wars we fought . . ."

"Sure, Dad."

"And how I had to ditch my plane in the Sea of Japan, and how I decided not to go back to the Soviet Union . . ."

"I don't understand that, you know? I don't understand how anyone could give up his native country and go live somewhere else."

"Oh, you had to live there in Russia to know that, son. But after I ditched the plane, I was picked up by a Japanese freighter and went to Japan, to the port of Hakodate, and there I lived for a while . . ."

"Dad?"

". . . before I went to Shanghai and got a job flying mail upcountry for the Kuomintang. Have you ever heard of that government, run by Chiang . . ."

"Dad, I have to go."

"All right, son," Phil said, lowering his head a little (in sadness that his son could not possibly understand at the time). Alan climbed into the odd little vehicle and drove off without looking back. He could count on what he would see if he turned around—both parents on the front porch waving goodbye.

"Be careful!" He could still hear his father's voice in his ear. "Watch your step!"

He did neither, throwing himself into the Bohemian life at the university and outside it with a gusto he had never known before. It was as if once having admitted to himself that he couldn't bear life at Lafayette and had to return home, he left the Perth Amboy household forever. Within months he had put the dormitory behind him, too, broke off his relations with a fraternity whose members had solicited him to join (though he remained friends with some of these fellows for a long time after), and moved into an apartment on the fringes of the campus with Jim Mohan, the incisively smart son of an Irish tugboat captain from Camden, and Bill Jones, a black student from North Jersey who was the most fastidious thinker Alan would meet for many a year. The apartment rang with the noise of people chanting their favorite poems, with folk music from the phonograph, with arguments about Kafka versus Thomas Mann, the puzzlements of Gertrude Stein, the greatness of Norman Mailer, the existential needs of the modern voyager in the world, ethics, poetics, and sometimes the giggles and moans of young women from the women's college on the other side of town, and the air sweated the sweet smell of bourbon and marijuana . . .

"Talk to your father," Tillie would say each time she called to inquire after his eating habits and such. "He misses you."

"Hello, Dad?"

"Hello, Oll-an. How are you doing?"

"I'm fine, fine."

"You're studying hard?"

"I'm enjoying myself, and what I study I study for the love of it."

"Well, that's all well and good but remember if you're going to get a good job when you finish college you're going to have to work for your degree."

"What's a good job, Dad?"

"Your mother and I hope that you'll go to law school, Oll-an, you're so good with words."

"Aw, shit, Dad."

"Oll-an, watch your mouth. Why the foul language, son?"

"I'm not going to law school. I'm going to be a writer."

"Don't be silly. Don't you know what a life that is? There is no money in it, son, and you have to earn a living."

"So what are you doing at your typewriter all the time?"

"I am telling my story. And besides I have a way of earning a living, which I should remind you pays for your stay at college, too."

"You want a receipt? You want to know every time I get an A on a French test?"

"Alan," Tillie broke in, "I'm listening on this line and can hear every word you're saying. You're not being very nice to your father."

"Oh, shit!"

"Oll-an!"

"Listen, I better hang up."

"I think you owe your father an apology."

"I'm sorry. Okay?"

"Okay. So you got an A on a French test you said?"

"Actually, no, I flunked it. I'm flunking the whole course as a matter of fact."

"You're what?"

"I'm flunking my French. They wanted me to translate Hemingway stories into French. I told the instructor I wouldn't do that. I'm not going to turn some of the purest, best English I know into French. What for?"

"What for? So you can learn French."

"Not that way, Dad. I'll go there and learn it. But I'm not going to ruin Hemingway with some dipshit exercise."

"Watch your language, I said."

"Should I hang up? I'm only speaking English, you know?"

"Not the English I learned."

"That was years ago. If you learned it now you'd talk like this."

"I don't think so."

"Look, Dad, I have to hang up now."

"Very well. But study your French. Go back to the teacher and talk to him about . . ."

"Dad!"

"Just do it. You need to make compromises sometime, son. Let me tell you how I . . ."

"Dad, I really have to go."

Tillie spoke up with a "Goodbye, dear."

"Oll-an?"

The young man braced his feet against the wall and gritted his teeth. Here it comes . . . here it comes.

"Yeah?"

"Do you need any money?"

"Sure, Dad."

"I'll send you a check."

"Alan, when are you coming home?"

"I'm not sure, Mother. I have . . ."

"Oh, Teel, he doesn't want to think about such things now. He's got to study. He's got his French to do. He has to concentrate on his studies."

"What about reading your father's story?"

"Oh, Teel, you heard, he's busy."

"Have to go now."

"Goodbye, Alan."

"Goodbye, Oll-an."

"So long."

And Alan said in his mind, *So long for a while, that's all the songs for a while,* the theme song of a show that he heard in his head now and then along with a thousand other lines and snatches of music (and, increasingly, poems), making of his brain the kind of collection of odds and ends of language high and low and middle, of noise high and low and accidental, of images ugly and beautiful, that comprises the street part of a makeshift American education, the process so informal but the result so important if you are going to feel a part of the life of the country rather than above and beyond it. Taken to the extreme he knew—and they talked about this in philosophy class—you had both to create and to destroy, to love and to hate, and unless you were out of control you didn't want to find yourself committing an act of destruction, but in theory, at least, it was possible to consider knowing everything about the present in the same way that history—he was studying history with a little better conscience than he was studying French—showed you as much about the past as was possible to know . . . all this thought, all this argument, all this reading in turmoil.

When his friends Mohan and Jones graduated Alan took over the apartment and the editorship of the campus literary magazine as well. Jazz in New York and the life of letters in New Brunswick: these became the young man's passions. Studies became secondary, perhaps as it should be for Alan, since his mother's way of putting it, "in one ear and out the other," seemed apt to describe his relation to his courses. He rarely went home now and never spent time with his father when he did. He was, you might say, adopting himself a family from the great orphanage of the world.

Or at least New Brunswick.

For example, one day while he was sitting in the office of the literary magazine, high on the fourth floor of a remodelled Victorian house of the kind that served many a department and committee on the Rutgers campus before modernization turned most of the acreage red and brick and ugly, in walked a lean, young fellow with a sharply carved face, short brown hair, and the wiry delicacy of an athlete.

"Who are you?" Alan challenged him, staring at the Long Branch High School sweatshirt the fellow wore.

"My name's Pinsky. I'm a poet."

He was right. The son of a Jersey Shore optometrist, and grandson of a roughneck New York club fighter, Pinsky used his natural intelligence with the swiftness and power of a boxer. Like Alan, he was raised as a sort of Jew—but literature, language, poetry was his native religion and began to surface soon enough through the junk-knowledge that had been piled on top of it.

Peter Najarian showed up soon after. Pete was a fatherless boy from Union City whose mother worked a sewing machine in a dress factory. If it hadn't been for literature, for painting as well as poetry and fiction, Najarian might have become a fairly adept hustler on the North Jersey streets, a middle-level criminal whose wide-eyed sense of wonder masked a keen ability for staying with the problem until he solved it. Najarian made a cult out of his Armenian background—made his background his foreground—and wrote about it, even as a beginner, with true lyric power.

Another interesting individual, somewhat older, appeared in the magazine offices one evening with a Bible in hand, quoting scripture to help the editors see the misery of their blaspheming. This was Henry Dumas, born in Arkansas, raised in East St. Louis. He had a shy young wife, and a new son named David, and was fresh out of the U.S. Air Force and ready to educate himself and reform the others.

"No more four-letter words or you'll burn in hell," he warned the editors.

A month later he returned, this time with Bertrand Russell's history of philosophy under his arm. He wanted the boys to see that careful thought and philosophical method was more important than writing poems or stories.

"Think," he urged. "You had better think before you write."

A few weeks later he was back—with a sheaf of stories under his arm.

"I'm a writer now, too," he said, and asked us to read the pages. One of the stories was so good that it won the fiction contest that year (though Pinsky pointed out some time later that it was taken nearly word for word from a story by William Melvin Kelly). Dumas went on to write and publish many stories and poems, only to die prematurely in a shoot-out with a subway patrolman in a Harlem station.

Over at the university newspaper things were both more frenetic and more calm. One of the editors, a tall, two-by-four straight boy with a crew cut, Digby Diehl, became Alan's friend. And Alan got to know David Rosensweig and Robert Wiener, too, a pair of journalists in the making. And the head of the independent student organization, Robert Rosen—who wanted a seat on the student council with the rest of them and created a group, of which he happened to be the only member as it turned out, in order to demand representation. He got it.

Alan's studies did not get much better after he flunked French.

"What are you studying now?" his father asked him the next time then spoke on the phone.

"Chaucer," he said.

"Oh, what's that?" Phil asked.

Alan explained.

"That sounds interesting. So are you doing well in your other courses?"

Alan didn't know whether or not to talk about such matters, particularly since he was flunking yet another course, this one because he had refused to read *Middlemarch*. No one should have to read a novel that long, he had said to the instructor. Read it or flunk, the instructor had said. Alan flunked.

"I guess so."

"You guess so? Oll-an, you don't know?"

"Education isn't just courses, Dad."

"I know that, I know that. But if you are going to law school you need to make good grades."

"Who said I was going to law school?"

"I thought you told us that. Didn't he, Teel?"

"I remember," Tillie said, coming in on another line.

"That's funny. I don't," Alan said.

"When are you coming home?" his mother asked.

"I don't know," Alan said.

The odd thing was that he was feeling more and more at home away from home, with his roommates, with his friends, and, miraculously enough, with his professors. Some of these, such as Paul Fussell, preferred to hold him up at arm's length and scrutinize hard, as though Alan were some curious exotic creature the man found digging among the Jerusalem artichokes in his garden. Others, such as Francis Fergusson, opened their offices to him with a generosity the boy had never known before in strangers. One man, John McCormick, took him in like lost, or found, family. These strangers became his friends, as much as teachers (because in these days, as Fussell once remarked to him, he was virtually *unteachable*), his student friends his brethren, and some of the adults new fatherlike mentors to the young man.

When John McCormick took in the aging Canadian railroad man with bad legs and bad memory who was his father, Alan was amazed. Here was a grown man, one of his prized professors, who was caring for the old fellow as though the elder were the child.

"You've read the *Aeneid*, haven't you, Alan?" McCormick said.

Alan nodded.

"Well, that's what happens, you carry your old father Anchises out of the burning ruins on your bloody back."

That night after Najarian cooked dinner for him and Pinsky and Pinsky's friend, Ellen Bailey—ah, Pinsky had such good taste in so many matters even at the age of nineteen!—Alan curled up with a copy of the *Aeneid* he had stolen earlier from the university bookstore and continued his education.

In his younger and more vulnerable years, Alan's father gave him a piece of advice that he had been turning over in his mind ever since.

Alan loved the opening lines of *The Great Gatsby* and had been turning over those lines in his mind ever since he first read the novel at Rutgers. Sometimes late at night in his toll-takers booth at the New Jersey Turnpike where he had found a job after graduation—the object being to save enough money to head for Europe within a few months—he read over again certain passages from the well-worn copy of that book (and read his way through, among other writers, Thomas Wolfe and Proust, odd bedfellows in his continuing education). The fact was that he would have to emend Fitzgerald's statement. In his younger and more vulnerable years—now, at this moment, here, in this booth, and on the street in Perth Amboy and in New York where he took his days off to watch movies and try, without much success, to find girls—his father gave him very little advice about anything, and when he did offer some Alan spat on it.

"Live a little before you try to write," Phil told him.

"Don't tell me how to write," Alan said, pushing off from the porch and pounding down the steps toward his odd-shaped little car.

"Where are you going, Oll-an?" Phil asked. "Come here, I want to talk to you."

"I'm going down the to shore," the son said, thinking to himself, who the fuck is he to tell me how to write.

"And what are your plans? Come here, for heaven's sake."

The man never used foul language, the man never invoked an oath stronger than *shucks*. It was as if he had learned all of his obscenities from a sanitized television comedy hour.

"What, Dad?" Alan said, taking a few steps back toward the house.

"You want still to go to Europe?"

Alan nodded, watching the cloudy sky above the stunted little maples of their street.

"How much will you need?"

"I'll have enough saved from the turnpike," Alan said.

"Oh, are you keeping a little back from every toll for yourself?"

"That's not a joke, Dad. You can get arrested for that."

"I can't joke?"

"Joke."

"No, no more jokes. So you'll have enough?"

"Yes."

"I'll give you a little more. So go now, go to the shore. You've got a date?"

"Sort of," Alan said.

"You don't want to tell me?"

Alan shrugged the question away. He simply could not begin to talk with his father and he doubted if he ever could. It seemed all so embarrassing, like the old Biblical injunction against looking upon thy father's nakedness. Should the father be allowed to look upon the grown son's? Alan could not begin to reveal his own confusions and doubts to himself, and so he could not possibly talk about such matters with his father.

"Have to go, Dad."

"Have a good time at the shore, son," his father said.

That day Alan went down to the water and watched the Atlantic surf crash against the beach, but it did him no good; no true thoughts broke through. And that night in his tollbooth, in the long intervals between automobiles, he set down the book he had brought with him, a Russian novel this time, Lermontov, about heroes and the true stuff of adventure, which happened to be much more interior, more psychological than he had ever before imagined, and some ideas flickered through his mind about his father's life, thoughts about the old man's stories, the tales about flying in those bi-wing airplanes, the long narrative he had heard over the years in bits and pieces about his father's old life in the old country, the war stories, the moment when in that storm over the Sea of Japan he said that he realized that he was going down, and further adventures in Japan and then in China, in Shanghai where he told how the Russian secret police—having discovered his presence there—tried to kidnap him out of his hotel room and bring him back to the Soviet Union because he knew military secrets—and how he had miraculously escaped from their car in the middle of traffic in the foreign section of Shanghai, and eventually secured a visa for travel to the U.S. where his father and brother were living—odd how he never never mentioned his father after that part of the story—and spent some time in Hawaii and then came to San Francisco, places that Alan had yet to visit, and then came to New York where he met his mother at that dance in Brooklyn. In those solitary nights in that booth, in the strange no-man's land of the toll plaza where between the hours of three and five in the morning few cars rolled through, he dreamed about travelling to Europe and writing books that would make him famous and admired, though he knew nothing about the terrible labor involved in the writing and the kind of life that he would have to lead in order to put out that labor, a life of strange rhythms that fluctuated between isolation and society, rhythms that could twist you in their torque like the currents off the Jersey coast out beyond the breakers.

I am wondering where you are, you never write," a letter from his father informed him. He also mentioned that the local Selective Service board was wondering, too, since Alan had left the country without informing them of his departure. "I listen to Berlioz's 'Harold in Italy' on the record player and think about you travelling in Europe."

This letter reached Alan in Greece, where he found himself blinking in brilliant light at ancient ruins on the edge of the sea. It was the first indication that his father had ever listened to classical music in years and years of talking about Glinka and other Russian composers. In his own record collection back home Alan had gathered a lot of jazz and some Dvorak and Beethoven and some twentieth-century American composers, Copland and Barber and the like. But as far as he knew, his father had never listened to any of these. Could he now be going upstairs to Alan's old room and rummaging through the box of records, choosing among them?

The letter went on, talking of the importance of taking a trip to Israel.

"You must go, you must see the land of your origins." Phil offered to wire cash for a ticket to the Holy Land.

Who but a fool would refuse such an offer? Alan was only barely not a fool. When the money arrived at the American Express office in Athens, he set off on a slow boat across the Mediterranean for Jaffa. He found work on a kibbutz near the Dead Sea, but stoop labor did not agree with him. Neither did the constant jingoism of the people, nor the visible discrimination against Jews with dark skins. Alan returned to Spain, where he had first arrived and had not been successful at writing stories. Wearing a Hemingway costume and attending every *corrida* in the province did not a writer make. Within the year he was back in the United States, living at home and working in New York City, where he spent most of his time after work. He rarely saw his father except to quarrel. They had a number of favorite topics that inspired them both to anger.

Writing was one.

"You should see by now that it didn't do any good to go to Europe," Phil said. "If you're going to write you can write anywhere. In a bedroom. In a urinal. You don't need fancy scenery outside your window."

"In that case I ought to stay here in Amboy the rest of my life," Alan said.

"Don't be so sarcastic to your father," Tillie said. She was watching, listening, more like a caretaker than a referee. Phil had been having trouble with his heart and he was on medication, forbidden by his doctor to get himself too worked up about anything, not if he wanted to go on lifting and hauling as he had to do in his business.

"I wasn't being sarcastic, I was being perfectly straightforward," Alan said.

"Don't knock Amboy," Tillie said. "You could do worse than live here. Your friend Joe lives here, your friend Barry . . ."

They fought about Israel, too. Phil had put a photograph of Golda Meir above his desk and this annoyed Alan no end.

"The killer grandma," he called her whenever he noticed that face.

"Alan," Tillie cautioned.

"I was there," Alan said. "You don't know what it's like."

And politics was always a topic that could inspire them to anger.

Alan worked for a couple of years as managing editor for a quarterly journal published in New York City called *Studies on the Left.* Surrounded on the editorial board by historians and political theoreticians, some who made sense, some who seemed to spin more air than wool, he tried to make himself into something of both historian and ideologue, but he just didn't think that way, and threw himself with more passion to the job of editing than writing.

"Can't you change the name of that rag?" Phil said.

"What's wrong with the name? It is what it says. Should we call it *Studies in the Middle?* We're not in the middle."

"I worry about you getting into trouble, Oll-an. I don't want you to have something like that on your record."

"Fuck my record. I want to have a record. I'd love to have that on my record. I don't give a shit about my record."

"And what about law school?"

"I don't know. I don't care. I'm not going to law school."

"What if someday you change your mind, son?"

"I'm not going to change my mind about something like that. If I did, I'd shoot myself."

"Don't talk like that. Do you know what it does to me when you talk like that?"

"What does it do, Dad?"

"It makes me vorry."

"Well don't worry. I'm not going to do that. I care too much about my work."

"What vork?"

"My writing."

"Are you writing?"

"I just said I was, didn't I?"

But he wasn't. He was lying. In France and Spain he had taken coffees and cognacs in all the right cafes, but he had not written much of anything at all. And upon his return to the States he had not written.

"Will you read my manuscript?" his father asked. "Just read it and give it a good going over?"

"I don't have time for that, Dad. I'm busy as hell."

"Just take a quick look at it."

"I said I don't have time."

"You have time for all your left friends."

"I don't have time for your manuscript. Do you understand?"

"I don't. I don't understand, Oll-an."

"Oh, for Christ's sake, just give it to me and I'll read it."

"You promise?"

"Just give it to me."

And Alan took the manuscript with its hundreds of pages of awful typing and misspelled words and scratched-out lines and put it somewhere in his small apartment in Little Italy in Manhattan.

"What did you think of it?" his father asked the next time he came home.

"It needs a lot of work," he said.

"You've read it all the way through, all the things about flight school and the war in Khiva?"

"I've read it," he lied.

"You've read about how I ditched my plane in the Sea of Japan?"

"Dad, I've read it. And I think that you ought to put it aside for a while."

"You do?"

"That's what I think."

"Well, if you say so. You're the expert."

But Alan was an expert on nothing except keeping his egotistical dreams of an artist's life alive during years when he had a talent for nothing much of anything.

He certainly had no talent for love. He had his passions, but he did not know how to harness these and travel along the high old way to real affection. All he did was make serious trouble not only for himself, but for others as well. It certainly added to the number of topics that he and his parents could battle over.

Phil and Tillie took a trip to Israel, and when they returned their son argued with his father all the more vehemently about the subject. Within the year they added another topic of contention, the gentile girl, the daughter of an air force general, whom Alan had met at a party in New York. She looked like a young Tuesday Weld, her red hair giving every indication of the fiery soul that lay within. The two of them moved in together and then decided to marry. Tillie attempted to go into mourning like a Sicilian peasant woman, but her basically sweet and loving nature triumphed over her worries about broken traditions, dreams gone awry. Phil grew moodier and moodier, not because of any single event but because of the deepening sense of mortality attendant upon his heart ailment. About a year after his first grandchild, Joshua, was born, he went into the hospital for open-heart surgery. He not only survived—he threw himself with new strength into the composition of his retitled life story.

Tales My Father Told Me
by Alan Cheuse

When Alan saw the new title of the new manuscript his father handed him, he lost his temper.

"How dare you use my name that way?" he said. "When I'm ready to have something published under my name, I'll let you know." And he refused even to read more than a page or two into the romantic adventure story that his father had told over the years. He had his own adventures, on a much smaller scale and in a decidedly lower key. Having gone with his wife and new child to Mexico, he had returned after a year with nothing to show for it except more empty aspirations. When John McCormick informed him that he was starting a graduate program in comparative literature at Rutgers, he signed up. If he could not write fiction he could at least teach it. And so he did his graduate work and took a teaching job and performed it well for nearly a decade before yielding to the pressure building within him to give writing another try.

Phil, meanwhile, had grown weaker and weaker in the heart, though he kept on revising—tap-tap-tapping away at—his book. And Alan lost heart, too, having made a mess of his first marriage, and losing Josh to New York and his red-haired mother. But then a few years later—look sharp! suppose another wedding! a wedding in the Green Mountains on the back veranda of Ann and Bernard Malamud's Old Bennington house.

A beautiful day in June, blood relatives and desired friends all present, Alan's new bride-to-be, Kentucky-born Marjorie Pryse, a gifted teacher and critic and writer, glowing with her own dreams. Alan moved forward to take her hand. A woman friend, a justice of the peace, performed the ceremony, which meant presiding over twenty minutes of poems and prayers that various friends had chosen to recite. Toward the end, a poet in his cups called from the back of the crowd, "Is this a wedding or the goddamned *Norton Anthology of English Verse?"*

Such joy and humor! Only Josh found anything harmful in the event—a garter snake that he discovered in the flower bed beneath the porch, though this reptile that he held up for all to see seemed quite benign at the time. Phil stood to the side of the crowd, his hair completely white now, some sort of shrinkage about his eyes. Alan watched him pay most of his attention after the ceremony to Bern.

Phil and Bern, two of his fathers, the former, the novice in his seventies, talking, talking his life story to the latter, an accomplished genius of American fiction. Malamud, always gracious, bowed his ear toward the older man's lips.

TWENTY-EIGHT

I AWAKEN AFTER A DREAMLESS SLEEP, DO MY exercises, wash and dress. Josh does all this more quickly. We hurry downstairs for a quick juice and coffee and then a rendezvous with guide and driver. Our guide is Svetlana Umerova, a broad-faced blonde who appears entirely Russian. But she speaks fluent Uzbeki to the driver, and I ask her if she learned to speak that well in school. She replies shyly that, no, her father is Uzbek, and that her mother is Russian, a person who came here as a child as part of a work relocation program to which her parents belonged, and she met an Uzbek child in school who would one day become her husband. (Svetlana's husband is also a western Russian, an engineer, like her father, in the cotton processing industry. She met him here.)

In our Volga we travel south out of Urgench through field upon field of cotton plants on either side of the road. Josh takes pictures from the car of men, women, and children standing and walking at the side of the road, of donkeys pulling carts, of small adobelike houses clustered here and there to make villages, the horizon a hot smudge of whiter than white air.

"They tell me—I have never been there but I hear it is so—" says Svetlana, "that this countryside is a lot like much of India. Have you ever been to India?"

I shake my head no.

"Have you travelled much?" I ask. (Our guide to Zhitomir had explained to me that she had led Soviet groups to India and to Egypt.)

"All over the Soviet Union," Svetlana says. Which is not, as Josh and I have begun to understand, an inconsiderable bit of travelling.

Facts: Svetlana's voice has a kind of innocent, breathless quality, as though she's always on the verge of asking crucial questions; the countryside around us is unlike anything that I've ever seen, with low bushes between the cotton fields, white smear of the horizon all around, the oriental features of the people on foot, here a man wearing some variety of headgear that looks like Rastafarian dreadlocks, there a man wearing a suit and carrying a briefcase; I am moving along now in this car with Josh and the guide and the driver, my heart pounding as though we're in a space shuttle heading into the dark blue of the stratosphere.

Khiva. The sign appears at the side of the road. I sit up even more attentively and notice the closer groupings of the adobe houses, with a clothing shop in someone's living room here, a barbershop there, and now we pass a little cafe (closed and shuttered) on the edge of what appears to be a small, artificial lake. We slow down enough so that children standing at the side of the road see us in the car and stare. I wave. A kid smiles, turns away. Girls in school uniforms wear braids that complement their brown, almond-eyed faces. Boys kick stones toward a donkey tethered before a cart. We pass a low building to our right that appears to be an old palace, as Svetlana continues her obviously often-recited talk on the empire of the old khans.

Josh and I look at the building.

"And there is the old wall of the ancient palace of Khiva."

Now say my father (and all of us) had been born into another line of history, and say that, instead of serving as he did with the Red Army Air Force, he had been a young cavalry officer with the bluecoats out in our West and had been, say, stationed with his troops in a place like Taos Pueblo, or some other similarly enclosed place of habitation built by the same people that he was warring against, and say that after his death I had come west to Taos, to the pueblo, to see the very rooms and places on the floor where he had bedded down . . .

Say that I went west with my son and we walked through the entrance of the pueblo and saw the Indian families going about their business, baking bread, mending tack, sweeping the walkways, plastering the houses, sitting before open fires conversing about the events of the previous day . . .

Say that *you* did this, entered the pueblo after having spent time in the more modern places of Albuquerque, Santa Fe, even Taos itself . . .

Say that *you* smelled the aroma of the stuff in the cooking pots, the odor of the bread, the tang of the dogs and the dung and other animals (these invisible to the viewer's eye), say that *you* listened to the sounds of voices in a completely strange language, saw designs and colors in the buildings and the way the buildings lay against the sky, these odors, colors, noises. The feel of the dusty ground under *your* feet, all this combined to make an impression unlike anything *you'd* ever felt before . . .

And say that *you* had come here because *your* father had lived such a life as to have fixed forever on his mind and heart this place as the single locus of his best early times . . .

Make even half of this true for yourself in your imagination, make it out of the pieces and epoxy of your own particular experience, and you will have some idea of the awe and the dread and the pleasure and the anxiety I feel as I pass through the old wall of Khiva into the narrow, canopied street before us, where the shadows well up in shaded places before us like deep, fresh, clear water as high as our heads and over.

Svetlana begins her lecture, about khans and religious schools and architecture and tile-making, painting and poetry—this is a place rich rich rich in visual magic, world-famous for its geometric designs in majolica tile, and a living center for the Islamic audience for centuries because of poets such as Alisher Navoi and the philosopher Pahlavan Mahmoud—and I'm stumbling about in sunshine and shadow, peering up at the beautifully painted minarets of the schools, at the prayer tower, searching for the rooftops where my father stood and surveyed the skies, the desert where he lay down on his bedroll and slept his nights away.

Josh takes picture after picture, of the kids with vaguely familiar faces, in the streets, the women in their brilliant cottons, of old men wearing calf-length gabardine coats and long, white beards, some with skullcaps on their heads, others with large turbans that give them the appearance of Rastas, he takes a picture of a photographer who is taking pictures of children from the new city and tourists who come to get their pictures taken atop a local camel, and he takes a picture of a German tourist who's atop the camel, and we enter the palace of the sixteenth-century Khan of Khiva, a territory which included thousands of miles of desert around the desert town, and he snaps photographs of the living quarters of the khan and his harem, the wives in favor living in the sun-drenched side of the courtyard, the wives in disfavor living in the shade (which meant in winter that they froze), takes pictures of the intricate floral designs in the majolica, intertwining florets and vines that have no beginning and no end . . .

And I'm trying to find a way up to the roof but the doorway is nailed shut, all these buildings are still under restoration . . .

And I try another door but that, too, is blocked by a thick wooden partition nailed in place . . .

Will I rip away the barrier? I decide against it . . . I don't need to climb to the actual height of the roof of this palace. I am there already, I have reached such heights that I can see for thousands of miles back into the time of my father's presence here, I can see forward into the near-present of what I will return with to our own country, I can see into the stratosphere where spirits soar, can see the ghosts of our parents, and their parents before them, even Navoi and Pahlavan Mahmoud, I can see, I think, the spirit trails where my father's comrades swept up into the air and roared away over the Amu-Darya toward the desert, the far bank of the river, and I can look down into the center of things, see the waters come rising, bubbling up, see my daughters and my children's children, and I know something about what it was like to have been that ancient astronomer who dug a deep well-like hole in the ground and lowered himself within, and climbed down, slowly bracing his feet against the mud-brick walls of the well, until he reached the bottom and could look up and see, as he had guessed he could, as no one had before believed he would, but he did, he could see them, the stars by day . . .

And, after we have left the palace, I see in the mausoleum of Pahlavan Mahmoud the brilliant tile, and his poems painted around the alcove where the urn with his ashes stands . . .

And in the charcoal factory I see men in blackened skull-caps make the fuel for the fires of the metalworkers who bang away at tin in the little houses along the narrow streets. Tam-tam-tam-tam, the music of the metalworkers resounding through the streets . . .

And I see school after school in various stages of restoration. So many many schools! The art of poetry, painting, philosophy, history, theology, mathematics, all taught here over hundreds and hundreds of years, the Muslims of Khiva, as scholarly as their Jewish cousins, but for the most part richer, and with far far greater political power in this part of the world for over a thousand years . . .

And Josh in his new blue cap strolls along the aisles of the Khiva bazaar, the only place in town that smells as the city in the old times must have smelled, the odors of oranges and apricots and plums and grapes, with cooking fires behind the fruit stall, an old man driving a wretched miniature burro in front of his cart that is loaded with charcoal . . .

And the old music of Uzbekistan rings out across the market from loudspeakers mounted on the old walls . . .

And a gaggle of young Khiva girls in their flowing robes move across the open space before the food stalls . . .

And I thought I had seen everything I had wanted to see here, in a single glance, but there is more . . .

I see a young air force lieutenant in his desert khakis, his boots highly polished despite the rising dust of noon, strolling through the market square, tilting his head in the direction of one of these young girls, girls newly liberated from the old ways of wearing veils and keeping to themselves behind the closed walls of their fathers' houses. He scans their faces as a girl slyly passes her eyes in his direction, dark, round eyes fixed like carved chunks of charcoal in an olive face: their eyes meet . . .

Yes, the familiar voice, absent for a little while, comes to my ear. *Yes, it was like that.*

And armed with his few words of Uzbeki he advances toward them, and the other girls fade away toward the fruit stalls, leaving their shy companion temporarily stranded, alone.

Yes.

He'd been hurting from the pain of losing his comrades and friends, aching for some simple sweet and tender affection from a woman who asked nothing but the same from him for he would be far away soon, and who knew but that even tomorrow he would crash into the dunes and end his life in flames.

Yes. And she smiled at him as though watching from behind that absent veil, something promising, something gay and spirited and full of desert sun and laughter.

Yes.

Do I have half-brothers, men only a little older than I, in tea shops or working in the cotton fields, in the laboratories that attend on the cotton industry, soldiers, scientists, street sweepers, engineers, women teaching school, managing factories, engineers, soldiers?

I watch for familiar faces as we walk slowly on the shaded side of these narrow streets toward the teahouse that Svetlana wants to show us.

I see my face in every person I pass, and in no one. I am the stranger, the half-brother I am seeking.

I'm carrying a glass from the hotel bathroom in my pack, the tea glasses in the teahouse remind me of it. I had wanted to go to the banks of the Amu-Darya outside Khiva and scoop out a glass of that river water my father describes in his story, and study its muddy, swirling potion, and sip a toast with it, me and Josh, to Phil, but Svetlana tells me that the river swerves about thirty kilometers east of the town at this point.

I think about how I chose not to break down the makeshift door to the staircase leading up to the roof of the khan's palace. I didn't need to. My visit here is not symbolic, it is real.

I don't need to commit symbolic acts, the breaking of the door, the climb to the roof, drinking the waters of the Amu-Darya.

I decide to return the glass to the hotel room unused. Not necessary, I tell Svetlana. I didn't realize the river was that far away from the city. But why did I want to go? she asks.

"I had a friend who lived here for a while many years ago," I tell her. She looks extremely interested. "A flier, an adventurer who fought against the horse soldiers, the desert fighters of the next to the last Khan of Khiva."

"Against the counterrevolutionaries?" she says.

"Against them, I guess so."

It is cool but not truly dark in the teahouse. The air within is clear and every object seems to stand out in the shade, like images carved on obsidian: the grey-haired man in white shirt behind the counter in the center of the room brewing tea in the only samovar we've seen in operation since the train from Helsinki to Leningrad (which seems a lifetime away); the small boy in T-shirt and shorts helping to serve; the wooden beams of this clay building, tan in black light; and the glasses with the cool juice of apricots, a drink as muddy as my father's Amu-Darya; and the glasses with the steaming tea.

We sit on the rug on the floor opposite the counter, enjoying first the cool drink and then the hot, freshly brewed tea, the taste of which seems as dark and yet distinctive as the air around us.

Over in the far corner of the room I spy an old, white-bearded fellow in skullcap and long coat just sitting down with a group of men gathered cross-legged around a small, beautifully carved central wooden table.

On impulse I leap up and ask Svetlana to come with us so that she can introduce us.

"D-a-a-d," Josh grumbles, wanting to sit still and rest after the hours of walking in the sun. But I urge him to his feet, and the three of us cross the shadowy room.

The old, white-haired man with the long, white goatee is sitting with three darker fellows all wearing skullcaps and shirts made of colorful rough cotton. One of these men smiles at Svetlana as we approach.

"Good afternoon, comrade," he says, motioning for her and us to join them.

She makes apologies, explains that we have to get back to Urgench to catch an airplane, but says that we, the two visitors, wanted to say hello.

The man smiles, extends a weathered hand in greeting, asks us to make ourselves welcome to Khiva. Do we like the place?

We do, we do, we explain, Svetlana translating in her fluent Uzbeki.

"This man is also my guest," says the local elder, nodding toward the man sitting cross-legged on his right, the white-haired, white-bearded fellow in the sheepskin headpiece whose slight oriental cast gives him an air of wisdom even beyond his obviously advanced age. "He has come a long way."

"From where?" we ask.

"He has come all the way from Dushanbe."

"Dushanbe?"

Svetlana fills in—Dushanbe, the capitol of the Tadzhik Soviet Republic several hundred miles to the southeast, in the Pamir Range of the Hindu Kush, bordering on China and Afghanistan.

"We saw your mountains from the airplane on the flight from Tashkent," I say. "Tallest mountains in the world, I think, yes?"

The visitor nods, pleased that we know something, however scant, about his home territory.

"Okay, Dad," Josh breaks in, "let's stop playing Mister International Traveller and go. My stomach's getting to me."

"Just a minute."

The local elder converses with our guide in Uzbeki, and she turns to us.

"He would like you to sit down and take tea."

I look over at Josh, squirming while standing still.

"We have to go," I say. "But thank him for his hospitality."

The elder from Dushanbe speaks to his host and then looks up at us, squeezing his sun-creased face in a smile worthy of a Halloween pumpkin, showing us the large, empty spaces where most of his teeth used to be.

True to my profession—and now I realize I have to add, as well, *and my father's son*—I wait for some intimation of our shared travellerhood, an epiphanic burst of heart music, some sense of an ending of this particular quest.

The local elder nods, and addresses Svetlana. She says something in return.

"They want to know where you and your son come from."

"From the United States," I say, nodding toward them.

They nod in return and say a few words.

"The man from Dushanbe . . ." Svetlana purses her lips.

"Yes?"

"He says that he does not know where your country is, but he is sure from the look of you that you have come a long way, too."

Somewhere outside in the town a record or tape of the local music makes the air begin to quaver with a mixture of sadness and hopeful ululation. A cock suddenly crows right through the layer of undulating sound, though it is certainly not sunrise and not yet evening. A donkey brays, too. And I feel as though all the particles of my life hang suspended in the liquid light of this teahouse.

There is a bright burst of children's voices, as though someone has just released a flock of doves or cast a handful of pebbles onto the taut surface of a drum. I still have many questions. I still have many things to see and do. *Yes*? And I still feel uncertain and not entirely satisfied with any single thing.

But I know a little something now (though to say that I "know" assigns to the almost entirely unutterable, the nearly completely ephemeral awareness that I'm living with, a palpable and substantive presence that I'm not entirely sure it can sustain). As sure as I can say that I have passed through this antique town of mosques and minarets and markets, an old oasis between deserts as ancient as any place on the surface of the earth, as sure as I can say *we have been here!* I understand that just as life made it difficult for me to progress before I came here it now seems possible for me to move along. One can move through time, through a lifetime, aging but never maturing, and one can travel tens of thousands of miles and always stay in the same mental place and so really never leave home. *Yes.*

If anyone can be said to ever have a home on this planet of wonders moving through space and through time, if the rest all comes to nothing, and even if the gospels are mistaken and all will be for nought, and even if the prophecies are skewed and all of us, not just some of us, come to very bad ends, even if our watches stop and love turns to dust and our children, ah, the lovely fruit of the earth whose futures when we think in a dark mood can make us hold our heads in our hands and whimper and gibber like helpless, stupefied apes, and even if our children turn their faces from our lights and wander through deserts vaster than the Kara Kum, even when we call out to them, try to call them back in our best and smartest voices, even if they wander away from us still, *yes,* we can say that we at least halloed to them, hailed them, spoke our love to them over miles and years, we can say, each in our own way we can say . . .

Yes! say it!

We can at least say . . .

And who knows but it might be *more* than least? a *little* more than least . . .

At least . . .

If you go there, and you must try to go there, save your money and plan your trip, pack your bags and suffer the little discomforts and indignities of travel, the bad food, the danger, the heavy load of foreign pressures coming down on your brain . . . put home out of your mind for a while and give yourself over to the voyage, the air, the sea, the train, horseback, camelback, jeep, the bus, walk across the sand in your tire-soled shoes, however you go, whatever your mode of motion, wherever it is you are going in your dreams you must plan to travel there now . . . to whatever point on the map means the most to you because of fathers mothers brothers sisters children uncles lovers . . .

Make up your mind now to take the map out and plan the route to wherever it is you have to head for, so that you can say sooner than later that at least . . . at least . . . at least . . .

We have been to Khiva.

TWENTY-NINE

I ONLY WISH WE COULD MEET ON BETTER OCCA–sions," said Oll-an's brother at the airport. He talked a great deal during the car trip to the house, but Oll-an merely slumped back quietly in the seat. The landscape around him did not help—the snow-covered roads, icicle-bedecked buildings, so cold and frigid and unlike the South where he had been living with his wife and his young daughters.

Poor Tillie! She and Oll-an clung together in the old living room, patting each other, weeping for a short while, lapsing into silence. Twenty times an hour she narrated for him the last minutes of my going—my waking up, my request for a sip of water, the way I turned my face to her, then looked away as if at a sound in the night outside the house.

The funny thing was, I hadn't gone all that far. Apparently we have to stick around, souls like us, to help the ones we've left behind. Like teaching children how to ride two-wheelers or use chopsticks, it's not all that easy. But we try. Try, Teel, I said to her, over and over. Try, try. I worked all night, with little success. All I did was stir her up so that around one or two in the morning she sat up in bed and tried to speak to me.

"I know you're there," she said. "Are you there?"

Oll-an meanwhile had gotten into the liquor cabinet, something he hardly ever did unless it was a special occasion.

"Daddy," he was sobbing through his drink, "Daddy, Papa . . ."

Oh, Oll-an I wanted to say, who isn't afraid? When I set out on my own long trek away from home, didn't I cry out in the taiga in the Siberian night? Didn't I call out for my own father, that brute and deserter? And if you're thinking now, Oh, if I could have him back again in the world of the living I'd even listen to his talk about the moon and about writing, about Israel and time travel and video phones that let you speak between the inner planets and the far far stars, about the future and about the past, all those adventures, all that young manhood stuff. And if you're thinking this, then good to think it, and make your peace, and sleep after a while, rest and sleep.

Toward morning, as they say in stories, he slept. And he awoke in an odd state, in disbelief of my absence.

"Well, Sonny," I had to say to him, "it's time to face the music."

He didn't hear it that way of course, but merely shivered in the chilly wind that suddenly blew through the overheated house. He sat up, as though he'd heard a ghost! I said to him, accidentally letting some of it slip through, it's just the way I always had to wake you for school in the morning. I wanted to pat him on the head, give him a hug, all the things I did to him when he was a little kiddo.

I'm going, I said, and he felt it again as a breeze. Leaving this place.

Here was Teel, sticking her head in the doorway of his old room.

Neighbors began to arrive. And to each one, or to small groups, Teel described the sequence of events of my going—waking, asking for water, taking a sip, and the rest. And each of them to Oll-an said that they hoped to get together next time on a better occasion. And they said prayers, though what good these did me I can't say. No earthly act could help any more, and prayers belong to the earth. You know, I was never much for religion, but if they helped you, Teel, Oll-an, Shel, then fine. Then came the cars, the drive to the hall, more prayers. What a good man I was, they said, which proves to me that anyone living must be praised as good since I was just an average son and father and husband, no better, no worse, than the billions come and gone.

It was raining as they drove to the graveyard, raining even harder when they reached it. A cold rain. And this icy water poured down on Oll-an's head, better to cleanse him, but too much would also wash the earth away. He was looking down at the sodden beds, the barren patches where grass would spring up in a month or two, thinking, unaccountably, about his daughters' gerbils, about work he had to do, about *my* manuscript, oh, that long story I wrote for him a few years back about my early life which he took and tossed in the trunk of his car or stuffed somewhere in a drawer or box.

Read it, I tried to urge Oll-an. At least now he would read. I saw him thinking it, knowing it.

And the cold rain rained down.

Cover your heads, Teel said. Cover your heads and pray.

And Oll-an was thinking he would read my story now, and now that it was too late he would tell my story, perhaps even find the money to take a trip to my old native grounds.

If you won't pray for your father then at least pray for me, Teel said.

Oll-an refused, though his brother prayed. Nice boy. Teel wept into the rain. For what good? Oll-an was thinking. And he was right, because I was long lost to prayer, as if they ever worked for such matters as someone's going, and Teel had her friends, but Oll-an, he had only his own childhood to mourn, and the new worry of leaving someday his own children behind.

Thumpk! the pounds of dirt hit the top of the wooden casket. *Thumpk!* a fist pounds against the door! Did a voice cry out to enter? or did it beg to be released?

Thumpk!

And the cold rain rained. And, Oll-an, your mother wept bitter tears. Yet when you turned to her she accepted the comfort you offered, and you two became one grieving creature, and I, released now from my own passionate watch . . .

Dropped . . .
Breaking the links . . .
It's a kind of physics . . .
And dropping I felt a rising too . . .
How I've always loved to fly . . .
But how also like a whale diving and then sounding . . .
A shuttle ship shuddering at launch . . .
The moon!

I come and go now rather easily, settled as I am among these outer spaces, conversant with my dear descendants back down on earth, pondering also the future of voyages further out.

All's pleasant here, like eating every meal at the finest restaurant and your taste buds never tire. I've seen my brother Joe, I've met my mother, I've even seen my father across the distance but haven't yet flashed to his side to surprise him, though in time I'll do it, I know, I'll apologize to him and he'll apologize to me, but such events mean differently here than over on earth, in earth, back down on earth, yet I do wander and look through crowds for a glimpse of one former soul, my *father's father,* and perhaps even for *his father before him,* though how I'd recognize any of them I cannot say, so many shrewd and ornery beings from out of the long, deep past do swarm here, the Frenchman—Napoleon's sergeant who tarried in Russia after his wound—traders and cameldrivers, herdsmen, craftsmen, warriors, firemakers, wizards, and the first who walked erect all hairy, flintknives in hand, ape-Adams, our primary fathers. Don't ask how or why, because here all questions are answered before you raise them. So much to see, to ponder.

Whoever made this planned so well. For whatever reason, all of it fits and pleases. Except for one itch, the one I'm scratching now. The sad—yes, sadness here, too—the sad fact that after a while, recollection of earth falls away, the way hair falls out in old age when you brush it or run a comb through its former lush and thickly curling waves. So you must exercise this muscle as I've been doing in order to keep a count of all those acts and faces and things that meant so much.

Go out, I say to you, Oll-an, and search for me if you care as you seem to. The last place I want to be caught dead in is here in this rain-soaked park. Read my story. Make up a trail from its pages and follow it. Go on a trip to my home regions and to the distant points I travelled through on the way to find your mother, your brother, and you. Go to Khiva, son! That will release me. I'll meet you there in the marketplace, where the obsidian-eyed women peek out over their veils and the air holds more spices than moisture. Take Josh with you, why don't you? We'll see how much has changed, how much has stayed the same. I'll leave you then, but you can finish the story. I'll have spoken to you at last in my pages and you will have helped me speak. Most of all you will have listened well. That way we won't have to wait for eternity for the chance to meet again, as my own father and I had to do.

It's funny, Oll-an, the urge that comes over me now and then to talk with you, to tell you stories, such a simple longing—mourn *with* me, not *for* me, son—for everything past, mothers, fathers, children, dunes, winds, dust, feet, camel flesh, earth, even shit (pardon my language), fire, mountains, channels, lakes, rivers, oceans, woods, plains, houses, forests, moonlight, starlight, starfire, rain!

EPILOGUE: LISTENING TO GLINKA

These scenes and incidents had the strangeness of the transcendental, as if they were snatches torn from lives on other planets that had somehow drifted to earth. Only nature had remained true to history and appeared in the guise it assumed in modern art.

Doctor Zhivago

I'D NEVER BELIEVED IN GHOSTS OR VOICES IN THE head until my friend, John Gardner, died and the day after—unless you are going to be razor-edge rational and dismiss this next with a shrug of the shoulders and say that I made it up out of my grief for John—while I was pushing a lawnmower across a large swatch of high grass down in Knoxville, Tennessee, (which is another story I can't get to telling here for the distraction it would bring, as to why I was there and not heading up for his funeral) John appeared to me. I blacked out the hot, midday sun and saw him standing at the edge of the lawn, just in front of a little patch of woods. He said a few words to me, assured me that he was feeling no pain.

"You go on working," he said, hands jammed into the pockets of his baggy blue jeans and giving a toss of his long, white hair. *"All you guys go on working."* And then with a

little shrug he turned and walked off into the woods. The sun burst back on me full-force, and I heard the roaring of the power mower in my ears.

How do I account for this? I don't know. The same thing happened again the next day while I was driving on the interstate through Knoxville, my two then very small daughters in the back seat. The light began to fade, and I had the sense to pull over onto the shoulder before I found myself once again in conversation with John, who stood just outside the car, telling me basically the same news as the day before.

"I'm going now," he said, *"but I want you guys to go on working. That's the only thing that matters."*

He waved, and shuffled away from the car—and all the light of day, the heat of the southern September afternoon, the noise of my car's engine, the roar of passing interstate traffic broke upon me like a wave, augmented by the screaming of my girls in the rear seat. They had been terrified, as I had no apparent reason for suddenly slowing down and pulling over onto the edge of the highway, car after speeding car zooming past, shaking our station wagon in their wakes.

So when my father spoke to me in my head—did you think that I was inventing those conversations? did you think that they were a mere *literary device?*—I wasn't surprised. I was only reassured, particularly when we flew in Soviet airships, of which before the trip I had heard only horror stories. The crowding, the lack of concern for the amenities Americans have become used to in commercial aviation, the bad heating, the lack of good pressurization. All that turned out to be true. And so when you put a naturally nervous flier into these situations you could expect that his fears might increase.

Not mine. Because all the time I heard my father's voice in my head, assuring me that these boys in the cockpit were the best anywhere, that he had grown up on Soviet aviation, and that he knew how they were trained.

As we left Uzbekistan and flew east over Siberia on our way to Irkutsk, and later as we flew above the Soviet-Mongolian border in a flight headed to Khabarovsk, I sat back calmly and revelled in my altitude, latitude, and longitude, made serene by the presence of my father's ghost, or spirit, what word can we attach to it? We saw something of Siberia, and then spent a day or so in Khabarovsk, and then took the overnight train south along the Ussuri River, Russia's troubled border with China, to board a Soviet steamer at Nakhodka and sail across the Sea of Japan, around Honshu, the big Japanese island, and disembark at Yokohama, to stay with friends for a few days in Tokyo, before flying back to the States.

I don't know how all this narrative has set with you, dear reader, but from the point of view of the one who has lived it through, lived through both the life and the writing of it, I look back on all this with as much of a sense of completion as, say, a patient who has survived major surgery and now stands repaired–or, and of course you may be thinking this, and why not? like someone who has just emerged from years and years of intense analysis with a feeling of new well-being and redoubled resolve to work hard in the world and at the same time try to never miss another beat of the life within.

There were just a few threads left dangling from this weaving–one of them being the memory of my father raving now and then about the music of the mid-nineteenth-century Russian composer, Mikhail Ivanovich Glinka.

"Oh, Glinka!" he said with a sigh that we usually hear reserved for exclamations of old loves and lost paradise. "You must listen to Glinka! You're getting an education, don't you ever find his music? Don't they ever play his music in this country?"

When he died, and I took out his manuscript from the carton where I had stored it, I vowed that I would face it head on and do something with his story. And now you can see what I did. But as we were sailing out of Nakhodka, and I stood at the stern for a long while, hours it was, watching the Russian mainland (I almost wrote *homeland*, and isn't that funny?) recede further and further to the west, watching the calm surface of the Sea of Japan as it was churned into a ploughed field of constantly shifting waves and currents in our wake, waters where my father drifted, lost, for one cold and deathly night, I heard him say one more thing to me beyond farewell.

The sun was racing along ahead of us, sliding high in the sky toward the islands of Japan, and beyond that, toward Hawaii, and the California coast whose cliffs of brownish rock and sand appeared, in retrospect, to have been broken off only lately and suffered the separation of these thousands of miles of glistening salt sea from their counterparts on the Russian coast. As I was mulling over such matters, my father's voice came to me one last time.

Don't forget to listen to Glinka.

I squinted back toward the fading cliffs of the Russian coast, where the Sikhote Alin Mountains come down to the water's edge. I waved, and he was gone, and I was at sea for several days, alone with my son and myself.

All this by way of explanation for why, on an afternoon in late autumn in New England I'm sitting in the music room of an old mansion now turned to purposes other than housing one extremely wealthy family, headphones covering my ears, listening to the symphonic music of Glinka.

And oh what romantic music! Glinka travelled to Spain and came back in the mid 1840s with the sounds of *seguidillas manchegas* in his head, and the rhythms of wild Spanish dances, and as I spin my way in my brain through these Spain-drenched selections, I laugh with the pleasure of love and affection for the young Fishka, who listened to these pieces as a boy and felt the exotic churnings in his blood, and for the boy that I was, called by some mysterious piper to the coasts of Spain myself those many years ago.

I am surprised, very surprised, that this is what the music sounds like—and then comes the varied "Kamarinskaya," the piece that the liner notes tell me is the source of all musical Russianness in the future, an inspiration to Tchaikovsky and Rimsky-Korsakov, all of those composers who came after—full of big, broad, full chords, darkened with the pessimism of the Russian bleakness of soul that you can see almost palpable in the air in Leningrad of a rainy afternoon or evening, and then lightened by the sudden optimistic intrusion of the final resolutions, the hope if not of heaven then at least for a natural cycle that will take the Russians out of winter into spring, out of darkness into day.

I'm reminded of those Moscow days when the wind would come up and blow in a reminder of late autumn, of something like the day it is today, blaring with sun but cold and windy nonetheless. I'm whirling with my father in my spirit, in my blood—this soaring, surging orchestral fantasy, the plaintiveness of the longing, the gaiety of the ever-turning propensity to waltz, to fly!

So that's what he listened to and loved, I say to myself. He was so much like me when I was that age—but then I stop and remind myself that I came after him, not the other way around.

When we arrived in Irkutsk, capital of eastern Siberia, we took an excursion to the shores of nearby Lake Baikal. The day was beautiful, sun-soaked, though the wind off the water was a chilly reminder that winter was on the way here, earlier than in most places.

Baikal is a deep, deep lake, some two miles deep along much of its distance, and the other facts about it are just as astonishing. It holds one-sixth of the world's fresh water, for instance. And a thousand miles from the cold, salt Arctic sea it hosts, among other animals, a species of seal. And it's so clear one can see a piece of white canvas floating at a depth of seventy-five feet.

Baikal has, according to our guide, its own climate, and Soviet scientists have a little discipline among all the other environmental sciences known as "Baikology," the study of this lake and its micro-environment, its ecology and all the rest of its nature, including the special weather that occurs in this region, and its peculiar seasons within the all-embracing climate of greater Siberia.

I think that each of us, if we let ourselves, and I for my part have tried to do it while telling this story, could regard our own hearts with the same kind of study and amazement.

ELVIS PRESLEY BOULEVARD: **$7.95**
From Sea to Shining Sea, Almost
MARK WINEGARDNER

"The great American adventure . . . just to get in a covered wagon, or the car, and head out across our amazing country, to see what happens."—*The Los Angeles Times*
"His instincts are remarkably honed, and his eye and heart are surprisingly sensitive."—*The American Geographical Society*

———— ♦ ————

ZOO STATION: **$7.95**
Adventures in East and West Berlin
IAN WALKER

"Fascinating . . . reminds one of Tom Wolfe, with its keen feel for details and nuance."—*The San Francisco Chronicle*
"Walker's accounts of the misfits drawn to West Berlin's underworld are hard-boiled and hilarious."—*The Seattle Times*

———— ♦ ————

MUSIC IN EVERY ROOM: **$7.95**
Around the World in a Bad Mood
JOHN KRICH

"A kind of ultimate travel book, very American. That is, more S. J. Perelman than Bruce Chatwin. I like it enormously."—Susan Sontag

———— ♦ ————

HEIDI'S ALP: **$7.95**
One Family's Search for Storybook Europe
CHRISTINA HARDYMENT

"A perfectly enchanting book."—*The Washington Post Book World*

———— ♦ ————

NIGHT TRAIN TO TURKISTAN: **$7.95**
Modern Adventures along China's Ancient Silk Road
STUART STEVENS

"A wildly hilarious ride through an amazing, surreal land. The best travel book I've ever read."—Beth Henley, Pulitzer Prize–winning author of *Crimes of the Heart*

———— ♦ ————

ALL THE WRONG PLACES: **$7.95**
Adrift in the Politics of the Pacific Rim
JAMES FENTON

"Brilliant reportage . . . a riveting collection of Fenton's crisply audacious chronicles of war, unrest and revolution in Vietnam, Korea and the Philippines. . . . Fenton's elegant writing gleams. . . . Great travel writing."—*The Boston Globe*
"Vivid and intelligent. . . . His style is all those things 'good' reporting isn't supposed to be: anecdotal, digressive, subjective, polemical; but because Fenton knows how to break the rules, it is also enormously successful."—*Kirkus Reviews*

◆

BEHIND THE WALL: **$18.95**
A Journey through China
COLIN THUBRON

"Superbly written, sharply observed. . . . This probing account illuminates the social and spiritual temper of contemporary China."—*The Washington Post*
"Thubron is transcendentally gifted . . . one of the two or three best living travel writers, in some ways probably *the* best."—Jan Morris

◆

IN TROUBLE AGAIN: **$17.95**
A Journey between the Orinoco and the Amazon
REDMOND O'HANLON

"O'Hanlon belongs to the Peter Fleming school of travel writing: self-deprecating, funny, perceptive and ludicrously brave."—*The Sunday Times* (London)